POLITICAL SPIRITUALITY
IN AN AGE OF ECO-APOCALYPSE

POLITICAL SPIRITUALITY IN AN AGE OF ECO-APOCALYPSE

COMMUNICATION AND STRUGGLE ACROSS SPECIES, CULTURES, AND RELIGIONS

James W. Perkinson

First published in 2015 by PALGRAVE MACMILLAN® in the United States—a division of St. Martin's Press LLC, 175 Fifth Avenue, New York, NY 10010.

Where this book is distributed in the UK, Europe and the rest of the world, this is by Palgrave Macmillan, a division of Macmillan Publishers Limited, registered in England, company number 785998, of Houndmills, Basingstoke, Hampshire RG21 6XS.

Palgrave Macmillan is the global academic imprint of the above companies and has companies and representatives throughout the world.

Palgrave® and Macmillan® are registered trademarks in the United States, the United Kingdom, Europe and other countries.

ISBN: 978-1-137-50700-6

Library of Congress Cataloging-in-Publication Data

Perkinson, James W.
    Political spirituality in an age of eco-apocalypse : essays in communication and struggle across species, cultures, and religions / James W. Perkinson.
        pages cm
    Includes bibliographical references and index.
    ISBN 978-1-137-50700-6 — ISBN 1-137-50700-4   1. Human ecology—Religious aspects—Christianity.   2. Sustainability.
3. End of the world.   4. Religion and politics.   I. Title.
    BT695.5.P43 2015
    201'.77—dc23

                                                           2015002538

A catalogue record of the book is available from the British Library.

Design by Amnet.

First edition: July 2015

10 9 8 7 6 5 4 3 2 1

Dedicated to the ancestors—of my blood, of this soil,
of all life here where the river goes round.

Contents

ACKNOWLEDGMENTS

This book began in eleven different hours, teased by breezes and haunts untold—those faint inklings that show up when the day is young, the body again poised, however brief and wrinkled, before a morning sun. Each chapter has a different germ, a spur or hand from a different turn of the calendar and muse. But the rhizome of life remains constant. I have a mother now in her second century, who pushes on past mission and love, cruising before the night, with courage and laughter still on her brow. A father gone to the other side, flickering into view on occasion in dream-time struggles to purge the pain and desire of day. Grandparents long singing their German, Irish, Dutch, and English tunes over deeper runes and darker hues, not knowing, I think, they were, as we all are, born of ancient Afrique. I only slowly now even know to seek their counsel, coming not in word but silhouette and shadow, a grammar of loam. And then there are the scents, the tremors of heart, the slight stealing light at the edge of a book or tool, the cicada-din on summer's back—all the giftings of that chorus of prehuman labor and savvy, from squirrel to sparrow to thunder and iron and far constellations. All of them—inside this flesh, breathing or feeding or holding forth against gravity's pull. I age, and owe more than I can account, to more than I can name. Though I do name those tribal ones, those shunted-aside ones, those indigenous precursors of the race—so beleaguered now, nearly disappeared, who yet teach—here the Ojibwa; in New Mexico, the pueblo and (strangely) the Tzutujil; at a distance, the Aeta, the Hadza, the Huarani. I know these only by report. But they speak! I have buddies of the streets here in Detroit, cohorts in conspiring, pushing back on the emergency of the hour and paying small prices. I have "exemplars" who do not know they are such—poor friends of color, surviving the times, in spite of. Kin of the mind whose writing and repartee is a warm fire when the year permits a momentary gathering to listen and drink and pontificate. Friends old and new, from coasts distant, watersheds verdant or drying, woods north and colder. Carnival folk in Philly; Chicago adepts scattered northwest and across an ocean; a monk, growing forgetful near a lake. I name you by your place and gift, your kindling in my own existence, carried like a beat in the bone. And most of all, I croon to the one next to my typing hand on this couch, who huddles in the cold of morning under my covers, sharing secrets and smells, idiosyncrasies and fears, smirking at a world crazy and hard—my throb, my love, my lifemate. To all—there are not words adequate. But there is resolve to remember. Thank you.

THE POLITICS AND ECO-LOGICS OF "SPIRITUAL" COMMUNICATION

The assemblage of reflections gathered here has been pulled together in the season of waiting, which runs from Advent to Epiphany. Such a designation invokes a Christian sense of time; given calendrical shape under the aegis and impress of empires Western and European. I do not intend to stay entirely within the lines of that particular tradition, but neither shall I wander all that far in what follows. Christianity is both the soil in which I grew up personally and the spiritual juggernaut under which modernity has pressed its claims globally. It has both nurtured and steamrolled—and most often steamrolled precisely in the process of pretending to nurture. So much so that now one-third of the world's peoples are caught in its conventions of practice. But here, I am primarily interested in its edges rather than its core— the places where a continual temptation to a monolithic absolutism has regularly been met with indigenous struggles to live close to the ground and with grand local style. It is that theater of encounter— a thread of struggle running the entire length of Christianity's time on the planet—that gives rise to the "across" in my chosen title. In what follows, we will track a continual battle between imperial logics of centralization and control and grassroots effervescence that proves uncontainable. And this will prove to be the case whether talking specifically of spirituality, more generally of culture, or in the widest possible frame, between species human and other in ecologies as varied as Mideastern desert or Amazonian jungle. But it is perhaps apropos to begin with a retelling of Christianity's most ubiquitous tale in a way that signals the intention here. Simultaneously the single most commonly celebrated religious ritual on the planet and capitalism's most "hallowed" rite of selling, Christmas convenes a scene of stark "signifying" that has all but been lost in the feel-good frenzy of our contemporary mock-up. Reading its hints against the grain of its central thrust points the way this work will proceed.

The Ensemble at the Crib

Of late for me, the tale arises with suddenly clairvoyant detail in a harsh setting. It is Christmas Eve in snowbound Detroit, beleaguered city, ravaged by half-century of white flight, corporate pirating, poverty long the plight, foreclosure the new rite of plunder, homelessness swelling. I was schooled in this tradition from my birth, German industriousness in my mom wrestling for years with Irish bluster in my dad, finally resolved into Presbyterian austerity in the church of my upbringing, whitewashed walls without a hint of mystery in any corner. Christmas Eve for me, growing up, was a bright splash of noon, not the titillating breath of a living night. But now a little motley crew of us, urban activists and ghetto poor alike, huddle in an inadequately heated, winter-shrouded Episcopal ark called St. Peter's, an upside-down ship of sanctuary in the Big D whose candlelight whispers with augury and ghosts.

It is night not only in diurnal cycle, and in the collapse of Motown, but as "sign of the times." For the handful of us gathered, the epoch increasingly appears one of apocalypse—a growing intuition that civilization itself may have been a wrong turn for our species, 5,000 years in the making, now emerging clearly in its all of its hell-bent fury to put an entire planet of life and matter up for sale in the market.

Whether Alaska king crab or diamonds from down under, salt from the desert sea or chicken grown in a cage, water from the midstate aquifer bottled by Nestle or an entire city offered to Koch Brother cronies on the platter of Emergency Management strategies—this whole menagerie of creaturely beauty reengineered into commodities destined in short order for a fate as garbage is quickly now taking us off the edge of the planet. Our best science in this dark hour has us facing a warming of four degrees centigrade or higher by century's end and the possibility of extinction. We are now looking straight into the barrel of a gun that one terrified business exec calls "the death of birth."

I am charged with offering reflection on the text of the hour on this eve. How tell the old, old story in such a global night, huddled against the cold, in a city of American Dream-fame, discovering its

late role as canary-in-the-coal-mine of industrial demise? The sheer
size of the travesty we have unleashed has me turning past the text to
the deep past to ask when we have ever managed to live otherwise.
The answer is—most of our time on the planet.

The crisis of our time has left my wife and me, for more than a
decade now, entertaining the idea that indigenous folk the globe over,
more often than not, had it right. Human life is not about some phantasm called progress, but about living beautifully and nobly in concert
with four-legged and winged and finned kin as well as with rivers and
mountains, soils and trees, grasses and insects, winds and waves and
seasons, in a local symbiosis of reciprocity. Across the ages, *hunter-
gatherers* have known how to carry on better than most, but *subsistence agriculturalists* also have managed cultures of immense dignity
and well-thought-out sustainability over long courses of time. From
the few remaining such groups, there is much to be learned, even if
the hour is catastrophically late.

But the biblical text—in the main and in this night's particular
lectionary selection—is preeminently a text of shepherding folk, of
pastoral nomadism, rooted in memory of Abel, whose blood yet cries
from the ground after having been killed by older farming brother
Cain, who likely memorializes the catastrophe that settled mono-crop
agriculture represents in history in seeking to domesticate plants and
animals and everything else in sight, including human animals. Cain
also becomes the first city builder, erecting the great Machine called
Babel's Tower as archetype of the human project of subjecting everything to technological control and remaking.

In such a reading of our time on the planet, pastoral nomadism
emerges as the first social movement in history, herders taking their
flocks and exiting empire to live on the land beyond the reach of the
managers. Against this backdrop, the biblical tradition can certainly be
read as seeking continuously to reconvene the possibility of a herder-
like exit from imperial ways and return to something more sustainable, learning from local plant and animal life as if such were actually
the "messianic flesh" people needed to embrace as their "Savior." The
pastoral nomad social movement named "Israel," recapitulated in the
prophets, reanimated under John the Baptist, given preeminent form
by Jesus, appears to invoke just such a return to being apprenticed to a
"saving" species of plant or animal to relearn how to live on the land.
Moses had his bush; John his camel; Jesus his dove.

The Christmas text (Lk 2:1–20) picks up with old Joseph and pregnant Mary on trek from their Nazareth village of tenant farmers and
day laborers to "be enrolled," under decree of Caesar, in the house

of their origins, tracing back to the time of shepherd David. This is empire exercising its "discipline of sight"—making a native populace "legible," controllable, manageable. (In our day, we might think NSA data-mining, Global Tracking System chips woven into clothing and inserted under the skin of children, drone warfare and domestic surveillance writ large. We too are being enrolled in ever-widening circuits of monitoring.)

Undoubtedly anxious, perhaps even terrified, Mary breaks water under the bureaucratic duress. Motel 6 is filled, as is the local youth hostel. Tradition has it she camps out in a cave—likely one of the rocky caverns around Bethlehem that shepherds used as corrals. In short order, she has her newborn in a "manger," feeding trough for domesticated livestock, enslaved creatures whose own wildlands grazing has been reduced to slopping beheaded grain from a wood or stone container.

Meanwhile local herding folk, out on the hills with their flocks, reading the stars and weather, tending to the night cacophony for any hint of danger, schooled, not in texts of Torah but in the sensuous spells of the wild holiness that is their "bible," are struck with an apparition, an emergent power of the outback, taking shape on the rocks, whispering omens, filtering light into a strange miasma of significance. They hear, are terrified, then comforted. Offered "good news." An event has taken place.

There is a sign. A child, *offered up in a feeding trough for animals.* And of course, good city-dwellers that we are, well-schooled in empire's delirium, we are sure the trough is ancillary to the meaning; it just means "humble birth." But what if it actually meant what it signifies—a newborn presented as divine offering in a food tray for animals—only one of which is our own species. That child will later say, "Eat my flesh . . ." Indigenous folk across the globe have everywhere understood food as god and vice versa—living flesh given and circulating up and down the food chain. Typically they would trace ancestry not to a human progenitor but to that plant or animal that most enabled their metabolic survival in their ecology. They might be Corn-People or Whale-Beings or Agave-Humans. Or in the Mideastern desert, Camel-Folk. In any case, here the exchange is a bare hint, under imperial duress: human child and grain bin held together in new life. Indeed, the adult-to-come will later say of himself, "Unless a grain of wheat falls into the earth and dies . . ." Subsequent church history will cite Isaiah to the effect that the ox and the ass know the score here in a way that humans don't, and depict them as the first real consorts of Jesus, interacting with him in *their* feeding bin (Is 1:3).

And many nativity scenes will also throw in camels. How indigenously dare we read?

But back out to the shepherds. For them still in the hills, an intimation of song—maybe Pythagoras's "music of the spheres" (whose natural resonance Pythagoras himself actually learned from nomadic Celtic or Scythian shamans) or some other wind-rock-chiming symphony of that particular ecology, whose recurrent meanings Palestinian herders spend their lives divining. "Angels," the city-bound evangelists will call them. But we need remember, so they will say about the Voice that later addresses Jesus on march into Jerusalem for his final showdown with the Powers, a Voice that most hear as "thunder" (Jh 12:27–30).

It is shepherds who are the magi of Luke, readers of the stars and rocks and rivers and storms of the seasons, the little people among whom memory of this tradition of shepherd Abel and nomad Abraham and herder Moses and all of the upstart, renegade women around them continues to be lived. It is shepherds living out on the land who are the only ones in Israel who grasp the hint of this peasant birth, who keep ear to the wind, eye to the night sky, senses on alert, who hasten to the site, treasure the strange omen—god as food for animals—and then return to their herder tasks, to watching for the very animals whose care has just been verified as a divine concern.

Empire, down the road, will reduce that care to a single species—our own—and render every other creature subject to savaging and extinction under our hand, not realizing that when the bees go, we go, when the plankton go, we go, when the rivers dry and the aquifers are all bottled and the mountains decapitated and the air fried, even the elites themselves will draw their last breath.

And there it is. Christmas. Read from beyond the pale of the city, inside the city. Under the imperial eye, elaborating written enrollments, lists of names, for the task of extracting surplus products and controlling revolt—a sign is given. It is illegible to the Powers. A mere shepherds' tale, a hilltop happening in the dead of night, mists shimmering, winds wandering, stars flickering, a child born to a teenage mother in the care of an old codger, outside the city in a cave with an animal feeding bin as their only cradle, and herd members their "family." Soon enough Herod will kill to erase the sign.

AN ENSEMBLE OF REFLECTIONS

The book here will go forth under this sign. Though admitting manifold meaning, the manger ensemble is at least significant of new life struggling for breath under the regime of domestication. In Lucan version, it presents enslaved grain and enslaved herd and enslaved human, "laboring" together in hope. But its scene also invokes older musings. For those schooled in Jewish tradition, ox and ass lingering cribside brings old man Job into the frame (Job 39:5–6). Drafted as wise "heathen" into Israel's quintessential tale of unjust suffering, Job calls Divinity to account with a fist of anger raised skyward, demanding face-to-face confrontation. He is finally answered. Directed to a panoramic display of wild mystery, he is vigorously queried: Where were you when the earth was founded, the sea bounded, the rains fathered, and the grasses given free range over the steppe? (Job 38–41). The rapid-fire rebuff lifts up every imaginable form of wild creature, simply "being itself." And squarely in the middle of the litany, wild asses and oxen are named as particularly bequeathed a gift of freedom—"divinely loosened bonds" to go feral up the mountainside or down the valley—and away from the regime of forced labor for humans (Job 39:5–12)! The language is unmistakably Jubilee. This central biblical trope of release encompasses not just humanity, but land and all of its shackled denizens. And it lurks in the wings of the Christmas story as a countersign of imperial presumption. For Job in agony under the suffering of unjust imposition, this ensemble alone is the "answer" to the demand to see divinity face-to-face. Not miracles, but the wild, in all of its teeming rage of beauty and eating. Learning broadly to read such "minority reports" and "bestiary insurgency" inside the biblical text was the effort of my most recent work, titled (less than fortuitously) *Messianism Against Christology: Resistance Movements, Folk Arts, and Empire.*

The book to follow here is offered as a companion text to that effort (much as *Shamanism, Racism and Hip-Hop Culture: Essays in White Supremacy and Black Subordination* functioned as companion for and follow-up on my first book, *White Theology: Outing Supremacy in Modernity*). The work finds its immediate tack in the recent interest in Political Theology. But given the growing turn in this country away from institutionalized religious commitment (the Pew Trust study of recent fame highlighting the coming age of "Nones") and toward a more generalized and postmodern mix of practices and interests typically styled as "spiritual," the work proposes "Political Spirituality" as a theme for investigation. The book consists of ten essays, first delivered as papers at various academic conferences, now retooled under this basic concern, seeking to challenge a spirituality that all too easily in our time "samples" tradition like a hip-hop dilettante without ever getting off the fascinating surface of global culture to confront the profound crises we now face. The motive force for each of the chapters is a deep concern for sustainability in the face of eco-disasters like climate change and population overshoot as those are compounded by political economy calamities (emerging from imperial responses to terror and corporate insistence on privatization of virtually everything "under the sun"—including water and air). The text articulates a deep suspicion of our growing cyborg fascination with a kind of "techno-messianism," while at the same time exploring some of the artistic innovations and meanings emerging both in industrialization and digitalization.

The organization of the essays begins and ends with personal testament—in the opening, exploring a childhood experience of a "tree revelation" and in the conclusion, discussing my continuous work with a spouse-partner from the Philippines in seeking to reintegrate, in our respective journeys, some measure of indigenous experience and wisdom. In both cases what is put front and center is the question of recovery of relationship with local ecology in general, and retrieval of a fast-disappearing capacity to listen to other species and the organic "surround" in particular. Which is to say, the central issue for the entire line-up is *communication*—two-way exchange across species, cultures, and religions—and the central trope offered to facilitate such, that of learning how to read and "be read by" one's environment and relations. Chapters 2 through 9 represent a historical progression that is itself also largely a matter of "sampling," beginning with the spiritual tradition that has most shaped the West (the Bible) and ending with what is effectively a postmodern mode of spirituality the West has most recently conferred upon global youth (hip-hop culture in general and "scratching" in particular—here analyzed as a postmodern mode of Filipino *babaylan* healing). In between, the exploration ranges across a number of historical developments. These include: Christianity put in perspective as a practice arising in an imperial environment dependent on settled agricultural; a colonial enterprise of missionary Christianity spinning off white supremacy as its most damning modern legacy; an "up-take" of colonial Christianity by subordinated communities innovating *guadalupanismo* and *vodou* underneath the surface of an imposed Mariology; and a hoodoo-influenced wrestling of blues culture into urban aesthetics and industrial techtonics by way of jazz improvisation. At each turn (in each chapter title), the "crossroads" is offered as a deep trope of folk culture, coming straight out of Africa in tales of the trickster of the road-fork, gatekeeper of choice and opener of the way, who is also the god of communication where the lines of the cosmos cross and tangle. Each chapter invokes a basic conundrum of our time on the planet.

And there is then once again (as in *White Theology*) a kind of chiastic structure at work. The outermost circle pairs off personal testament from two different stages of life as the beginning and end of the work. The next concentric circle juxtaposes the biblical tradition and hip-hop culture (two chapters each) in probing (what I would consider to be) some of the more compelling spiritual possibilities of each, respectively. And the center-most pairing puts together an "anti-indigenous" European Christianity in the social forms of empire and supremacy (characterized in two successive chapters) with creolized reactions to those developments innovated as "spiritualities of the oppressed" (in two chapters about various subordinated communities "doing judo" on their own domination inside modernity). Unlike the biblical use of chiasm, the structure here does not imply priority as much as interlocution. Within their respective "circles," the chapters riff on one another—Guadalupe and *vodou* on supremacy, jazz on incarnation, DJ-ing on parable, hip-hop on Jubilee. At one level the chapter topics represent what could appear to be a somewhat wild smorgasbord of writings. But at the deepest level, it is precisely a concern for "the wild" that shows up in every chapter as the unifying theme across the whole work, and integrates the material by again and again teasing out indigenous memories and insurgent energies available for living otherwise in quite disparate times and contexts.

Given the emphasis on communication and reading, it is also perhaps requisite to offer a bit of readerly assistance. As outlined above, the whole can be read sequentially. But given the text's origins as a number of separate reflections, the work can also be sampled a chapter at a time, in any order. Obviously, that facility means occasional repetition of concerns and insights (but in each case, with differing emphases and expressions). In aid of such an inclination, I offer here chapter summaries that telegraph subject matter a bit more explicitly.

THE ENSEMBLE OF CHAPTERS

The first chapter opens reflections phenomenological and personal. It camps out on an early childhood experience of grief and beauty in the face of a sudden "wild" disclosure to outline the profundity of the interlocking crises facing the globe today. The potency of that early experience was at once alluring and terrifying, a kind of communication from the larger ensemble of life. Its import, in words it has taken a lifetime to formulate, was one of "archeology," posing (in what Derrick Jensen calls a "language older than words") the fundamental wonderment of being human: "Why are we here? What does it mean to be alive on a planet teeming with a billion-fold community of other life forms?" Embedded in the question is both politics and spirituality. The essay here will focus especially on the issue of communication—across species as well as cultures—to argue that we face today a crisis of attention, of what may well be an eco-systemic demand to recover our entire sensorium as the organ of communication with a planet going up in flame and a biosphere plunging into massive rates of extinction. At stake in such a communicative dilemma is a deep and desperate need to break through the "containment" of human physicality in modern notions of rationality grounded in liberalism's idea of the body as a relationship of ownership and "nature" as the extension of that proprietary relationship into the surrounding ecology by way of labor. In wrestling with a broader notion of communication relevant to that experience, Paul Shepard's writings on the distinctiveness of human epigenesis serve as the baseline from which to think creatively about the ways indigenous cultures educated child bodies in local taxonomies of flora and fauna and then in adolescence rescripted those bodies in a poetics of initiation that broke open experience towards multiversed communicative interaction with the local surround. In constructing a theoretical reflection on such, Norbert Elias's theorizing of the modern body, Teresa Brennan's notions of the transmission of affects, Donna Haraway's idea of "cyborgs" each have purchase in the set of ideas offered, though the concrete experience of "initiation rites" as ritually elaborated by various indigenous cultures provides the primary data from which to rethink our responsibility to the planet today. And while the question is a general one for a world ever more radically colonized by the globalizing effects of Western culture, the hegemony of the West dictates prioritizing our focus on those traditions—particularly Christianity—that have most shaped Western presuppositions about human "being."

Chapter 2 moves back into the biblical tradition to "forage" for perspective. Within the gospel recordings of the Galilean Jesus movement, "how one reads" became a critical issue for public engagement and practical commitment. The essay here will center on the battle of interpretation outlined in Luke's account of the so-called Good Samaritan parable to underscore struggle over the meaning of Sabbath-Jubilee as the primary axis of conflict between the upstart rabbi-organizer of Nazareth and the comprador elites upholding the Temple-State and living well off the fruits of the appropriated field labor of Palestinian peasants. How Sabbath-Jubilee stakes out a forager memory (gathering manna in the Sinai desert) at the heart of the biblical tradition will anchor a much broader consideration of the stakes of "reading" religious texts in relationship to ecosystemic contexts. With sustainability as the urgent question of the hour, this biblical tradition of remembering a time of "living on the land" will be juxtaposed to contemporary anarcho-primitivist theory to articulate a deep question of land politics. In fleshing out the way the land "speaks" in biblical texts, the Genesis remembrance of the murder of pastoral nomad Abel by tiller Cain will be explored as giving the tradition one of its more fascinating tropes for listening beyond merely human agency—in this case, tracing a cry of blood, swallowed by soil that figures indigenous disappearance by imperial agri-business across the broad swath of history. Here is an invocation that reads our religious traditions back into their indigenizing re-visions of empire, exiting cities, leaving palaces, reschooling renegade resisters in the subsistence and nomadic skills necessary to a genuinely sabbatical partnership with the land.

Where the previous chapter dealt with the question of reading Sabbath-Jubilee in relationship to the biblical memory of land struggles, in chapter 3 we focus on a single set of seed-parables in the gospel of Mark, teasing out their potency from a permaculture perspective. Of particular note in Mark's rendition of the stories is their setting in a situation of soil-pedagogy for beleaguered peasants, under surveillance from dominating elites. The parables are displayed there as explicit counter-wisdom to market calculations and the imperative to hoard. But they are also "food for thought" about the power of the wild. The mustard seed parable in particular hints an agency beyond that of farming technology, playing on the prodigality of a spice-weed that seemingly sows itself. The slippage, woven into the telling, between shrub and tree—a nuisance-weed that suddenly morphs into a towering cedar—invites all manner of imaginative construction. Whether the point is cautionary (do you secretly hope that the destiny of "the kingdom" is that of becoming a mighty power like Babylon or Egypt?) or provocative (this is a "movement of the little" that grants "shade" and nurture in ways empire promises but never delivers) remains a matter of reading. But it can also be read "beyond the text" in an even broader compass of evolutionary logic in which invasive plants do represent a strategy of nature repairing its breeches in pushing towards something like climax forest ("big trees"). Here the reading begins to ferret out an "underground logic" of the messianic as harboring a subjectivity that is eco-systemic in extent.

Chapter 4 then waxes panoramic, offering a dialectical reprise of Christianity centered in the question sustainability. Situating the tradition in a wide-angle overview of human historical "development" running from hunter-gatherer existence, through settled agricultural organization, to modern industrial and technological innovation has the effect of underscoring Christianinty's basic social character. It emerges as a movement clearly shaped by the imperatives of an advanced agricultural society. This most consequential religious player on the world stage of today (at least in demographic terms) takes its major dialectical orientation not from a forager logic of engagement with a local eco-community of other life forms, but from the imperial surround of a peasant village-economy within which it signifies historically. Its primary focus is human communication, even though its sources of "revelation" admit profound input from plant and animal life. The bush of Moses and the dove of Jesus are underscored in the tradition as primal "media" of interdiction—in one case, interrupting the nomadic circulation of an octogenarian herder in the Sinai outback and in the other, driving a newly initiated peasant-laborer into the wilds of Judea for vocational "testing." In thus locating Christianity as itself formed in an agricultural ethic, the writing will tease out some of the resulting blind spots. The tack taken will involve listening deeply to indigenous cultures still partially embedded in an economics of reciprocity with their local ecologies as well as to hybridized traditions such as *vodou* practices or *ayahuasca* churches—often dismissed as heterodox—to articulate a constructive notion of Christology open to plant and animal forms of "incarnation." The core argument is that images of the means and media of salvation must move beyond a merely anthropocentric logic to recapture the ultimate significance of other life forms for human destiny.

Chapter 5 seeks firm ground in the face of high water. Taking off from the mounting force of ecological blowback such as we see in a storm like Katrina, this chapter opens perspective on the emergence of modern racial formation as the "ideologic" of conquest that has reorganized planetary ecosystems and cultures since 1492, with increasingly devastating effect. Working with Jared Diamond's genealogy of modern European ascendency over the globe, the argument sketches out the birthright and career path of white supremacy, as it has been elaborated as the apology for European march around the planet, licensing a Cain-like project of subjecting indigenous practices to Abel's fate, and doing so (at least thus far) without divine redress. Grafted into the project have been philosophical conceits as old as Plato's Great Chain of Being and theological certitudes as all determining as Calvin's supralapsarian projection. Even today, the argument will assert, neoliberal forms of globalization have as their subtext a certainty of superiority animating the drive to commodify an entire planet that primarily references white wealth and power. It began in early modernity as a mode of Christian supremacy that gradually birthed white supremacy—in the process decimating indigenous cultures. But beneath that great white overlay of "civilization," the claim will continue, lies buried an unkillable wild virtuosity, destined either to find social forms worthy of its vital mutualism or to escalate its search for such into ecologic comeuppance that will have the last word. As emblem of the stark difference—and intriguing possibility for "recovery"—marked out by indigenous knowledges not yet entirely eclipsed by white technologies, the essay will close with analysis of the adventures of conquistador Alvar Nuñez Cabeza de Vaca, on an intelligence-gathering mission along the Florida panhandle in 1526 until shipwrecked and stranded among the First Peoples of the area following a terrifying killer storm in the fall of 1527. Wandering westward for eight years after, Nuñez underwent profound "reprogramming" at the mercy of ecosystem harshness and indigenous wisdom alike, emerged from a winter-time ordeal of being lost in the wilds to native acclaim as shamanically appointed healer, effecting cures among his local companions in spite of his own disavowal of any requisite powers. This unwitting "re-baptism" of a white Christian conqueror in local native knowledge, mediated by ecosystem exigency, will stand as a "sign of the time" of our modern eco-crises that yet begs reading.

With chapter 6 we key in on the way an early Christian memory of female agency serves as an opening in the canon of domination for colonized peoples to insert ancestral imagery and deploy an alternative epistemology serving their own political existence. The appearance of a teenaged Mary at the beginning of Luke's "gospel to the Gentiles," gives laconic testament to a choice for motherhood answering to no male counsel, buttressed by support from an elder kinswoman that issues immediately in revolutionary rhetoric anticipating the downfall of power and the uplift of the poor. How this Mary becomes an iconic opening for indigenous re-imagining in the popular Catholicism of colonial and postcolonial Mexico, and anchors an entire menagerie of possession cult activity in the *vodou* practices of Haiti during and after slavery, will focus the inquiry. Gayatri Spivak's interrogation of the (im)possibility of subaltern speech and James Scott's notion of the difference between hidden and public transcripts supply the angles of approach by which to ferret out the polyvalence of meanings anchored by these icons of popular religiosity as they are danced and drummed, played and parroted in street contest and rural fest across the colonial landscape.

In each case, the claim will be that "what you see is not what you get," but rather, "what you see depends upon 'how you read' and indeed, 'how you let yourself be read by'" the phenomenon you are engaged with. Each of these "archetypes" is analyzed as the synergy of a collective and subaltern performance, enacting a kind of "geomantic contestation," a folk-agency, gathering up local custom in a picaresque ribaldry virtually indecipherable for official authority, reveling in renegade pleasures even as it suffers impossible contradictions. Not least among those pleasures is subaltern inversion of the strategies of domination by engulfing limitation in a voluptuousness of feedback. And it is precisely that interruption of the presumption to "know and control" that will be offered as crucial to the project of study. Looking out from the eye of Guadalupe or Ezili is a question of deep ancestry and "thick" ecstasy, asking the observer of such "performances" in kind: "Who possesses you and to what end?" The question here is a species of the broader issue of "ecological re-entrainment" that focuses this project. How recover communicative relationship with— and accountability to—the wildness that animates environments and bodies alike?

Chapter 7 entertains an unlikely commonality between *vodou veve* drawing in the ritual space of Haitian *peristils* and riffs of sound orchestrated in after-hours jam sessions in the jazz clubs of New Orleans or Chicago. The possibility that myth-work might be traced through handicraft on horn and floor will exercise imagination here. Embroidering texts of life in the tight corridors of a death sentence is not confined to narration. Cornmeal invocation and bent-brass incantation open momentary horizons for bodies-in-motion (in dance) to innovate a world otherwise than masters would allow. Myth coordinates contradiction into a hypothesis about living. In its textures, absurdity is relativized into meaning, rupture into resilience. Its animating feature is the break in existence occasioned by a radical advent—whether of new technologies of domestication or new lords of labor. Charles Long's comprehension of myth as making do under the duress of threatened demise will supply rich provocation with which to probe the gap in our own existence. What breaks out in late nineteenth-century second lines, dancing on the back of death in New Orleans, goes astral under the fingers of Miles, channeling cemetery haints into sonic haunts of urbanity. In one sense, this is the conjuring of the spirit of industrial metal and mineral into a two-step strut of defiance against the order of the factory. Mythic America confronts its own anti-myth, stealing forth in oblique horn squawks. Whether this human-possessed squall of technique, bending Euro-symphony into an improvised "sounding" of the underbelly of the country, also hints a new-god birth is the core inquiry. The long line of mythic advents from Earth Mothers to Sky Fathers congealing out of social ruptures teases the question: is the techno-fracture of modern existence combusting a deity adequate to the crisis? And how might we divine such?

Bringing the historical inquiry into our colonial legacy fully into the present lands us squarely in the presence of the cultural initiative most powerfully circling the globe today. Hip-hop wraps the world in a sonic Esperanto of shared syncopation. One of the innovations most notorious and indicative is scratch-work on the wheels of steel, taking the intersection of vinyl and needle into the ether-sphere of cyborg elocution. Chapter 8 samples the initiative. Afro-diasporic in genesis, the beat has augured deep under the surface of youth culture around the planet—showing up in one of its more radical incarnations inside a Filipino ensemble of turntablist impressarios on California's regularly quaked coast. Seismic in geologics, the place is also host to a seismic art. Among the talent, the fly-fingered wobble-wonk most infamous is a DJ by the name of Qbert, whose ethic of sharing product with his cohort goes against the beef and bite culture of MC-ing, and opens a collective exploration worthy of comparison with indigenous inclinations. Here, Qbert's aesthetic of cruising the volatile edge of techno-vibes, searching for sound-creatures adequate to the images that first assault his mind as shapes, takes us back to the old notion of shaman-flights in spirit-worlds invisible to the eye. To what degree Qbert can be lined up at the new end of a genealogy tracing back in ancestry to island healers who resisted colonial masters, opens a provocative question. *Babaylans* by name, some of these mystic hunters tracking soul loss and communal health found themselves impaled alive as crocodile bait on river banks, when their ways proved too resilient for Spanish overlords. Grafting insight from rainforest plant shamans into the mix, we will entertain Qbert as a postmodern variant of the mystic impulse, fathoming undercurrents of healing inside the machinery of industrialization by way of synesthetic elaborations of what does not submit to measure and profit in our time. Divining the "divine" outside the name, in electric skronks of sound, might seem beyond the compass of our concern for a dying planet. But just such a dive into pirated energies pulled up from the mineral underbelly of the planet may help open re-imagination of an older symbiosis.

After nearly a half-century of echoing some of the deepest contradictions of our current postindustrial condition, hip-hop has clearly established itself as an emergent phenomenon of tricksterism. Chapter 9 takes up the sound and mirrors the attitude. Insinuating itself by beat and style into local youth cultures of every stripe and orientation, the medium now hosts political visions as contrary as green anarchy and neo-Nazi nationalism, Palestinian intifada activists and Israeli Zionist militants, and boasts spiritual commitments as diverse as Jesus radicals and Nation of Islam conservatives, atheist "Nones" and Native American traditionalists. The essay here does not so much seek to describe the proliferation of the phenomenon as articulate its potential contribution to a "re-wilding" of Christian spirituality, in particular, that, ironically, might help open the latter to its indigenous forebears. Taking off from the imagery and lyrics of the recent Jay Z/Kanye West release called "No Church in the Wild," the analysis adopts the idiom to spin out a challenge to culture and church alike. The focus here is not hip-hop's surface features but its subtext and grammar. As a creature of urban decay in the deindustrialized South Bronx of the 1970s, the sonic apparition that emerged carried a full charge of its gritty surround. Here is wild memory gone digital, sounding out the eco-blight of its cradle with a temerity and hunger that remains unchecked. From its "Wild Style" beginnings under a Bambaataa beat, through its mid-90s "2pocalypse" of coastal battles, to its current underground duress, stressing local struggle for a better world in a thousand different theaters of youth activism, hip-hop, like no other religio-cultural aspiration of the time, has given texture to the untamed and game to the strain of DNA not yet capitulated to a drone-future of complete control by the corporate state. Certainly co-opted by the latter, in bed with the dollar, and too often treading the mill of "getting over" through bling, booty, and hollering, the culture nonetheless continues to channel something old and irrepressible. Reading its hidden transcript of wild bluster and ecstatic posture—even, when necessary, against its own drift—the exposé here continues the work of exhibiting ancestral memory and eco-systemic upwelling inside formations modern and compromised. The argument here is finally one that asks of all our attempts to exit the imperial script and "de-colonize": "How far down into the murk of the past must we go?" And it will insist that is it not enough to blow hard for mere inclusion in the Dream and join the middle class in scheming to continue the rape of the planet. The need is rather to listen at the level of the heart, gather energy from the groin, ferret out the pain of the ages, be summoned by the heavy gauge of planetary demise, go wild in cries and desires, and recover the possibility of having a future in concert with the rest of life.

Our final walkabout loops around to the first. Chapter 10 brings the historical discussion back home toward the kind of theorizing of personal experience with which the book began. Here the focus is on the task of receiving deep challenge from human "others" as the necessary concomitant for being reschooled by the ecology of otherkind itself. Once again the motive force grows out of increasing recognition of the limits and failures of the project of modernity from the point of view of indigenous experience and lifeways. At one level the issue is one of romance. Often accused of fetishizing the "noble native," my own comeback is often to invert the charge. The crises we currently navigate—casino finance ripping apart local economies, neoliberal fundamentalism pushing austerity for the sake of corporate "liberation," US "green-zone" imperialism generating terroristic blowback from its relentless extension of invasion and drone-terrorism, and now levels of environmental blowback that threaten the viability of the species itself—effectively challenge academic theory and middle-class dreaming to face the romance we actually "live." Technology, development, and growth are the fetish forms that have brought us to the edge of the cliff. What might it take actually to listen to peoples and cultures not yet entirely engulfed in the reigning delusion that business-as-usual can continue? Part of the question here is one of "reverse hermeneusis": how take in critique from those positioned subaltern to one's own position and programming? The reflection tacks back and forth between this white male's experience of being "rearranged" by black challenge on the ground in Motown and a Filipina partner's quite different experience of struggling with the fraught politics of the postcolony in the islands. The former has meant resolve to remain involved in black-led struggle against white power prerogatives while continually embracing ever-deepening awareness of personal failure and compromise and internalizing a different habit of being. The latter has opened into recognition that Filipino resistance to Spanish colonialism and US imperialism all the way up to present has often come at the expense of indigenous survival or flourishing (in the particular case here, Kapampangan lowlanders pushing indigenous Aeta out of their homelands in the very effort to take over Clark Air Base from the United States). For each, the task has meant living and theorizing in a crucible of contradiction where "innocence" is impossible. Precisely at the juncture where struggles for inclusion in modernity on the part of populations of color meet the delirium and destructiveness of modernity itself, the deep question of the hour arises. How discover that the Dream is really a Nightmare and re-orient toward what has actually worked for our species on the planet?

FROM SYCAMORE TREES TO HUMAN DESTINY: READING THE WILD AT THE CROSSROADS OF GLOBALIZATION AND APOCALYPSE

Thenceforth natural things are not only themselves but a speaking.

—*Paul Shepard*, Nature and Madness

The only way to begin this writing is with a form of confession. The planet is in trouble. It is not a time simply to "do theory." The signals are unmistakable for anyone willing to look. An interlocking quaternary of apocalyptic forces—peak oil, climate change, species extinction, and population overshoot—ride in upon us relentlessly like horsemen from the end times. M. King Hubbard's modeling of the peak production of modernity's primary energy resource accurately predicted the decline of U.S. oil production in the mid-1970s and served notice that such a global peak was in the offing (no matter how ferocious the attempts to enter Faustian bargains of self-delusion with our zooplankton and algae ancestors whose viscous bodies are the lifeblood of industrial civilization). There were only so many trillion trillion deaths in the planet's oceans over the millions of years leading up to this one, and the supply of "black gold," however tweaked by new technologies of extraction, is limited. But, as climate change denier Richard Muller (2012) has acknowledged, even if that peak is pushed out a few decades hence by tar sands fever, it will not much matter at today's rates of CO2 emissions. Political gridlock, corporate constitution in the imperative of growth, and all the reigning idolatries of short-term gain interlocked with take-no-prisoners advertising and its consumer culture offspring, translate into a depressing scenario. The recasting of human interaction as cyborg in social media fora—granting "full metal jacket" forms of isolated connectivity devoid of organic modes of vulnerability and measurably eroding our evident capacity for empathy and self-limitation—only compounds the issue. All of this coalesces into an accelerating rush toward the tipping point of unstoppable warming that does not seem remediable in our current possibilities of self-editing. Peak oil concerns may well be eclipsed in short order by peak air and peak water realities.

PLANETARY EXTINCTION?

Meanwhile, in the last century we have altered a long-standing balance between species extinction and new species incubation rates, which has us plundering the biosphere's generative capacity—and shredding its ecodiversity—with rapacity. As one commentator now argues—it is like constructing an ever-ascending tower to house our species ever closer to technocracy's vision of a high-rise heaven by ever-more furiously pulling out the bricks lower down to build with ever-increasing alacrity the next layer above (Quinn, 2007). The future of such an enterprise will remain "bullish" until the brick that is one too many is finally pried loose. And, slum cities of multiple millions cropping up almost overnight across the planet's global south, skyrocketing total population numbers toward nine billion (or more)—only deepens the thickening gloom! National governments make common cause with transnational finance and privatized militance—creating ceaselessly revolving doors between boardrooms, west wings, pentagons, and bedrooms, and erecting insurmountable lifestyle buffers between policy deciders and the effects of their decisions on those slum-dwelling denizens. The entire ruling apparatus appears increasingly as one cartel, under the dollar, invisibly ensconced behind state-of-the-art security and ruthlessly secessionist on a planetary scale—until the wrong technology falls into the wrong hand of rage and a nuclear winter or biotoxic horror is visited upon everyone.

In the face of such a dilemma, how might one say anything meaningful about "communication" that was not sheer twaddle? I do not pretend to know how to answer such a charge, except to say that the problem of secession identified here as promulgated by ruling class elites vis-à-vis everyone else, is even more radically the problem between modern humanity writ large and the rest of the biosphere. The question on the table of academic deliberation at least—if, indeed, not of every other area of human endeavor—is simply this: What does it mean to be human? We have evolved a form of knowledge production that resembles a hive of worker bees tending feverishly to their respective honey holes without a clue that the entire comb has been cut loose from the tree and fallen into a north-flowing river just south of Niagara Falls, New York. The interlocking crises should push us to stop in our tracks and recognize that continuing to do the same thing over and over again in expectation of a different result is indeed, as Einstein opined, the practical definition of insanity.

The logic of expansionist civilization inherited from a 10,000-year-old turn toward monocrop agriculture, driven by imperial demand for ever-greater technologies of control and ever-larger citadels of accumulation and unleashed on a planet of finite resources, simply cannot be sustained.[1] And as one scholar writing on these issues offers: "What can't be sustained . . . can't be sustained" (Jensen, 2008). We keep dodging the feedback from the biosphere in hopes that the social structures we have cantilevered over the limit of the planet's carrying capacity (Heinberg, 2014) will somehow find new support from some unforeseen technological innovation. And thus we will not really have to stop and do something different. I have no crystal ball and so cannot infallibly gainsay that hope. I can only say that for me—and a growing host of others who are trying to look reality in the eye without blinking—the ecological blowback is stark and demands radical rethinking of our entire career on the planet as a species. It means stripping down to the pith, reimagining the root, asking the unanswerable questions all over again: Why are we here? What does it mean to be alive?

"Human" Communication

Communication is everywhere—a grand phenomenon of nature taking place at every level of the cosmos: from bacteria sending out chemical "shouts" to their environments in search of return signatures indicating like-configured bacterial explorers in the same neighborhood to quasars and microwave hum from the primordial event of big bang yet sounding across the expanding bubble of the macro-space we naively call the uni-verse. Our own particular frequency of exchange within that grand cacophony is immensely narrow and tiny, embedded within an implicate order of ever-recalibrating waves of information and energy that makes Pythagoras's music of the spheres but a minute intuition of the whole. And yet something as human and vernacular as black church's call-and-response or Inupiat throat singing turns out to be a rough imitation of the ultimate conversation, both a riff upon and a model of what is going on intergalactically. Perhaps more to the point, we need to attend to the researches of E. T. Hall and William Condon from early in the history of the discipline of communication studies to the effect that the call and the response are actually happening simultaneously with each other, as the ever-emergent phenomenon of entrainment, and not as a cause-effect progression of linear events, threaded onto a line of time like beads on an abacus (Leonard, 1978, 14–22). There is indeed a temporal priority that invigorates our own genesis on the planet. But it is one in which we are the dependent beneficiaries of the grand concert of life forms who have distilled tested and true survival strategies in syncopated interactions with local ecologies for a millennial millennia of centuries before we arrived, late and now lost, on the many-layered scene. As a recent twist in the shape and thrust of spiraling strands of DNA coating the planet in strobing signals of photon exchanges and electromagnetic pulsations, we are "bathed" in communication. We find ourselves awaking on a stage not only set for, but composed by and of, an unfathomable quadrillion of others, whose very existence is lived literally through us, as indeed we live through them. The fundamental structure of what "is"—and the primordial communication echoing forth *from* and *as* that structure—is the metabolism of everything by and with everything else.

It is "eating and being eaten" all the way up and down the phylum. It is our destiny to become food for other life forms and our vocation to compost other life forms into the peculiar beauty and singular significance we mysteriously embody. But our mystery is no more than that of any other composite of this writhing codification of information called life. And that seems to be the great forgotten import that our strange eco-autistic affliction of self-reflection has somehow effaced from our otherwise quite formidable consciousness. We have incarcerated ourselves in the markings of our minds and the languages of our lips—like some huge Alcatraz of the imagination fogged in with words upon words upon words—forgetting that we are far more than a mere ocular substrate for the products of Maybelline and its parent corporation or the advertising orgasm that finds its most coveted stimulation in that part of our anatomy. Indeed, the 65 to 92 percent of our "being" that is communicating other than through our voice box is coparticipant in a nuanced and throbbing dance at every level. These range from the atomic and molecular inside our own bodies, where we ricochet around as minorities in the ecodiversity of bacteria living there, to the balletic stages of New York City and the robotic streets of South Central, whence we turn for relief and healing from our automaton-existence inside the corporate state, on out to the moon tides and sun flares that choreograph our blood beats and punctuate our body rhythm with novelty. Just where we should be directing our attention, inside this living vibraphone of communication as a species priding itself on some measure of self-consciousness, is no mean question.

I would argue for something quite prosaic and yet disturbingly profound in what I take to be an apocalyptic situation. Journalism scholar Robert Jensen suggests that we are today a species "out of place," trying to occupy a niche for which we are ill-equipped genetically (Jensen, 2008). Thus far relatively "hard-wired" by our Pleistocene inheritance to value morally and pay attention emotionally to what is about 100 yards around us in any direction, and bearing a cranial size capable of dealing with fewer than 150 relationships socially with any kind of complexity and nuance (what anthropologists are now calling the "rule of 150"; Wells, 2010, 118–119; 205), we are in trouble. Our wet dream of representative democracy among 300 million political actors in this country alone, or equitable living and sustainable dwelling among seven billion co-tenants of a militantly globalized economy, seems patently delusional in its ceaseless projections of progressive attainment. If we just try a bit harder. Run a little faster. Consume more rampantly. Kill a bit more efficiently. Grow more exponentially—we'll get there! Technology will indeed save us!?

Dialectical Identification

Maybe. But I find my deepest responses evoked by a range of voices insisting the only way forward is by taking deep stock of where we have already been—and that by way of radical apprenticeship to where we still remain: as one animal species among millions of species of other life forms. We are not yet able to eat our computers or drink our motor oil. And the research continues to indicate that our mental health declines in inverse proportion to the layers of machine we introduce between our bodies and those of our photosynthetic cousins outside our windows, whose green-producing miracles as the lone "self-feeders" ("autotrophs") of the planet—creating living matter out of hard rock and sunlight—literally creates the envelope of oxygen and animation upon which we all depend (Rasmussen, 214). (Seeing living plants outside one's window has measurable effects on health beyond that of observing a Screensaver depiction of foliage, according to recent research; Williams, 2012). All flesh *is* finally grass, as the Hebrew prophet Isaiah once raged, and thus it is no great wonder that for indigenous cultures the globe over, "grass" itself is the great primal godess to which all the rest of the pantheon offers homage.

And thus begins to re-emerge a perhaps strange suggestion in the face of collapse. Learn the language of an animal. Talk to a plant. Recover a sense of one's destiny as irretrievably intertwined with other life forms, whose communication and commensality is the very material and meaning of "being" alive. If I were "God," I'm not sure I would have arranged it that way. Warped as I am by my schooling in industrial culture, my lifestyle trajectory is more that of the "Borg" of *Star Trek* fame than the blue-skinned hunter-gatherer creatures *Avatar* names as "*Na'vi*." At least that would have to be the assessment if one judged by how and where I actually live, as compared with how I might fantasize or speak. But the returns today on industrial culture and its agricultural fore-parent are so far dismal. "Civilization," in spite of its vaunted achievements, has never not been built on coerced labor and violent exploitation, and has almost nowhere proven durable on the face of the planet in a 10,000-year career (Rasmussen, 1995, 41). The environmental "communication" of our time—really a compound form of feedback from . . . fish, and fungi—is at the very least the word, "Stop!" Ventriloquized through a human imagination such as mine it sounds thus: "Halt and listen! You are not the only being present here. We have something to say. Indeed, we have been talking all the way along the time line and you used to be able to hear. In fact, you cannot be *you* if you cannot hear *us*. If our very pheromones are to your anemic postmodern nostrils only so much stench, as Agent Smith snorted over the sweating head of Morpheus, then indeed *Matrix* is right. You have already become merely a Smith-clone; your organic metabolism of other organic bodies merely the fat and grease and calories of the great corporate machine whose algorithms have effectively 'eaten' you."

If human identity is fundamentally dialectical, gradually constructing itself in a crucible of negotiation with its quintessential others, then we could track human development as having "progressed" over its time on the planet through three gradually shifting moments:

1. a primordial indigenous identity as *living animal* worked out in our varied ecologies of origin (African savannah, Gobi desert, Amazonian rainforest, etc.) in languages populated by immense vocabularies of the flora and fauna regularly encountered and known in reciprocal modes of exchange in those ecologies;

2. a recent (10,000-year-old) agricultural experiment in which identity is increasingly fabricated by elites, sequestered away from plant and animal encounters in moat-protected "castles," as an ideological bribe and hollow palliative foisted on their laboring populations who create the wealth they hoard and consume, in which violent contact with other *human* cultures, encountered in the relentless project of expansion, becomes dialectically decisive for one's own sense of self, offering images of the despised and racialized "stranger" as the negative foil for identification, the savage sign of what one supposedly is *not*;

3. our current fetishization of the machine, emerging as the second and third and fourth skin of the human organism, the hardened carapace of urban concrete and suburban steel whose belly we inhabit like futuristic Jonahs without a beach in sight, the plastic and glass and vinyl cocoons in which we eat and sleep and watch our manifold screens, the molded alloys we drive, the silicon and plasma through which we communicate, the titanium and chemistry we splice into our ailing bodies, the GMO foods we wittingly or not eat, the whole spectral mass of re-engineered biosphere now rising up before us as messianic *cyborg* whose indestructibility is sold as a secret religion to our children through their wide-eyed consumption of "Transformer" toys and "Terminator" stars, against whose overwhelming engulfment we can barely find momentary escapist relief in recreation with a re-engineered "goofy" called a "pet" or visitation with an enslaved anomaly in a "zoo." I increasingly encounter students now who confess to closing their blinds at home because they are actually *afraid* of trees and grass. The cyborg is here. The question now is where is the human?

Personal Intimation

My own life trajectory has been one of continuous pilgrimage into deep encounters with cultures and people different from myself. I am a white male middle class heterosexual by background and conditioning who has lived the majority of his life in the inner city—mostly in Detroit. Without question my most profound educational formation has been "ghetto" street life over the course of four decades. There, low-income neighbors checked, challenged, embraced, rebuffed, and taught me, in what has amounted to an ongoing rite of initiation into another way of being a body, under protocols of rhythm and percussion, signifying and rhyme-spitting, dozens-playing and "jiving," that broke down the codes of bourgeois morality and presuppositions of supremacy I had internalized growing up, and opened a way to experiment with being "something else." The process continues today. Most of my academic work has entailed theorizing in both religious studies and communication studies discourses about race and racism animated by that personal trek across the boundaries separating black from white. And then late in the day, I married a Filipina and found myself confronted all over again with the need to undergo yet another regime of border crossing. This time it was into a culture structured in what one Filipino ethnomusicologist called a curvilinear tonality of communicating—both strangely similar to and yet confoundingly different from the percussive sensibility I had slowly internalized in inner-city Detroit. And yet again I have had to embrace a recurrent experience of awkward failure and apologetic chagrin as I seek to submit to a new protocol of embodiment in service of expanding my capacity for radical joy and the sweet tang of intimacy.

But now, even later in life, yet a third demand for journey has emerged with a vengeance. And that is an inverse climb back down the phylogenetic tree—in relationship to all of those plant and animal and fungi ancestors whose prowess and potencies have recombined in sexual and metabolic processes over multiple millions of years to produce "me." More specifically, such a trek requires entertaining the nurture and pedagogy of nonhuman genealogy. In encounter with indigenous cultures here and in the Philippines, and through wide-ranging reading in a newly emerging literature going by the name of anarcho-primitivism—asking deep questions about the impossible viability of civilization as we have thus far known it—I become more and more aware that "human emergence" over the vast reaches of our time on the planet has typically entailed profound apprenticeship to a given plant or animal "relative" in relationship to an intact local ecology. That relationship effectively became our earliest (and continuing) sensorium, in which "identity" was learned dialectically through symbiotic communication and reciprocal commensality. And given that evolutionary history, I must now confess that I am so far in my own life's unfolding a "not yet human" human being. Rather, I face in the mirror each morning, an immature configuration of cells, fizzed up in a thousand commercialized discourses to hanker after books and french fries, lattes, and hot showers. I have attained middle age without yet having been "initiated" into the living matter which is our living *mater*, and cracked open to the vital insurrection of wild-spirited animation that is simply the way things are in nature. And I stumble now toward old age with inconsolable longing and inchoate aching for that early boyhood level of awakening that first caught sight of the stunning magnificence and intolerable beauty of life and loss in this world.

My first real inkling of what it might mean to be alive outside the womb came when I was but five years old. On a summer late afternoon in an open acre behind our house a towering sycamore suddenly breathed on me with its ever so subtle pungency of dry-heat scent. A looming solidity hovered in the cicada-keened shaft of light, cutting through its leaves and my skin with a vast Something, indefinable as taste, insoluble as hunger. I suddenly knew the strange touch of beauty and grief that haunts every moment of actually *seeing* into a thing, without explaining either it or oneself, of stumbling across an invisible line into an immensity of presence that simultaneously provokes immense melancholy because it cannot be possessed or kept from sliding into the eclipse of night, any more than my own being could be. The moment was one of abrupt voluptuousness and galactic sadness all at once, a huge, wild beast of response that broke surface in my young body like an unsuspected whale from the depths, carrying me over into the body of the world around me as if there was no barrier between. Today in my adult voice, I would argue that such experience is simply what it means to be a child and suddenly "see" into the sheer magic of the natural world—a quality of experience every one of us is designed *for*, in some version or another, but which becomes increasingly remote or even impossible as machine culture gathers us into itself relentlessly. Indeed, many adults I know today would say, "Oh come on, Jim, cut the New Age crap, it was just a tree, not a snort of cocaine!" But that is the entire point: there is no such thing as "just a tree." That is "just a concept." The real thing is . . . !? What is a tree? Do we really *see* it? Can *you* make one? In any case, it was a moment I would never recover from, however much it might be covered over as the years rolled on. Rather, it was something I would grope for—usually unknowingly when late afternoon sunlight takes on a particular cast. In all the seasonal drifts to follow—lurched by my various choices into a living concatenation of such seeing and its losses—I remain irrecoverably aware, before and beyond words, that life is an uncloseable hole of grief and beauty into which one falls incessantly. Or else runs from and dies coldly.

But that suddenly sentient tree of my boyhood would also show its terroristic side—the terribleness of its wildness—only a year or so later, when during a thunderstorm, it would just as suddenly drop an arm on the head of a seven-year-old friend of mine, running home from the rain straight into the path of the descending branch. The falling limb caused a concussion and shattered any illusions of deference to things human that such a newborn lover as myself might be tempted to predicate of its majesty. The tree was, after all, committed merely to being a sycamore, surging up in infinite slow motion in its own great photon love, hosting the million-fold drama of life and death composting within and composing its own bark and branches and roots and shade, without favoring any. And I was merely a human being, suddenly awake to what was so much bigger than me, trying to walk forward in this little sliver of reality called my body, *without* a society or community around me to give orientation or meaning to that experience. I could hardly tell anyone, as the moment did not come contained in the thin coin of words and grammar. It came as an entire world, pouring in through my pores, without fanfare or business cards.

COMMUNAL PRIVATION

But the ghosting of the experience remains a "ghost," a haunting—questing for a body worthy of its intensity. I now recognize its real subject—the only interpretive body capable of giving "human" texture to its significance—is what anthropology would call a band community, small enough to know all of its members, tempered and tuned to a given ecology over multiple generations by its own locally born mythology and ritual practices. The culture of such a community historically encoded all such immensities of touch and smell and sight and sound in a shared fabric of meaning. Its carefully tended root was the other life forms providing the second womb of existence in that particular place in the world. Its imagined destiny was literally the overhead canopy of observed infinity whose night-revealed face we can no longer grasp as light-blinded, machine-bound urbanites. And while the reality of such communities is rapidly being extinguished today, intimation of this kind of ancient hunter-gatherer existence still lives inchoate and writhing-with-longing in our cyborg-saturated psyches.

But the best we can do is Facebook. Or Twitter, as we head to the mall, trying to reproduce in mere sound bites that longed-for connection in all the intimacy of its richly sensate detail, transacting through smell and sound and feel with a local living ensemble of kindred living beings who really are "all our relations" (*mitaquwe oyasin*, according to the Lakota). And the resulting absurdity of trying to erect deep meaning on top of displaced matter, ripped from its living context and incarcerated in commodified paper and price tags, leaves us numb with boredom. We grow desperate with emptiness in the midnight hours when we can no longer fend off the whispering demons of our loneliness with whatever happens to be our latest addiction. We have become an autistic species, imprisoned in the machinery of our own image and making, wailing in fevered silences and deadened satieties for something whose loss we do not even know *to* grieve any longer, much less *how*. I am a wild child of an animal locked inside a tamed and terrorized adult, uninitiated in the body of my ecology and ancestry. I look helplessly to a machine-surround of enslaved matter—a house in a city, navigated by a car, flooded with neon, covered with cement, coded in digits—to provide what only *wild nature* can give. I am made for a living texture that matches my own, as stunningly beautiful and ferociously mortal as my own heart and flesh. A tree!—not a computer—has been the source of the most profound communication of my life.

But I have had no school capable of educating me into the nuances and epiphany of all its subtleties. I have no community ready to introduce me into a lifespan of reciprocity—in a local human-tree symbiotics of community and communication—that would grant over time, to my entire sensing anatomy, the knowledge of what it means to live and die in such a place, *as part of all of the other living and dying going on in that place*. A computer can give me information about all of that living. But it cannot give any sense to all of the dying, including my own. Computers don't die; they just freeze up and are thrown away, to bleed the toxins of their recombinatory chemistry and metallurgy into somebody else's environment. And thus it is that they teach me about myself—silently intimating that my destiny is a huge warehouse called Florida, where I will be stacked up with 10 million other failing flesh machines, whose entire significance of slowly disappearing is keeping Nike and Callaway in profits.

To the real question mark of existence, there is no textbook answer, no longitudinal data gathering and academic shifting of communication theories, capable of rousing the sensitivity and passion adequate to what is actually going on. There is only the possibility of shivering before the unutterable eloquence of what is alive, and keening before its inevitable destruction and loss. Living grief continues to throb—un-honored and without a mythological idiom or ritual forum adequate to its communication—under our machine skin. Our ancestry calls, the bear calls, the loon cries, the moon woos . . . But we just open another Budweiser, flick the channel-changer, and settle into our couch—sure the only message worthy of our attention is the electronic face appearing there, speaking imperial English. There is no word left inside this machine for what we actually are. But if that is the only place we can now look for the communication that does matter, because we no longer know how to communicate in any other way, with any other living intelligences, it doesn't matter. We have already become extinct. The rest is just history.

THEORETICAL REEXAMINATION

But there remain a few communities on the planet that some scholars would actually esteem—rather than lament as Hegel did—for their ability to exist "outside" history, as we know it. History of religions legend Mircea Eliade (however we might evaluate his politics) is one who queried our Western certainty that historical discourse and narratives of linear "progress" are evidence of advancement, in favor of folk around the globe living closer to the ground and more intimately involved with natural cycles and seasonal rhythms (Eliade, ix, 95, 153–154). The late Yankton Sioux lawyer/activist/ theologian Vina Deloria argued that Native Americans lived not "in" history, but inside mythologies, pursuing not "clear and distinct ideas" as Europeans have fetishized ever since Descartes, but "visions" (Deloria, 1999, 105, 119, 126, 143, 157). These wide-angle "pictures" were quested for in wild settings, carried for a lifetime, interpreted in a community. They were lived as a gestalt of meaning, ritualized and elaborated through generations inside an ecology of shared being. There, the lines of demarcation between humans, animals, plants, spirits, ancestors, rocks, mountains, trees, rivers, stars, and Earth itself were understood as permeable and temporary, admitting both intercourse and communication. Such relations demanded both respect and the risk of crossing. Indeed, indigenous cultures the world over bear similar witness—to the degree they remain conversant with their respective habitats and resistive to Western epistemologies and the penetrations of globalized capital. They insist human being is contingent upon and constituted by interaction and communication with the living envelope of "otherkind" that is its larger "body" and real community, into which ancestors transform and from which new generations arise.

And in many ways today, science and theory are now beginning to confirm the intuition, pushing us moderns to face the degree to which we inhabit a paradox. At once physically intimate with our surroundings while profoundly alienated psychically and culturally—many of us today find it at least mildly shocking that we remain vulnerable to the waters we drink and become, the soils we absorb in our greens and metabolize as muscle, the air we transfigure into both flesh and spirit, even as such exchanges fade from our ritual appreciation or conscious attention. Lacanian feminist Marxist Theresa Brennan, for instance, takes on the continuing Enlightenment predilection for autonomous understandings of humanity by working to return a calculation of nature's immense efforts to Marx's "labor theory of value" (Brennan, 1993, 124 ff, 210 ff). One of her books focuses on the role of pheromones in human consciousness, going so far as to argue that we will not fully grasp the latter until we comprehend the effects of the former in galvanizing our repertoire of attractions and repulsions and inflecting our agency (Brennan, 2004, 9–11, 68–69, 112).

Cultural critic Norbert Elias diagnoses modern experience as malady. He offers a kaleidoscopic history of embodiment, tracking the degree to which—as I hinted in many of my comments above—we are incarcerated in an entire somatic *habitus*, increasingly closing us off from more organic transactions with each other and with "animality" in general. For Elias, this modern habituation reconstitutes us as what he calls *homo clausus*. We emerge in history as the great enclosed ones—increasingly walled off from the Bakhtinian "grotesque body" of the Middle Ages, which was routinized and licensed to exchange substance with other open bodies in regular ritual happenings like the Feast of Fools or May Day celebrations (Mennell and J. Goudsblom, 1998, 269; Bakhtin, 1984, 11, 27, 32, 84). Instead we stake our lives on a huddled existence inside an "individualized" identity. This individualized body is largely unexercised in intense emotional expression. Schooled in bourgeois niceties and decorum, "civilized" into a cosmetic appearance and a physiognomy of politesse, the modern individual seems capable only of the momentary "intensities" Lyotard might theorize, but devoid of the durable ferocities of grand passions and fierce living (Lyotard, 194). (Extreme sports might indeed be theorized as a postmodern reaction to such.)

And especially suggestive for this line of argument is the Spanish colonial trope of *reducciones*. The vaunted Jesuit communities called "Reductions" (in centuries-long missions in South America) committed their pastoral energies to pulling natives out of their jungle habitats and "reducing" them into "civilized" morality under priestly surveillance and Inquisitorial torture. Within such a disciplinary enterprise, native body and psyche alike were ramified as the quality-control products of the well-oiled machine of Euro-domination (Dussel, 1995, 68–69). But inevitably, the discipline cut both ways. The "reduction" of indigenous identity to a dark and disfigured shadowing of Euro-whiteness, as black theologian Willie James Jennings argues, worked the topside of the colonial divide as well (Jennings, 2010, 58–62, 78, 82–83, 96).

On the other hand, techno-feminist Donna Haraway gains contemporary fame as the diva of postmodernist cyborg thinking, exploding modernist fictions of individualistic agency and autonomous dwelling. Her work constructs a comprehensive re-visioning of reality as thoroughly hybrid across multiple borders of technology, metabolism, fecundation, cross-pollination, defecation, and organo-mineral exchanges writ large (Haraway, 1992, 298–99, 313, 331). Rather than the supposedly autonomous individual, her "unit" of analysis reveals itself as a caterwauling tricksterism of interpenetrations under no one's ultimate control and direction, untheorizable under a single sign, eluding in extent and complexity alike, the regime of human thought beholden to scientific experimentation.

INDIGENOUS RECAPITULATION

All of these theoretical initiatives offer insight relevant to the argument being constructed here. But it is especially to the cogitations of anarcho-primitivist pioneer Paul Shepard that this particular slant of challenge owes much of its heat. Shepard—intrepid interdisciplinary voyageur that he is—is deeply unimpressed with modern humanity. Where we continuously (and now ever more desperately) hum the mantra of progress, he sees profound immaturity and pathology, a culture as self-harming and autodestructive as it is lethal for its planetary home. But while the evidence of civilizational dysfunction piles up exponentially over the course of his life, Shepard never waxes pontifically strident about its "original sin." He rather traces a slowly generating aberration—an animal, wired into a two-decades-long process of epigenesis[2] as necessary to arriving at mature ontogenesis at age 20 or so, that gradually stumbles away from what would educate and rouse its robust flourishing. Ranging across biology, genetics, zoology, anthropology, psychology, ethology, history, theology, poetics, and myth, Shepard begins his academics with works like *Environ/Mental: Essays on the Planet as a Home*, treks through *The Tender Carnivore and the Sacred Game*, ruminates *Nature and Madness* and *The Others: How Animals Made Us Human*, to end with *Coming Home to the Pleistocene, Traces of an Omnivore* and *The Only World We've Got*. These wildly synthetic achievements—whose reach and depth at once astonish and provoke—defy easy summary. Here we will settle for a focus on *Nature and Madness* to convey the flavor.

In that work, Shepard outlines the trajectory. We began, he muses, as a species living in "stable harmony" with nature not merely out of reverence or incapacity to do otherwise, but for a "deeper reason still"

(Shepard, 1982, 4). The change that began 5,000 to 10,000 years ago, Shepard reads as "madness," a failure or mistakenness that is not easily accounted for. Neither the result of necessity nor the eclipse of old gods—this creeping irrationality emerges largely unconsciously. Observably, it fosters a sense of mastery, a growing willingness to extirpate nonhuman life, a wrenching apart of the "ancient social machinery that had limited human births" (Shepard, 1982, 4). The expansion of material demands—covering the land with the destructive "progress" of civilization—he comprehends not as cause but conse-quence of the change. But he also insists that what once was, yet germinates within us, as what should be.

The capacity of "relic, tribal peoples" to live at peace within a given local world, treading lightly as guests rather than masters, Shepard chalks up to an ontogeny "more normal" than our own and does so precisely in the face of charges of sentimentality and romanticism (Shepard, 1982, 6). He judges such a lifeway the product of natu-ral selection. Group members proceed through an entire calendar of stages, outfitting them with an orientation toward the world as mys-terious and beautiful, imbuing everyday life with spiritual significance, and mapping passage by means of ritual celebration experienced as integral participation in "the first creation."

Played out along an individual life, those stages find their first moment in the "infant as person-to-be" nestled in the arms of a nur-turing mother. From the very beginning, this newborn experiences the surround of plants and animals as the "stuff of a second ground-ing . . . in some sense another inside, a kind of enlivenment of that fetal landscape which is not so constant as once supposed" (Shepard, 1982, 7). Here, in this bright new world of texture, smell, and motion, says Shepard, "there are as yet few mythical beasts, but real creatures to watch and to mimic in play," each of which "seems to embody some impulse, reaction, or movement that is 'like me'" and by which, when enacted in play, "comes a gradual mastery of the personal inner zool-ogy of fears, joys, and relationships" (Shepard, 1982, 7).

At puberty, however, the immediate givenness of that original tax-onomy of living forms is cracked open in the ordeals and testing of ini-tiation. Under wise guidance of elders, this primal and originary world is reentered at a new point of ingress as disclosing a kind of infinity of meaning and possibility. Here the ones coming of age will learn that those early experiences were effectively a language. In myth and ritual, these natural things are revealed as "not only themselves, but a speaking" (Shepard, 1982, 9). This is a world from which there is no graduation. Adolescent initiation opens a lifelong process of study and quest into an ever-expanding dimension of significance and creativity. The beloved world of childhood is not left behind as illusion or mere metaphor, but is deepened as a tangible domain of poetics—numinous, analogical, endless as thought itself (Shepard, 1982, 9).

And this then is the basic claim of Shepard, repeated and reinforced throughout his life's work. Within its compass, modern society is read as an anomalous achievement. It tends to reproduce human beings at one very deep level as children in adult bodies, stuck between worlds, grafting infant impulses and childhood fears and adolescent grandiosity onto adult projects, outfitted with ideology and armies leading to all the destructive consequences we've witnessed growing up around us over the last 5,000 years. But in tracing such, Shepard is far from hopeless himself. All of his work is an attempt to outline a possibility.

He ends *Nature and Madness* with an article of natural faith. Beneath civilization's facade lies a primal impulse. Not an animal or barbarian as humanism would have it, but a human birthed into a sense of reciprocal validity waiting to happen. This "secret person" knows the rightness of dwelling in a setting of natural rhythm, play with living creatures, the schooling of the wild as a discipline, the joy of simple tools, food as gift received with art and gratitude, the plentitude of natural phenomenon as living metaphor, the relief of life in face-to-face community, ritual initiation and lifelong mentorship in moving from neophyte to elder through carefully crafted and tended stages (Shepard, 1982, 130). The spontaneous response to these is immediate—even in the broken forms they assume in contemporary society: animal fascination twisted into pet-love and zoos and cartoons; body poetics reduced to machine algorithms; pubertal idealism subverted into the perverse logics of national or racial or religious fundamentalisms rather than ecophilosophic flowering (Shepard, 1982, 130). The task is not one of creating something new, but recovery of what is very much alive and waiting. Its advent does not require a strained metaphysics of reconciliation with the earth, but of something "much more direct and simple."

That directness may be as simple as the smell of a tree and late afternoon light. The deep demand of a humane response to the state of the planet today may in part hinge on what most would consider an oblique and archaic consideration: a return to ancestries human and other. What if there really is no other way to achieve health and a viable future than to do so at the level of a local ecosystem, with its teachings of skin and feather, soil and weather? The writings to follow here will explore this intimation from multiple angles across various disciplines.

PART I

THE QUESTION IN THE BIBLICAL TRADITION: COMMUNICATION AND RESISTANCE

Chapter 2

Cain's Offering and Abel's Cry:
Reading Sabbath Jubilee
at the Crossroads of Farming
and Foraging

As indicated in chapter 1, sustainability has emerged in recent years as perhaps the burning question of our time, pointing to the interlocking crises sweeping toward us from the future. Peaking reserves of global oil deposits, potentially runaway climate change, species extinction, water table depletion, and population overshoot threaten the viability of our species on the face of the planet. Eco-scientist James Lovelock of Gaia fame is convinced that the planet is already in the process of eliminating us as too dangerous to the homeostasis necessary for biosphere continuity. Geo-engineering writer Gwynne Dyer, though less totalizing in his alarm, is another scientific voice beginning to break the silence about the growing terror in the science community that our current political gridlock will not be able to loosen and respond before the tipping point into unstoppable warming is reached. Certainly no one can be certain of time lines or magnitudes of catastrophe; but that major upheaval is in the offing seems irrefutable. What is patent is that our addiction to consumption and our fetishism of growth as our primary economic values are beginning to show their true character as the inverse of sustainability. Unleashing (as we have) a logic of infinite and relentless expansion, putting every possible resource up for sale in the market as rapidly as possible, in a context where such resource stocks are, in fact, limited, is a formula for disaster. Of course, part of the problem with facing into such a scale of calamity is one of comprehension: how organize our perceptions and focus response? Or more specifically for this chapter—how mobilize a religious tradition like Christianity to catalyze response outside its historic role as acolyte to the destruction? Whether seeking perspective on the situation or seeking counsel from a spiritual tradition, the issue is at one level a question of "reading."

APOCALYPTIC READING?

In response to analogous crises in the past, many of our religious traditions developed *apocalyptic* reading practices—symbolic articulations of the monstrous unease that stirs in the waters of repressed consciousness when large-scale systems of injustice begin to "achieve" world-ending levels of destruction. Most of these visions arose historically in reaction to urban-centered empires whose cooptation of spirituality to valorize oppression represented what *Guns, Germs, and Steel* author Jared Diamond has called "religion as kleptocracy" (Diamond, 1997, 269). Against such operations of plunder, apocalyptic speech functioned as a kind of "street intelligence"—at once both "revelation" and "mask"—rendering state violence legible in spiritual terms for people struggling to survive an impossible situation. It simultaneously "unveiled" the machinations of power and divined an alternative mode of justice and community. As a genre, it provided tools for folk analysis and inspiration to endure for beleaguered minorities, even as it hid the critique in code.

Christianity is merely one among many religious traditions to have developed such a critical apocalypticism—though at this point in history, it has become more notorious in having leveraged more apocalyptic *collapse* for other societies on the planet than any other tradition. Historian David Stannard, among others, for instance, has detailed the extent of genocide actively pursued under Christian auspices in the European colonization of the Americas. In the name of a new millenarian hope, conquistadores and puritans precipitated the effective "disappearance" of some 95 million indigenous peoples of the Western Hemisphere over five centuries (based on newly revised estimates of population densities at the time of contact in 1492), and initiated a project of African enslavement that annihilated another 30 to 50 million persons in the process of delivering 10 to 12 million bodies to the auction blocks in the New World to labor the conquered lands into productivity (Stannard, 1992, x, 11). Certainly, much of the Native American die-off was due to disease (some of which may have been actively and knowingly transmitted by European Christians in an early mode of biological warfare). But the remaining percentages were "cleansed" from the desired lands by genocidal policy and homicidal practice.

This was "apocalypse" as state plan. Its genocidal practice was promoted by its way of characterizing native culture. As former Methodist pastor Colonel John Milton Chivington once ranted, for instance, before wiping out a camp of more than 150 Cheyenne Indians primarily composed of women and children at Sand Creek, Colorado, in 1864: "nits make lice" (Stannard, 1992, 131–134). It did not matter that this same group of Cheyenne were on record as having agreed to peace and were flying a white flag of truce alongside an American flag of supposed "protection"—if the adults were "read" as vermin, the children must be butchered without regret or hesitance! The sentiment was by no means anomalous. Christian theological evaluation of native peoples provided all too easy rationale to see Indian folk as mere pestilence. Just before the massacre, this same colonel—executive board member of Colorado Theological Seminary (later to become the University of Denver and Iliff School of Theology)—had vented publicly, "I long to be wading in gore" (when having trouble finding Indians to slaughter who were not already "reserved"). Indian body parts "culled" in the ensuing orgy of mutilation on that November day of 1864 became "war trophies," brandished in Denver bars by Chivington's forces. This was a not unusual "ritual" practice of U.S. troops fomented even by future presidential office-holders like a William Henry Harrison or an Andrew Jackson (Churchill, 1997, 185–186). That such an atrocity as Sand Creek—emblematic of the reality of apocalypse suffered by Native America as a whole—would be lauded as one of the great military triumphs of the Indian wars, by no less than Theodore Roosevelt, only underscores the consequences at stake in the ideological struggles that make conquest possible in the first place. How we "read" and deploy our various traditions of meaning-making—both religious and secular—is no mere academic pastime. It has everything to do with who lives and who dies, as well as with who gets modern streets or towns named after them (as in the case of Chivington today in the area of Colorado Springs) and whose names and faces disappear from history. "Reading" Christianity as a system of meaning-making—in the face of such a history of apocalypse, as well as before our own moment of impending doom—shall focus what follows.

HOW DO WE READ?

"How do you read" is, in fact, one of the more telling responses recorded within the Christian tradition itself, to the reality of history's traumas and disappearances. As recorded in Luke's gospel, it memorializes a sharp rejoinder by peasant resistance movement leader Jesus. On his way from a campaign of organizing oppressed small farmers and day laborers and "outlaw" turf-gang members in the outback of Galilee to a high-noon showdown with the powers that be in urban Jerusalem, he is brought up short by a legal functionary. This latter had been sent by the temple-state hierarchy to entrap him in a damming sound bite that could be used against him in the kangaroo court that would compel his eventual arrest and execution (Lk 10: 25–37). The question posed by his interrogator was the seemingly sincere inquiry, "Teacher, what must I do to inherit eternal life." The text, however, frames the interlocution as one of "testing," an honor-shame riposte that camps out on the fact that the plotting on Jesus' life had already begun in Luke's gospel with his inaugural address in Nazareth, six chapters earlier. In Luke's chronology, Jesus had already long been laboring under intense surveillance as a marked man by the time of the so-called (and actually misnamed) Good Samaritan parable initiated by that eternal life question. In a cryptic story line lionizing an unclean "half-breed" Samaritan, the parable served as pointed comeback to the subtle invitation to risk compromising himself in front of his peasant-rabble following by engaging in a proof-text "battle." The lawyer's question sought to initiate an exchange where each would lob verses at the other like grenades to see who would be "blown up" first. Jesus' hard-faced counter-question, "You tell me . . . how do *you* read," itself begs reading as riposte, sharp-witted refusal of the lair of the question, in favor of a sumo-wrestler-like circling and sizing up of the opponent. "Where you coming from, Jack," we might transliterate for the streets of today in urban America, "Show your colors, and I'll show mine!"

How one reads the tradition is at one level the entire issue for the ministry of Jesus. It underscores a battle of interpretation that can be more sharply specified as a mortal struggle over the practical meaning of one particular strand of the Torah writings. Again and again, it is the Sabbath-Jubilee continuum of teaching that is put at issue by Jesus' words and actions. This particular "freedom and release" strand of the tradition had been given trenchant purchase by Israel's prophets for relief of the painful existence of the *am ha'aretz* "mud people," the impoverished peasantry in Palestine who—as most peasantries in most places in history—were dying early and ugly and often under oppressive royal or imperial rule. In Jesus' context in the first century, it was the particularly heavy hand of the Roman *imperium* that was doing the damage, economically mediated into Judean and Galilean reality by local comprador elites, living well off the fruits of the appropriated field labor. Jesus does not abrogate the Sabbath-Jubilee traditions as some evangelical Christian readings of our day would intone. He rather radicalizes their requirements as necessary for a simple realization of justice and a basic humanizing of a populace otherwise deformed by predatory social relations. "How do you read" will indeed serve as the watchword for what I want to sketch out here, focused on this same Sabbath-Jubilee emphasis. I propose an overview of the biblical tradition, answering to the emerging question of sustainability, pushing us to review some of our most basic assumptions about the texts. We will read the Sabbath-Jubilee tradition within the large-scale horizon of a 10,000-year-old project of domestication of life forms on the face of the planet, in counterpoint to the urbanized vision of life promulgated by agrarian empires as "civilized" norm for human "being."

From Where Do We Read?

In elaborating that overview, however, it is apropos first to tip my hand. I come to the vision I trace by way of a growing movement of the moment sometimes referenced as "anarcho-primitivism." The name (problematic as it is) invokes a recent "deep ecology" turn in both theory and practice. While easily mistaken for Jean-Jacques Rousseau's "noble savage" fascination derived from the reports of "state of nature" indigenous communities circulating in Europe because of colonial contact with Native America, the vision I hold is politically informed by early modern Leveller (or Digger) rebellions against the closing of the Commons in England, and more recent Luddite and Romantic and Amish reactions to industrialization. It equally entertains the witness of "marronage" communities of "tricultural isolates"[1] such as the Seminole Indians of Florida or the Ishmaelites of the Midwest in the United States before they were eliminated by the nascent republic. More recent additions to the list of inspiring counter-examples would include Zapatista agitation for autonomy in Chiapas, Mexico, resisting NAFTA policy for more than 20 years now; alter-globalization efforts to challenge the neoliberal juggernaut displacing or destroying the few remaining (relatively) intact indigenous cultures left on the face of the planet in the name of development and debt. Closer to home, but no less compelling are the "slow food," community urban gardening, and food security movements that have emerged in recent decades in various places, seeking to anticipate peak oil emergencies, exit the unhealth of so much of our agribusiness food production, and radically relocalize collective human "being."

The growing body of literature that reflects this perspective derives from two primary postulates. The first is that "civilization," as anthropologist John Gowdy notes, has almost nowhere over its 5,000-year stretch of urbanizing history shown itself sustainable, but rather continually over-reaches the carrying capacity of its environs, fractures into civil war, and then collapses or is forced to relocate elsewhere (Rasmussen, 1995, 40–43). The second, equally startling claim is that the antithesis to civilization, hunter-gatherer culture, far from the "solitary, poor, nasty, brutish, and short" lifestyle characterization popularized by Thomas Hobbes in the seventeenth century (never having himself been to the New World or met a forager in person), actually represents what anthropologist Marshall Sahlins in 1966 famously dubbed "the original affluent society" (Sahlins, 1998, 5; see as well, an entire library of anthropology, some of whose more widely read authors include Claude Levi-Strauss, Joseph Chilton Pearce, and G. Reichel-Dolmotoff). Band-society cultures of forager-hunters, as it turns out, typically have their productive function down to about three to five hours per day, often realize remarkable forms of social and material equality across their membership including in gendered roles, relatively rarely break out in organized violence, and frequently elaborate comprehensive mythologies that ensure sustainability by way of ritual sanction and "sacred" conservation (Lee, 1998, ix–xi; Gowdy, xii–xxix).

The 1966 "Man (sic) the Hunter" Conference at the University of Chicago where Sahlins and others presented their findings marked a kind of intellectual watershed. Not only have numerous creative scholars weighed in since with quite serious investigative works (John Zerzan, Paul Shepard, Derek Jensen, Daniel Quinn, David Abram, and Gary Snyder are the best known), but a kind of postmodern hunter-gatherer youth movement, in versions Christian and punk, urban and country, has also more recently emerged. Sahlins's summary of the anthropological findings of the conference has largely held up despite critical challenge in the ensuing years. Lawrence Keeley's claim to the contrary, for instance, that "primitive" societies engaged in regular (and often quite vicious) warfare and astronomically high levels of homicide relative to their numbers, turns out, on careful investigation, largely to describe primitive *agricultural* proclivities for violence

(Wells, 2010, 193–194). Among hunter-gatherer groups referenced in a separate study by geneticist Spencer Wells, a full 30 percent never or only on very rare occasion erupted in anything like war (and even when they did so, often engaged it in largely symbolic forms of violence). These "live and let live" organizations of human "being" yet remain a counterwitness to the claims of many moderns that predatory violence and social domination are hardwired into the human psyche.

In addition to those arguing that indigenous lifestyles anchored in intimate symbiosis with local ecologies are so far the only human social form that gives evidence of sustainable longevity on an evolutionary scale are those like Jared Diamond, Robert Jensen, and Wells, who note the ubiquity of civilizational collapse. The history of brutality attending agricultural and industrial social orders, everywhere erected on slave labor (or the equivalent thereof) and pirated resources, points to the grave difficulties of shared decision making or reciprocity of relationship beyond a tribal-sized unit of 150 or less (Jensen, 2008). The evidence so far, according to evolutionary psychologist Robin Dunbar, is that this limitation of reciprocal communication to the "rule of 150" may reflect an epigenetic boundary correlated with the human (neocortex) brain-size, "set" in its basic parameters, during our Pleistocene adaptations (Wells, 2010, 118–119).

Very close in vision to this positive revisitation of hunter-gatherer experience, but nuancing its backward evaluation to include small-scale pastoral nomadism and daring to live it out in the San Pedro River's Cascabel watershed of southeast Arizona, is a cowherding collective known as the Saguaro-Juniper Covenant Community, beholden to Quaker maverick and visionary Jim Corbett, whose texts on "goatwalking" and "pastoral symbiotics" offer a provocative and careful examination of the herding traditions that alike underwrite Judaism, Christianity, and Islam (Corbett, 1991, 4, 8, 85, 88; and 2005, 108, 118–121). Here is an invocation that reads our religious traditions back into their indigenizing re-visions of empire, exiting cities, leaving palaces, reschooling renegade resisters in the pastoral and nomadic skills necessary to a genuinely sabbatical partnership with the land.

READING THE BIBLICAL TRADITION

Within such a theoretical horizon, I open the proposed overview of the biblical tradition in the shadow of modern debacles like the Sand Creek slaughter, reading such under the sign of Abel, "disappeared" pastoral-nomad brother of field-tilling Cain, who, in Genesis 4, might be said to figure the genocidal elimination of indigenous cultures across the entire landscape of agricultural "advance." The biblical Cain is stylized in Genesis as the author of primordial murder, the earliest archetype of violence, killing his flock-tending brother for no clearly identifiable reason other than seeming anger at not meeting the Lord's favor with his own offering of "re-engineered" seed-crop. But the event may well also remember an epochal conflict between lifeways. The immediate context is of course, "the fall," in Genesis 3. This is part of a composite "origins story" whose earliest beginning in chapter 1 is a staging of life's inception, for collective earth-creature "Adam," as a life of trust in (what Kentucky horticulturalist Wendell Berry calls) "the big economy of natural provision" that draws down divine approbation as "Good." It is followed in Genesis 2 by the story of the quest for control over the fruit production of trees. At stake is the knowledge of who shall live and who shall die in the primordial garden. Violation of the proscription on eating certain fruits issues in banishment outside the blessings of ready provision and a "descent" into tillage and toil. The resulting "hard labor" on the part of the males, as Genesis 3 asserts, is necessary to "reduce" fields to mono-crop yields they otherwise would not give up in their merely "wild" state. But it also results in increased dietary dependence on carbo-hydrates that begins ballooning fetuses into "hard labor" childbirths for the Eves whose hip width does not keep pace with their babies' increasing sizes (Myers, 2013, 115).

As best we understand, these texts may well remember, in mythic form, a sixth millennium BCE Fertile Crescent history around the time a Mediterranean flood breached the present-day Black Sea basin and gave rise to Noah-like stories throughout the region. At roughly that same time the earliest city-state-centered, monocrop agricultural societies of the area would have been expanding their domains, taking over land from hunter-gatherer or pastoral nomad bands living tribal lifestyles closer to the ground and more embedded in local ecology. And here perhaps is the real backstory to the Abel murder. Farmer Cain is also figured as the earliest city-builder, in a story trajectory that will then run straight through the Flood account to find its apogee in the great Tower Tale, Babel as icon of urban *hubris* erecting artifice as simulacra of the original garden.

This latter ziggurat-like construction recapitulates the sacred *axis-mundi* world center of a natural mountain abode of divinity (storm-ridden Sinai in the Moses cycle) as a now humanmade world-city. Its ruling denizens ascend the heights in technologized pride, eviscerating cultural diversity in the same way they destroy biodiversity, in a monolingual demand for imperial conformity—a monstrosity of language that has to be broken up by an act of the divine court. And all of this is mere preface to the particularity of the history to be told beginning in Genesis 12, a kind of backdrop against which the focal story will unfold in high relief.

The very first moment of the privileged narrative is then a simple command: leave Haran (after having already left Ur of the Chaldees), exit the city, go feral. This divine imperative to "wander" the region of subsequent promise as an Aramean *cimarron* (as Quaker goat-herding, desert-dwelling, sanctuary activist Jim Corbett reminds us is the meaning of the Hebrew word *'obed* [with an aleph])—is actually an order to go "wild" (Corbett, 2005, 108, 120; and 1991, 4). It entails fleeing the desiccating deformities of urban and urbane civility, whose epitome is the domesticated *'obed* (with an ayin) or "slave," in favor of a life lived with herd animals out on the steppe.

A case can then easily be made for a subsequent elaboration of the tradition as tracking the ongoing struggle between these two basic lifeways. One was committed to an agribusiness mode of "re-engineering" the biosphere—first in neolithic monocrop domestication, remembered as primordial "fall" in Genesis 2, then in urbanized imperial sovereignty organized first as Egypt, then Assyria, then Babylon, Persia, Greece, and finally Rome. These latter examples of agrarian state formation constituted a social form demanding acquiescence, enslaving labor, oppressing the "stranger," and aggressing continuously on tribal neighbors. It gave rise to the regime of ever-looming geopolitical "powers" whose violence was quintessential and structural and whose decimations of surrounding peoples was proverbial and epic. The other lifeway emerged in revolt against the first as a pastoral nomad style of living rooted in a wayfaring much less destructive (to either ecosphere or community), seeking continuously to exit the above-outlined form of organized predation. It was quintessentially *habiru*—outlaw and renegade, giving rise to early Israel as a Canaanite retribalizing movement of highland-dwelling feral peasants, making common cause with the nomad band of escaped slaves from Egypt who rolled into Canaan worshiping a no-name[2] deity of liberation. The ex-slave wing of this hill-farming league of tribes had been reschooled in a desert ecology under the hands of a retooled and reskilled Moses (as Ivan Illich might say). This former palace dweller had himself had to "unlearn Egypt" through 40 years of apprenticeship to the Sinai landscape in concert with his herd, before conducting his charges on their own 40-year initiatory regime of wandering and relearning the land. Primal, among the lessons encountered there, would be the economic injunction to limit their food-gathering to "one-day-at-a-time" (Ex 16: 1–36; cf. also 31, 12–17), as we shall see below.

This mixed Hebrew-Canaanite horde existed for roughly three centuries as what Walter Brueggemann calls a historic experiment in decentralized political decision making and roughly egalitarian land tenure (Brueggemann, 1996, 31). The experiment was known as "the kingdom or reign of Adonai-Elohim," a tribal federation under a hyphenated God, whose eventual choice to go monarchical is registered in the Book of Samuel as betrayal (I Sam 8:1–22). Under state domination, that older tradition of pastoral nomad savvy about labor and land will give rise to the impossible metaphor of royal leadership as a task of "shepherding" (e.g., Ezek 34:1–31). Within that Jerusalem-centered kingdom, Israel's minority memory of its own origins as *cimarron* and fugitive (Dt 26:5) will give rise to a millennium of prophetic and apocalyptic movements, and ultimately to the retribalizing instincts evident in the revitalization movements of both John the Baptist and Jesus of Nazareth. Beholden to Myers's reading, I would argue that we have, in this corpus, the first written tradition of an anticivilizational, counter-imperial, city-fleeing sodality of "rewilding" highland herders, continually trying to figure out modes of self-sufficiency outside the royal and imperial economies within which they were engulfed and by which they were oppressed (Myers, 2013, 111, 119). How do you read, indeed!

READING THE CRY

Within such a teasing out of broad themes anchored in historical regimes and prehistorical developments, Abel's murder remains a kind of narrative "fertilizer" of the tradition's actual and figurative loam. The *curse* of the land harboring the cry of the blood spilled in Genesis 4 could now be read as oil on the beach sands of the Gulf of Mexico or the Monsanto-bred living nightmare of terminator seeds taking over global fields while Roundup closes out the incorrigibly wild mustard-plant root whose seed Jesus lifted up as weed-metaphor of the "kingdom" he was championing (Mk 4:30–32). And the cry itself (*tsaaq*), specified in that text of Genesis as the living voice of Abel's ground-swallowed blood, is definitive of the tradition. It is the truth of the land where nomad bodies have been disappeared or domesticated into subservience and crushing labor. It is clearly demarcated in Exodus as the lynchpin of the entire vision (Ex 2:23–25).

The four-times repeated moan (*anach*, *zaaq*, *shavah*, *neaqah*) mobilizing divine attention and action in Exodus 2 is the galvanizing force (*tseaqah*) of all that follows according to the fiery Bush Voice in Exodus 3:7. It re-appears in the case law decisions of the rest of that book in connection with the widow, the orphan, the stranger and the poor denizens of Israel itself, where it is enshrined as the sonic plumb line (*tseaqah*) governing the viability of the entire nation (Ex 22:21–27). It takes on flesh in the prophetic movement as molten verbs and pyroclastic adverbs erupting from grieving lips hell-bent on exposing covenant-betrayal and oppressive policy during 400 years of monarchy (e.g., Is 40:6–8; Jer 8:18–9:11). It remains a grunt under the breath of peasants laboring cash-crops into imperial coffers during the long centuries of postexilic occupation. And in the early first century, it drives Baptizer John into the Judean *wadis* on a wild mission to retrieve the yet-writhing lamentation of Rachel still haunting those hills of ancient loss (Mk 1:2–4; Mt 2:17–18).

The cry could further be said to "incarnate" (if Christian terminology be warranted) in an upstart messianic outlier from Galilee named *Yeshua*, where it conjures pain from the belly (Mk 1:22–23; 10:46–52) and healing from the hand of the stigmatized majority (Mk 9:38–41) who were drawing hard breath and burying family members early (Lk 7:11–17, 18–23) under the police-state tyranny of Herod the Great's lesser sons. It waxes panoramic and planet-wide in Pauline 3-D vision, in Romans 8, of an entire creation groaning for comeuppance and freedom (Rom 8:18–27). And it is finally "gathered"—in the only kind of hunting empire knows—inside the great archetypal city of the end of the age, the Babylon concentration of goods and gore, pirated from everywhere, symbol of the destiny and reality of every city everywhere, beneath whose glitter and self-congratulation lies "the blood of all the prophets," indeed, "of all those slain since the foundation of the world" according to the Apocalypse of John (Rev 18:1–24).

Indeed that deep moan could also be divined in Muhammad's "*iqra*" sonority, the deep cadence of Arabic recitation whose precise tremors and tones conjure seventh-century bedouin oppression into haunting expression and launch a sweeping fire of justice-seeking across the sands of a continent, continuously and insistently structured in a rhythmic incantation that English words and Hollywood visual can never match (Armstrong, 136–139, 142, 144–146)!

Yes, that cry!—a great subterranean ululation, sonic arc of primal undulation, Abel's cry as the truism of the tradition, signifying all of the unrequited indigenous disappearance over a 5,000-year-long suppression. From Cain's younger brother to the Sand Creek massacre to the Koi San Bushmen in Botswana in the 2010 summer, barred from their ancestral well by a government covetous of tourist safaris and diamond mine profits, this is the real substance of so-called civilization. And it is registered in the calculus of the biblical prospectus as the inchoate protest of hard-pressed flesh whose unsilencing Revelation anticipates will convene the last court of appeal and convey the final evaluation of the Judgment of the Ages. So, yes, how *do* we read?

For the kind of counterimperial "Christian" orientation such as I am currently involved in—embracing Catholic Worker types and Liberation and Black Theology proponents—this "Abel-reading" gains lifestyle focus and social traction around the vision of Sabbath-Jubilee, rooted in an archetypal memory of the desert wandering of newly escaped slaves in the Exodus-event-articulation that ever after anchors the tradition. Delivered from Egypt under Moses's leadership, as the story goes in early Exodus, the proto-Israelites yet need to have "Egypt" cauterized under their own skins. Even before handed the ten covenant words that shall conscript them into a clearly demarcated relationship with the liberating Mystery (whose pillar of fire and cloud of smoke have guided them from the brickyards of bondage to the outback of Sinai), in Exodus 16, they are given their primal object lesson. Eating what was most likely a resin secreted by aphids on Sinai flora, whose gummy flakes are gathered by bedouin even today (as *man* or "honey dew"), they wax wry in humor and name it "manna"—roughly translated, "What the f . . . is this?" (Ex 16:1–36). More important, they are told "gather enough for one day (and not an iota more), and every six days, enough for two days only!"—an initiation of the Sabbath tradition that predates even the Sinai Mountain rendition of tablets and commandments. They are later warned that this is the preeminent sign between God and the people; not keeping its requirement means destruction (Ex 31:12–17).

It is worth pausing before this proscription. In Egypt they had been enslaved making bricks for storage cities for grain—the necessary architecture for Pharaoh's "food as weapon" policy by which he enslaved his own people with debt and dependence before similarly entrapping the guest workers in his domain (Ex 1:8–14; Gen 47:13–22). The lesson is provocative—a proscription asserting that among the people of this tradition the danger with economics is one of having *too much* (Myers, 2001, 12). Here is a basic vision: an economy of sufficiency, worked out in trust of the desert ecology as supplying "enough." Israel is *not* to repeat the predatory nature of an economy of hoarding. Rulers do indeed confiscate the surplus product of labor and sequester resources under lock and key, doling out subsistence with a demand for deference and acquiescence to royal policy and privilege. But not so Israel—in its most primal self-reorganization in the desert! And not so Jesus' own peasant resistance movement, centuries later (!)—laboring to exorcise a centuries-long appropriation of Torah-vision by imperial foreign powers, bent on remaking Palestine into a cash-crop periphery for whatever urbanized empire had most recently invaded and occupied that transit zone between Egyptian and Fertile Crescent domains of strategic power.

READING SABBATH-JUBILEE

The pedagogy of the prophet-rabbi from Galilee is given formulaic representation in the prayer his disciples ask of him in Luke 11. Like rabbinic followers elsewhere in Israel, they request the rhythmic chant that distills the essence of the teaching they are struggling to embody. In Luke's version—counter that of Matthew's more ornate incantation—the structure is skeletal and starkly clear: "Hallowed be the great name, give us today our *daily* bread, release us from (the stigma of) 'sin' as we release any who are (concretely and materially) 'indebted' to us, and lead us not into temptation (that is, into equivocation when called on the carpet and threatened by the political authorities ever seeking to suppress little upstart movements daring to challenge imperial organization and ideology)." The teaching is centered in the manna memory of not hoarding for even a single day. And given elaboration in the juxtaposition of "release from sin" and "release from indebtedness"! The word translated "forgive" in most English versions in Greek more broadly means "release."

Here too, we are not used to reading in actual context. There is sharp evidence that Jesus practiced a form of "restorative justice" in his table politics, gathering tax collectors and sinners at the same table of simple fare, outside the wealthy economy of banquet-going and ostentation to which he was also regularly invited (both to supply "hick" entertainment for village elites and as a means of surveillance and entrapment as already noted in the Samaritan Parable). At these latter, he regularly initiated polemical challenges (Lk. 7: 36–50, 14: 1–34, etc.). On his own turf, among the peasant crowds that flocked to his movement, he gains a street rep as a "glutton and drunkard," "friend of tax collectors and sinners," someone who simply liked to "party with the folk!" (Lk. 7: 31–35; Mt. 11:16–19). But not only that! Serious organizing was also in the offing—which drew down public censure on the part of the authorities (why do you eat with tax collectors and sinners?) (Lk. 5:32). "Sinner"—unlike in Paul's

revisionist theology "anthropologizing" the term to apply to everyone individually—in the gospels is a social term, designating those
who were publicly marked out as not keeping Torah. In the harsh
realities of first-century Palestinian economics, that censure was most
likely to fall for failure to pay the required Temple tithe. And the
reason for that failure, on the part of hard-pressed peasants, was most
immediately the requirement also to cough up Roman tribute, col-
lected by fellow countrymen whose own circumstance had grown so
desperate as to push them into the social suicide of agreeing to gather
taxes for Rome.

So here we have an interlocking "two-step" of desperation—one
oppressed group forced to prey on another for survival's sake, with
the benefit for rulers of keeping the cauldron of oppression and its
attendant angers internally stirred among the marginalized in a typical "divide and conquer" strategy. The gathering of these two groups
(tax collectors and sinners) in table fellowship is portrayed as definitive of Jesus' ministry. It is that for which again and again he receives
rebuke and threat from the authorities. It is indeed the social practice
for which he will be condemned to execution as a subversive once
he brings the same logic of "restoration and release" to the Temple
precincts, after clearing out the low level operatives of that particular
structure of exploitation. Jesus is represented as breaking the link at
its base, gathering the first line of predatory economic agents into a
face-to-face communion with their immediate victims around a table
of "freed up" food. At the same time, he teaches that "sin" is erased
for oneself by the concrete action of "debt" release of others, thereby
inverting the relationship between the terms that ramified the oppression. Though rendered in English as "forgiveness" (and thereby
depoliticized in its apparently "spiritual" emphasis), the Greek term is
actually a gloss on Jubilee "release" (Myers, 2001, 24). It is quintessentially and concretely economic, envisioning the undoing of domination in a freed-up circulation of goods and access to land.

There is not space here to trace the ubiquity of the release theme
running through the gospels. It shows up in relationship to everything from "released nets" in Mark 1 to "released fields and houses
and relatives" in Mark 10. It is the prerequisite for Galilean fisher
folk called to follow in Jesus' earliest moment of recruitment and the
prerequisite of discipleship-in-general late in Jesus' ministry while on
his way into Jerusalem. It affects personal tools of trade as well as the
basic economic building blocks of production and consumption and
labor in the first-century Palestinian economy. Suffice it to say here,
the trace of Jubilee shows up everywhere. In view is not merely the

big release of every 49 years, but the entire continuum of Sabbath-Jubilee practice outlined in Hebrew scripture. There, it is projected as a comprehensive discipline pointedly ramified every 7th day in observing the Sabbath, every Pentecost celebration carried out 7 weeks after Passover, in the 7th month Feast of Succoth memorial (spending 7 days out in the fields like a day laborer living in a flimsy "booth" or "tabernacle"), in the every 7th year mini-Jubilee of Ex. 23 and Dt. 15 (the Sabbath year release that frees up land, labor, and animals, and specifically vacates indebtedness), and in the 7 times 7 years Jubilee recapitulation, as classically outlined in Lev. 25. On paper, Israel was to live a "school house of the sevens." Sabbath-Jubilee was routinized into both ritual remembrance and economic practice across the temporal landscape of days, weeks, months, years, and generations. And it is adopted as integral by Jesus. According to the *Ben Adam* ("Son of Man") saying of Mk. 2:27–28, the tradition was "made for man"—a practice presided over by "the Human One" to "humanize" the movement and keep followers from slipping into perpetually oppressive social patterns (Myers, 2001, 25).

The battle over the core meaning of Sabbath-Jubilee is central to the struggle with the authorities that will ultimately decide Jesus' fate. It shows up, once we learn to read its very evident invocations in the original Greek, as the lodestone of both the teaching and the movement following. Luke will even style Jesus as a living, walking initiation of Jubilee liberation, in his way of framing Jesus' inaugural address at Nazareth in Luke 4 (concluding with the "acceptable year of the Lord"). The sermon there underscores the anointed one as "Jubilee incarnate," a personalized embodiment of the tradition, which is subsequently radicalized and intensified for his disciples (as in Peter's "forgiveness" of his brother not just 7 times, but 70 times 7 in Mt. 18: 21–22). In the movement, the demand for Sabbath-Jubilee release is daily and continuous, not just reserved for 7-day or 7-year cycles.

But the reading sketched out here is not merely about Sabbath-Jubilee in its radical import for human-to-human relations. The vision is fundamentally rooted in our relationship to land. It is a ritualized practice not only of limitation in "getting over" on each other socially. Even more crucially it enjoins a discipline of reapprenticing ourselves to a particular piece of Earth to relearn its own "manna" provisions in local context (which might be acorns if you were a Chumash Indian on the California coast or lake-growing wild rice among the Ojibwe of Minnesota, etc.). Not only does Sabbath-Jubilee demand a "hallowing" of the way time restores fecundity apart from human labor (to riff on British feminist Teresa Brennan's concern to restore nature's labor and rhythmic regeneration to Marxist calculation). It also aims at making every ecological space into a "holy" land, granting nurture even to sparrows and appraising lilies as more wondrously arrayed than any palatial ostentation or royal show (according to Lk.12:22–31; Corbett, 1991, 4, 8, 85, 88). "Do not be anxious about what you are to eat or wear!" admonishes the Galilean prophet—for us after five millennia of agricultural domestication and three centuries of industrial reengineering, a merely lyrical metaphor, impossible of serious following, but for peasant strugglers in first-century Palestine, a sharp invocation to remember their origins "living off the land" as manna-gatherers in the Sinai outback (Corbett, 2005, 220). Living without anxiety about food and clothes is simply the hallmark of indigenous living around the globe—what hunter-gatherer and pastoral nomad folk[3] regularly experience because they know the land and its rhythms of provision.

APOCALYPTIC READING

In sum, I am reading the biblical tradition under the rubric of apocalypse, as a literature that remembers renegade struggle in spite of being embedded in texts produced by scribes employed by Israelite kings. The genres are not alone "apocalyptic," but multiple and layered, and demand respectful exegesis on their own terms. Nonetheless, the reading strategy here does broadly embrace an apocalyptic sensibility. I approach the corpus as "code" in a situation of duress. Specifically, I read with an eye for struggle—peasant and pastoral nomad alike—laboring to keep alive practices and gestures that refuse entirely to conform to an imperial agenda. In relationship to the most radical questions of our hour—on the meaning of being human in the face of climate crisis and global breakdown—I read the tradition as a counter-sign to the evolutionary advent of imperial formations—a tradition that indeed roots its deepest immediate identity in the privileging of the "stranger" that Israel was before it was Israel (Exod. 22:23). This is the archetypal refugee-wanderer to whom Israel remains accountable in its covenantal obligations once it becomes "Israel": primal symbol of the ceaseless litany of displaced peoples across the entire history of so-called civilization, whose earliest progenitors are the Ur-exiting *cimarron* peoples given emblematic representation in the figures of Abram and Sarai. The key issue for me in reading then is the continuing quest, within this corpus, for the significance of the murder of herder Abel whose blood continues to cry from the ground as late in the tradition as the writing of the Hebrews epistle (where "it speaks still"; Heb. 11:4, 12:24), and Revelation's vision of the collapse of Babylon (whose walls and well-being "contain" the blood of everyone "slain on earth"; Rev 18:24). Such a reading requires placement of oneself back behind that moment of agricultural aggression upon pastoral nomad existence to listen for the wisdom of those who have been "disappeared" with him. A contemporary aphorism like postcolonial feminist scholar Gayatri Spivak's "Can the Subaltern Speak" echoes in these concerns in the form of Corbett's apprenticeship to one's own land as "holy," in which the deep question of an "otherness" that is "under" our vaunted texts of history and economy morphs into a Moses-like interrogation, "Can the bush speak?" But Moses learned to "see" and "hear" such phenomenon only at the far end of 40 years of apprenticeship to an African-related bedouin clan, indigenous to that desert land, whose practices and names mediated that apprenticeship. Pastoral nomads were in fact the first resisters of empire in history.

In this "apocalyptic reading" the issue is then clear. Such a land initiation and feral apprenticeship (into a "cow-man" or "goat-woman" or "manna-communion" or "bush-human" vision quest and "messianism," rather than the abstract "God-Man" compound of classical christological formulation) is definitive of the tradition. Comprehending its counsel is paramount if we would engage the desperation of the hour. Today, that counsel is quintessentially the gift and necessity of indigenous "First Peoples," globally, especially given their nearly completed disappearance. (Perhaps, for instance, we could read the burning bush experience as something like an ancient Sinai equivalent of *ayahuasca* visioning and training in the Amazon, in virtue of which Moses gained his sense of vocation and clarity about desert nutrition and desert survival for the later trek of fugitive slaves he would lead, without which the entire tradition would never have happened. And indeed we shall briefly foray into this rain forest experience in chapter 6.) And I take it for granted that Abel's cry shows up across the entire reach of violent imperial history as the adumbration of creation's cry heard by Paul in Romans 8. It is also the dynamic restlessness undergirding and mobilizing the downfall of the archetypal city in Revelation—the sonic unease or "noise" that is quaking the political unconscious of Babylon's elite and stirring oppressed peasantry and refugees. It is the inchoate energy inside the blood-cry of the prophets and everyone killed "from the foundation of the world" (Lk. 11:50–51) that is "stored" in every "Great City's" walls and coffers, technologies and commodities. The crisis of today has us faced forward to an immediate future of demise and asking after the planetary inheritance we are leaving our children. But I say, being accountable to the seventh generation forward is also being account-able to the earliest ancestors in the past. As such, I want to open the biblical tradition like a huge ear cocked toward that deep past, listening *through* the tradition of Sabbath-Jubilee to its far side, to the memory of an "other" way of being human that it so desperately tries to secure and memorialize in the face of imperial erasure, and to hear there its nuances and tremors, its terrors and ecstasy, its report on what it means to be alive, querying, finally, the deep meaning of our brief appearing on this planet.

CHAPTER 3

WILD WEEDS AND IMPERIAL TREES: READING A MESSIANIC PARABLE AT THE CROSSROADS OF SETTLEMENT AND THE WILD

It is like a grain of mustard seed, which, when it is sown upon the ground, is the smallest of all the seeds on earth; yet when it is sown, it grows up and becomes the greatest of all shrubs and puts forth large branches.

Mark 4:31–32

The seed parables of the gospels are "heirloom" for modern readers. They come across time, hard with unpacked dynamism. As bare kernels, they sit unmoving before the eyes. But given the right nutrients from without, they may sprout with a surprising prolixity. In what follows, I want to treat these little Galilean riddles like transportable spore, and see what they do in a plot of contemporary "compost." But it is important to say up front, my concern is not for the parables themselves as artifacts of history, but for the perspective they can open in a situation of crisis that increasingly engulfs the globe today. They offer commentary from their own time and space on the nature of the "messianic." Their home provenance was social movement. Their context was a tradition of prophetic dissent about oppressive politics—including things like imperial clear cuts of ancient forest (such as Solomon's hubris in chopping down the cedars of Lebanon for his building projects). In transplanting them for a present reading, however, I want to begin by paying close attention to their soil of origin.

Christianity emerged out of first-century Palestinian travail under Roman imperial occupancy as a movement transitioning from the countryside to the city. From a collective enterprise reflecting peasant struggles against metropolitan forms of exploitation in the Galilean hinterland, messianic Judaism quickly morphed into an urban outlaw movement (at least after Nero's 64 CE edict), centered among slave classes and traders, increasingly accommodating its vision to the politics of city life. In that transition, seed parables would quickly have lost their valence as a form of tenant-farming pedagogy in favor of a growing focus on "halo-ing" an individualized messiah, modeled on the hagiography and iconography of the Roman emperor cult. The Jesus fetishism that attends this imperial accommodation (and reaches its apogee in Constantine's takeover of the tradition as the new vehicle for imposing imperial "unity") effectively suppresses some of the signifying potency of the vignettes. Displaced from soil to streets, the "seeds" tend to free-float on whatever gust of interest momentarily launches them into the ethersphere of spiritualized interpretation. My concern is rather to reseed the stories in rural movement context, as folk riddles encoding "little tradition" wisdom and opening space for "thinking otherwise." Neither strictly exegetical nor systematically theological, my reading here is imaginative and constructive. It seeks to probe these parables for a bioregional sense of subjectivity rooted in older traditions of living more sustainably. At stake here is a vision of the messianic not only as a "movement" phenomenon, organized against the imperial "grain" (both figuratively and literally). It aims also at articulating a messianic "subject" inclusive of local soils and biome.

LIKE A MUSTARD SEED

My way into this imagination of a bioregional messianism is to sit before the soil riddles in question and let them speak "from below" and "on the run" as first of all, sayings animating a social movement. The "Parable of the Mustard Seed" has occasioned wide solicitation over millennia and, in its laconic brevity, has inspired commentary ranging from prosaic schmaltz to scalding critique. But as set in the earliest gospel (Mark) in a parade of polemical sayings underscored by activist scholar Ched Myers as apocalyptic brilliance in the key of peasant vernacular, the parable's political "chops" can hardly be gainsaid (Myers, 1988, 169–185, esp. 170, 172). The smallest of seeds, mushrooming into sky-kissing shrubbery giving even towering cedars a run for their money, has to be internalized with a guffaw and an eye-glint awake to its bite.

But context is everything here. Myers has the parable completing a lakefront time of strategic debriefing (Mk 4:1–34) on Jesus' first direct action campaign (Mk 1:21–3:35). His prophetic assault on scribal control of Capernaum synagogue space (Mk 1:21–28) and his torah-based Sabbath teachings (Mk 2:23–3:5) have resulted in death plotting (Mk 3:6) and public defamation charging him with channeling the quintessential Canaanite arch-demon, Beelzebul (Mk 3:19b–30). In response, Jesus has gone feral up in the lakeshore hills (favored haunt of those disenfranchised poor who have taken up social banditry to survive the tightening economic conditions in colonized Galilee) to select his inner circle and come back down lakeside to begin schooling the hungry crowds in movement reality (Mk 3:7–20; 4:1).

He concentrates his teaching there in a folk genre of agricultural *mashals* ("comparisons") seeking ready purchase in peasant heads. In his popular pedagogy, agriculture is made to speak politics, peasant imagination to disclose movement vision. The first bit of open-air reflection "plants" the crowd with an archetypal story of sowers and seeds whose surprising twist promises over-the-top yields (30-, 60- and 100-fold). Such wildly abundant harvests—in the dry-soil farming techniques of first-century Galilee where a 7:1 yield was normal (and a 10-fold crop considered "bumper")—would have allowed a tenant-grower not only to "eat and pay his rent, tithes, and debts, but indeed even purchase the land, and thus end his servitude forever" (Myers, 1988, 177). The asserted outcome is a hint. "Break-away yields" enabling oppressed farmers to quit their bondage to rapacious landlords actually grow out of particular "fields" of practice—the Jubilee way of debt release (Mk 2:1–12, 13–17, 23–28; 3:1–6) and neighbor care (Mk 1:32–34, 40–45; 2:15–17; 3:1–10, 11, 20, 31–35) already being emphasized in Jesus' nascent movement!

And the image is not mere hyperbole to feed the imagination of disgruntled crowds in the outback. A similar 100-fold increase—this time in lands and houses (along with brothers and sisters, etc.)—will be reiterated later for a dismayed discipleship band just before the march on Jerusalem (after a rich young ruler caused consternation by walking away from the Jubilee counsel of asset circulation and treasure-in-heaven in Mk 10:17–31). Meanwhile, the copiousness itself becomes real in actual movement practice in the loaves gathered after the archetypal wilderness feedings when Jesus is again "underground" and withdrawn after the death of John (in Mk 6:14–44), and occupied with preparing for his own final showdown (in Mk 8:1–21). (As indeed it will become "normal" in the communal goods-sharing practices when the movement goes public in Jerusalem after Jesus' own death, as Luke makes us aware in Acts 2: 44–45; 4:32–37; 5:1–11). And far from offering esoteric counsel suitable only to a select few (the "lamp under the bushel" image of Mk 4:21), the possibility is open to all.

But as quickly as he has gone idyllic in this opening episode of wilderness teaching in Mark 4, Jesus waxes polemic. In pointed critique[1] of two conventional wisdom sayings enjoining resignation to the system's seeming intractability, the Nazareth itinerant warns his hearers to "take heed" whose aphorisms they internalize! Cache phrases are inevitably socially located and ideologically freighted! These two reinforce the interests of the rich. "The measure you give is the measure you will get and still more will be added to you" counsels strict "market calculus" as the method of securing increase. While the corollary—"For him who has will still more be given; and from him who has not, even what he has will be taken away"—juxtaposes "winners" and "losers" and effectively asserts that failure to commit to aggrandizement will result in privation (Mk 4:24–25). Far from advocating such, Jesus is more plausibly quoting the two in order to argue against them (Myers, 1988, 178). The kind of carrot-and-stick ideological advice these "pop culture proverbs" actually offer only serves to break up any possibility of peasant solidarity and conform their thinking to the very mechanisms of their own oppression (even though it also ironically indicates exactly where the "more" actually comes from!). Take heed, indeed!

For Jesus, tabulating "returns" on movement practices like debt release is as impossible (and laughable) as trying to "measure out" light, as his sarcastic send-up has just hinted (the "lamp" saying literally references a two-gallon *modion* or "peckmeasure" in the Greek; Myers, 1988, 178). As counterpoint to this dangerous *realpolitik* of the market, the Soil Sage[2] of the Galilee outback counsels patient trust and resilient hope. The "good ground" will produce the bondage-busting harvest "of itself," according to its own fecund logic and timing (Mk 4:26–29). And even the smallest sowing of "spice" can issue in astonishingly broad-based vitality and "deep-shade" security (Mk 4:30–32).

Thus, against market calculus we are given (in 4:26–29) the quiet daily rhythm of the field laborer, not needing to know how the earth produces, but only *that* it does, and that "the sickle [will be] put in" when the harvest does come (a clearly "politicizing" allusion to Joel 3:10–13). William Herzog notes that the earth producing "by itself" here echoes the Greek translation of the Hebrew *sapiyah*, pointing to the free yield of the land during the Sabbatical and Jubilee years in Lev. 25:1–17 (Herzog, 2000, 196)[3] and that "the harvest" under imperial constraint, ripping from peasant hands all but a subsistence return, is a yearly debacle calling for just the kind of judgment hinted at in Joel.

On the other hand, against the "get bigger or lose what you have!" proposition—we have a grain of mustard becoming a shade tree. Even the tiniest of seeds may surprise.

In both cases, the context is the movement at hand. This is a "following" that refuses Jewish temple-state and Roman imperial dictates of business as usual, in favor of the Sabbath-Jubilee ethic of asset sharing destined to have results far beyond anyone's ken.

LIKE A TREE?

But this latter comparison begs deeper reflection. The mustard seed parable deadpans a kind of first-century Palestinian "magical realism" in having outrageous smallness suddenly issue in humongous greatness. But the humor only flashes if the cultural background is clear. This is a rural audience hip deep in growing crops and deeply hip to prophetic scripts of towering trees and their demise. Arboreal parables in both Ezekiel and Daniel use the loft and heft of mountain cypress—whose shady cover and leafy branches give safe harbor to all manner of birds and beasts—as code for large-scale political hegemony (Ezek 17:1–24; Dan 4:1–37). And far from celebrating the "supersized" cedars—on prophetic lips, these timber allegories caution imperial powers (like Nebuchadnezzar's Babylonian order) about the real source of their own lofty dominance (Dan 4:1–37)—or promise (for the power structure of someone like the pharaoh in Egypt) downfall (wherein the rotting trunk, supine on the soil, becomes the woody dancefloor for cavorting crows doing the two-step hustle on its toppled backside; Ezek 31:1–18). Thus we might lip-synch under the breath with Jesus' hard-pressed crowd: "Beware the mighty mustard you puff-chested, branch-swaggering, cypress-headed paragons of pride! It's up and coming! And you are coming . . . down!" But of course, the real addressees in this rustic lake setting are not the powers, but the struggling peasant head hangers themselves, who need reassurance that their nascent following of this throw-down dreamer of ever-waving fields of grain has at least a snowball's chance in hell of coming into some kind of fruition!

They are promised . . . what? Mark hails the mustard achievement as a "bush" victory: it becomes the "greatest of all shrubs!" he says in 4:32. This is a condiment plant (*brassica nigra*, or black mustard in that part of the world) whose branches at maturity, in real life, are hardly dense enough to harbor even one egg-coddling nest or provide refuge even to rabbits. Maybe it could host a hummingbird's heartbeat for the flicker of a second in its maximal nine-foot-tall featherlike wafts of foliage (what mustard, at best, actually attains at maturity)— but not much more. Yet Mark says "it puts forth large branches, so birds of the air can make nests in its shade." As already indicated, this is clearly a sudden intertextual reference riffing on Daniel's "Babylonian" call-out, in which the huge-branched, shade-spreading monolith of imperial power providing shelter for all manner of winged ones is put on notice that big size is what we might call an "organic gift," not a proud achievement, and is simultaneously and inevitably a setup for a big fall (big trees do not usually come down gently).

Mark's mustard promise straddles the discordance between these two images. Peasant humor in the mix would presumably titter at the incongruity, but how such notorious tinyness could leverage security and flourishing on par with the political big boys remains as magical as the 100-fold economic yields envisioned in the sower's field of the previous vignette. Perhaps it was enough in the moment that the promise was of a coming "reign" of littleness, capable of offering real refuge and nurture! But questions remain. Does "the kingdom" in this *mashal* ("with what can we compare the kingdom of God?" Jesus queries) take its cue from the epitome of current *kingship*, imagining its own goodness in terms supplied by the aggrandizements of empire? Or do we get confused in the comparison, forgetting that a big tree is not the same as a big military? Perhaps it is time to let the tree trump the sovereignty.

I imagine the parable's oral telling with a pregnant pause (over arched eyebrow?) in the story line before the herb suddenly "jumps species" and "blossoms" in tree-sized foliage: "It is like a grain of mustard seed, which, when sown upon the ground, is the smallest of all the seeds on earth; yet when it is sown it grows up and becomes the greatest of all shrubs" (and we are head-bopping along, right on beat with the teller in good call-and-response fashion, when suddenly he goes silent for a second and then says) "and puts forth large branches, so that the birds of the air can make nests in its shade!" Whoa. Where did that come from? (Well, obviously from Ezekiel, as we have already indicated.)

But perhaps it is a question. Is this what the kingdom is like— a little renegade movement that becomes . . . a big empire? Is that what we secretly hope? It *is* what Peter and the inner circle hoped (Mk 8: 32; 10:35–44). (And certainly, lamentably, Christianity in time achieved such! But the "kingdom" is not Christianity. Or at least so I would argue). Or perhaps inversely, the parable means to "burlesque"[4] imperial forms of securitization in favor of an alternative vision of confidence. Myers reads it as offering "firm apocalyptic conviction" that, however absurd, this "minuscule remnant-seed within Israel" would not only survive the forest-like "shadowing" ("surveillance"?) of "big trees," but actually "overthrow . . . the mighty Rome" (Myers, 180). His entire book is an exegesis of an alternative safety, built on a willingness to die in the cause of truth-speaking and justice-seeking, if necessary, rather than reproduce imperial structures of violent control of others (e.g., Myers, 405, 407–408). But however the little construct may codify subtle critique of the Roman police-state in celebrating a "seed-truth" about something like the power of vulnerability (or "weapons of the weak"), I want to take the reading a different direction. Borrowing from the license Markan riddle-making itself takes in spelling out soil conditions as "movement-obstacles" (as we see in Jesus' private *midrash* in 4:10–20 on the public parable of 4:1–9)—I want to let the spice story speak beyond its immediate inference in the geopolitics of first-century Palestine to a movement concern of our time.

LIKE A WEED

There is much to harvest here, for a mind willing to let the meanings germinate and grow. What if, like the arch-story of sowing (that Jesus claims, in 4:13, is key to understanding any of his parables), the mustard parable is a kind of arch-image of growing—what seeds do when humans do their thing right and soil is ripe. What if—giving license to what Fredric Jameson might call the "political unconscious" of the text—these three parables of Mark on sowing, soil, and seed are *all* read as indeed arch-characterizations—but now under the pressure of our own political times, ones that lead back from technologically controlled and imperially organized agriculture toward something wilder and more primal? (Jameson, 1981, 1).

Mustard is, after all, really a weed, wild in both provenience and propensity. In home use as medicinal or culinary around the globe, such has been found in undomesticated form "from time immemorial . . . as weeds in grain fields" (Oakman, 1986, 124). Pliny the Elder in the mid first century gives local Mediterranean flavor to the prospect:

> Mustard . . . with its pungent taste and fiery effect is extremely beneficial for the health. It grows entirely wild, though it is improved by

being transplanted: but on the other hand, when it has once been sown
it is scarcely possible to get the place free of it, as the seed when it falls
germinates at once. (Rackham et al. 5.528–529).

Biblical scholar Dominic Crossan will pronounce on that prodigality
to the effect that while garden cultivation of mustard was "dangerous," it was utterly "deadly" rampaging through a field (Crossan,
1991, 278). Accordingly, the Mishnah, around 200 CE, entirely
proscribed its use in Jewish gardens, decreeing careful segregation
out at the edges of larger field plots where its drive to intrude and
intermix could be controlled (Scott, 1989, 374, 380). Otherwise,
given its hyperkinetic reproductive cycle, it would take over. Mustard was designated a field "crop," suitable only away from personal dwellings, and even out there, was considered by many to
be noxious and invasive. And even today, in spite of our agrobusi-
ness technologies, a quick Google search will yield a California blog
lamenting:

> Black mustard is EVERYWHERE. You can't walk a wildland trail in
> Orange County without walking past THOUSANDS of black mustard
> plants. It is the single most pestilential invasive plant in the entire county
> (worse even than ice plant), and you can help yourself to all the seeds
> you want—the native-plants-now people will thank you for preventing
> its propagation. (http://chowhound.chow.com/topics/587681)

If we step back from these notations, and, like all good parable-
wrestling hearers (albeit from across the centuries), let the figure "figure," the import is tantalizing. In our contemporary context, asking
after the larger role of such a seed from a perspective concerned for
"the whole" (a good "salvation" word, at least in the Latin meanings
from whence we derive soteriological nomenclature in English), new
shades of significance begin to sprout. The whole today—as increasingly we are being forced to recognize—is an entire planet of ecosystems, each of which depends upon riotous diversity for the flourishing
of any of its given species, and each of which tends towards an "end"
of ecosystemic maturity. Permaculture recovery of the "design" of this
larger whole makes us aware of a *telos* in the growth of things that aims
toward profound interdependence and multi-functionality.

For instance, in commentary on the kind of concern for invasive
species evidenced in the California quote above, *Gaia's Garden* author
Tory Hemenway argues that much contemporary effort to preserve
native habitat is "misdirected and futile," absent "major changes in

our land-use practices" (Hemenway, 2009, 13). Taking a closer peek at "opportunistic plants" (e.g., mustard seed), Hemenway notes:

> In nearly every case, these plants are invading disturbed land and disrupted ecosystems, fragmented and degraded by grazing, logging, dams, road building, pollution, and other human activity. Less-disturbed ecosystems are much more resistant to opportunistic species, though opportunists can move into them if they establish at entry points such as road cuts and logging sites. (2009, 13)

In consequence, we make a mistake when we intervene to eliminate exotics because we think nature is making a mistake. The problem, he says, is us. The creation of "hybrid, fast-healing thickets" is nature's way of allowing disturbed habitat to stabilize. Opportunistic plants are in effect "pioneer species" that "crave disturbance . . . love sunlit edges . . . churned-up ground, and often, poor soil" (13). Indeed, some are nitrogen fixers, rebuilding soil fertility out of farmed-out fields and overgrazed rangeland. Cleared land and fragmented forests are, from an ecosystemic point of view, so many "open niches," begging invasion for the sake of healing:

> When humans make a clearing, nature leaps in, working furiously to rebuild an intact humus and fungal layer, harvest energy, and reconstruct all the cycles and connection that have been severed. A thicket of fast-growing pioneer plants, packing a lot of biomass into a small space, is a very effective way to do this. (Hemenway, 2009, 14)

These tangled edge zones result in what permaculturists call "recombinant ecologies," blending natives and exotics in a strategy for repair. But their aim is beyond themselves. The day comes when the new species is "'implicated' into the local ecosystem, developing natural enemies and encountering unwelcome environments that keep it in check" (Hemenway, 2009, 15). At that point the edge stabilizes into an equilibrium with the interior of the ecosystem and the life cycle of the exotics is enveloped and overcome in the much larger cycle of an ecosystem seeking its own maturity (mostly old growth forests, unless otherwise checked or deflected). A plant like mustard, it would seem, *does* indeed ultimately aim at becoming a tree. And likewise from this point of view, what is "exotic" and what "native" is merely a matter of perspective. Opportunistic invasives are a kind of "natural scream" (or "groan") that there is a problem needing fixing and simultaneously, a beginning remedy. That such hybrid patches attract just as many native pollinators and seed-spreading birds as surrounding natives renders moot the idea of demonizing certain species as "invaders." The issue is rather—what is trying to happen in the long term?

And here we circle back around to Mark with renewed insight and questions. While certainly not claiming Jesus (or Mark) had such a horizon in view, the deep intentionality at work in both ecosystems and texts provokes imagination. In the parable, for instance, the question of birds receives quite contradictory treatment from respective scholars. Crossan supposes that Palestinian peasants would hear the promise of aviary "shelter" as actually demonic threat (given the birds that eat the path-sown seeds in the sower story immediately preceding). While Myers sees the provision of leafy protection as a positive apocalyptic trope for movement nurturance and safety. Although Myers is probably closest to the overall Markan sense in its narrative and historical context (as a movement message struggling with its troubled relationship to an active rebellion against Rome in occupied Galilee of 69 CE), there is room here to imagine creatively. The role of birds vis-à-vis mustard plants from the perspective of nature's own "ultimate intentionality" queries the apocalyptic image with profoundly chthonic effect. Today we begin to grasp that a "heaven-sent" renewal of *Earth* may indeed require literal winged ones. And here also then is deep intrigue for David Abram's suggestion that the genealogy of our image and understanding of winged "angels" (a quintessentially apocalyptic literary invention) likely traces back to an older time of woodland environments and birds. In the forest world, actual bird species and their songs—long observed and carefully decoded by indigenous peoples living there—served as the original "messengers" from the "spirit world" of other life forms, offering clear signals about conditions in the surrounding forest and any dangers (such as predators) that might be approaching (Abram, 2010, 192–199; 1996, 12–13). But however birds may figure apocalyptically as demons or angels, or in indigenous cosmologies as shape-shifting shaman-healers or predatory sorcerers, their reality in most ecologies as a necessary and "salvific" part of the whole is just beginning to emerge with clarity.

THE MESSIANISM OF MUSTARD

Wild as such a chain of thought may be in its proliferating associations, the Markan mustard seed parable remains a scandalously "noxious" send-up from the point of view of settled agriculture and its ownership class. In its figuring, the kingdom is a *weed*—intrusive, hybridizing, dangerous! And a subtle difference in Mark's telling from the way either Matthew or Luke relate the parable hints even more provocation. As Crossan notes, these latter assign human agency to the sowing: "a grain of mustard which a man took and sowed" (Mt 13:31; Lk 13:19; Crossan, 1991, 278). Mark does not. His version simply says, "a grain of mustard, which when sown" (Mk 4:31). It is quite possible to read this as an undomesticated seeding. Here mustard may be *sowing itself* out in the fields. And if this is right, the real subject of the parable is the ecosystem itself. This would then be a kingdom image whose pedagogical scandal exceeds its own agrarian provenience. It would point back behind plowed fields to a growth unauthored—and unauthorized—by the human project of domesticating life forms. It would simultaneously point beyond such to a question of the ultimate role of wildness and things "uncivilized." And from such an assertion, numerous further implications could be entertained—a couple of which I want to play out briefly here in conclusion, as setting the stage for consideration of a future alternative to eco-collapse.

One has to do with the backward glance indicated. As chapter 2 detailed, in recent years, in relationship to our planetary ecological crisis, numerous scholars have begun to entertain a deep question about civilization as perhaps exhibiting not "progress," but a wrong turn toward something like an evolutionary dead end. Attending to the crescendoing "blowback" from environments around the globe— all of them laboring under a world economic system answering only to the imperative of growth—these anarcho-primitivist thinkers have argued that the late Neolithic turn toward domestication of plants and animals has unleashed a 10,000-year-long aggrandizement of expansionist human settlements, whose career on the face of the planet has virtually everywhere been one of domination (of the majority of their populations), decimation (of their ecosystems), and finally self-destruction (in the implosion of social order). The historical record is that civilization has so far not proved sustainable.

Given such, hunter-gatherer, horticulturalist, and pastoral nomad social organization have become the source of alternative visioning and questioning for these theorists.[5] Recognition that human beings seem to be hardwired emotionally to respond deeply only to happenings within a relatively small clearing around us, and hardwired socially to be able to deal caringly, in detail, only with about 150 or so human relationships, gives pause (Wells, 2010, 118–119). Social critic Robert Jensen asserts, in the mix, that democracy as we try to live it among 300 million (in the United States) or prosperity as we try to share it in a system driven to produce extremes of wealth and poverty, are patently impossible (Jensen, 2008, 2). We are trying to live in an artifactual ecological "niche" (created by our technologies of control) for which we are not genetically suited (Jensen, 2008, 4).

In asking what then is sustainable for human beings, it is hunter-gatherer societies that offer a kind of baseline. While not all such societies were themselves sustainable—many were, living for centuries or even millennia in the same ecosystem without devastating it. (Think of the Pomo Indians of Northern California dwelling in the same neighborhood for 12,000 years without having to go elsewhere. Or even more to the point, think Australian aboriginal peoples settled into the outback of the most inhospitable continent on the planet for 40,000 years without need of any of the outside input or the "help" that Euro-colonists of that continent have needed ever since they arrived in the nineteenth century.) They offer the only model we so far have for a human lifestyle that does not labor under the sign of a rather rude expiration date. And their pattern of inhabiting their respective ecospaces is patently as a "wild-honoring" species elaborating cosmologies and rituals whose lived effects conduce to preserve that space and its creatures as also "wild."

Within this framework, classical Christological discourse, for instance, stands indicted a priori as an ideological construct deeply shaped by settled agricultural presuppositions about human domination and superiority over other life forms (as we shall explore further in the next chapter). Here, theory edges toward the brink of a yet-to-be-accomplished "Copernican Revolution"—for those of us Western-trained and "duped"—concerning the real place of our species on the planet. We have accepted for nearly half a millennium that Earth is not the center of the universe; we have yet to believe human beings are not the center of the Earth. (Whereas this latter orientation has long been both the claim and the witness of indigenous peoples the world over!) Within this compass of things cosmological, what might it mean to say, "the kingdom of God is like a mustard seed"? If the favored figure of "the kingdom" is a weed—not a god in heaven or a man (gender intended) on Earth, but a growth underfoot—then here is a "note from the underground" of that image: the "reign" is ultimately about the "rule" of nature—prolific, wild, self-sowing; and the "god" in the equation—a "rain" of life forces interior to and commensurate with the whole, fecund and teeming, from fungi to elephants, on the ground of a soil so packed with multitudes that a cubic foot hosts a community solidarity 10 billion strong. And all of this under a sky serving as a protective window on an even wilder quanta of forces and energy, ballooning into an untold billion-fold of galaxies, zooming ribaldly off from one another into such a wilderness and darkness of space that entire blackboards of mathematical approximations cake up into mere chalk dust and blow away, just trying to keep up!

And the ultimate Copernican "revolution"[6] may well be not so much a going forward to something entirely new as a retrieval of what native peoples have long known: that all of our stories, any of our images, each of our varied words for this vast unthinkableness (like "God" or "Spirit") are mere tropes for the "teemingness" all around and within us, minuscule metaphors and tiny shards of seeing whose real dangers are not mistaking something "earthly" for the divine, but an idolatry working the other way around—imagining that the earth (and its unfathomable universe of dark matters and energies) can be dominated, commodified, diced, spliced and reengineered, used up and boiled down into entropic dissolution by self-aggrandizing human projects leveraged by a favored set of ideas, theological or technological, alike. "God" in its multiple-millennial-long career as an agribusiness construct, legitimizing hoarding of means among an elite and of meanings among a priesthood, is perhaps the primal technology of "civilizational" control—the Great Licenser of Hierarchy and Patron of Locked-Down Food, withheld or given for the sake of obsequiousness at the royal whim. "Divinity" true to the fact is wild, many, and everywhere—a Mystery unquantifiable in word or number. A weed, indeed!

And this leads into our final rumination—the second musing, focusing on the forward glance. The role of mustard is not to convert all living reality into itself. Of late on the world stage, within a permaculture ken about the thrust of things, it might be grasped as the repairer of an agricultural rupture, stepping into the breach of human intervention to mend the outer perimeter of ecosytemic heterogeneity. Its goal is beyond itself. Its healing power—the filling of a wound with fecundity. Its destiny is to be succeeded by a recovering prodigality of life forms. What if "YHWH's kingdom"—counter its 1,700-year "Christian" recodification as imperial and totalizing—were to be comprehended roughly thus: a limited function and tenure on the world stage of history; "sown" at the height of agricultural aggrandizement as a response thereto; "intended" in the mystery of proliferating cultural forms for the sake of recovery of a wild prolixity of articulations of ultimate meaning; serving to ground spiritual rumination in real struggle over real ground—demanding resistance to domination, serving the margins of weed-plants and "weed peoples," insisting that real change is necessarily organic and real growth sub-servient to the whole, anticipating its own fulfillment (and succession) in the enablement of a wild flourishing of multiple religious practices and cultural patterns and spoken tongues and danced rites? What if "God" *is* mustard and "the kingdom" an entire planet of thriving forest? If so, the deep question for our species is how long the reign-ing wildness will tolerate the arrogance of our will to homogenize and control. After all—we too are an invasive, certainly destined to be succeeded by something much grander. What if that "something grander" is actually an Earth no longer decimated by corporatized growth, rather than some imagined "heaven" descending from on high to make up for all our failures? Will it take our extinction to real-ize this kind of reign?

PART II

THE QUESTION AND THE CHRISTIAN
TRADITION: COMMUNICATION
AND EMPIRE

CHAPTER 4

SINAI BUSH AND JORDANIAN
DOVE MEET HAITIAN SNAKE
AND AMAZONIAN VINE: READING
CHRISTOLOGY AT THE CROSSROADS
OF EMPIRE AND ECOLOGY

God called to him out of the bush.

—*Exodus (3:4)*

The issue of sustainability—climbing like an Amazon smoke signal over a burning ecology—is the apocalyptic sign of the times for an entire planet careening toward calamity under the reigning growth idolatry of neoliberal globalization. While obviously part of a much, much bigger question, the chapter to follow here will focus its intervention on Christianity in particular, as a 2,000-year-old form of anthropocentric conviction that has contributed in no small measure to the crisis we now face. The focus favored will not involve thinking at the problem from merely a present, mainstream Western position, but will rather seek orientation from a depth-sounding of indigenous cultures still partially embedded in an economics of reciprocity and obligation with their local ecologies. Attention paid to what speaks from beyond the borders of mainstream (and Western) Christianity will find an inner echo in Christianity's own myths of origin, as well as in "hybridized"[1] versions of the tradition such as *vodou* practices or *ayahuasca* churches—often dismissed as heterodox—that have also worked out a creative adaptation of Christian orthodoxy to local ecology. The core conviction of the exploration is Christological: the idea that images of the means and media of salvation are a critical litmus test for a tradition committed to incarnational notions of divinity and anthropological responsibility for humans.

REPRISE

As outlined in chapter 1, part of the argument here is a long view that the human species has moved through three major experiments of dialectically negotiating its basic identity vis-à-vis a primary "other." For most of its time on the planet, we have crystallized our sense of self in relationship with plant and animal communities in hunter-gatherer lifestyles. Then, roughly 5,000 years ago, the constitutive other of our species began to shift away from the local ecology of kindred beings to that of human groups constructed as "strangers" and "enemies" in urbanized settled agricultural lifestyles. And more recently, we have witnessed another shift as the human lifeworld becomes increasingly enveloped in cybernetic machinery and subtly begins positing the cyborg as the new image of integral otherness. Obviously, orthodox notions of "salvation" ("wholeness") are beholden to the second stage of identity formation: the constitutive other of salvific hope is another human, the God-man (*sic*), Jesus of Nazareth. Recent popular culture media have begun creatively to explore our assimilation and eclipse inside layer after layer of built environment and technological *habitus* in filmic expositions like *The Matrix*, where the protagonist Neo functions essentially as a cyborg mediation of wholeness. The concern here is rather to explore incarnation in the other direction—invoking much earlier and longer-standing notions of referential otherness when plant and animal life formed the entire "surround" of human living.

The basic challenge emerges out of the history of urban imperial expansion upon, and conquest of, hunter-gatherer groups—a history of empire directly constitutive of modernity itself, but also long in process before 1492. This imperial initiative categorically vaunted developmental expansionism over reciprocal exchange between life-forms. It just as ruthlessly promulgated an ongoing disinformation campaign rendering foragers as "primitive," "savage," and subhuman—and thus easily *savaged by* the self-proclaimed arbiters of "civilization." As already noted, today the question of history's "real" savagery finds serious theoretical articulation in a growing ambit of scholarly work arguing that the historical record of hunter-gatherer lifestyle is patently more civilized and humane ("human") than anything civilization has yet managed. The axis of conflict—materially, ideologically, spiritually—between these two different ways of imagining and organizing human practice on the face of the planet is in part a conflict about the relationship between humanity and other life forms. To what degree are other life forms integral to human survival and indeed identity? Is the relationship best comprehended in terms of human domination, production, consumption, reengineering, domestication, and finally entropic discarding of other species? Or are other species actually kin and ancestry, inevitably constituting a dynamic surround of creative exchange that is necessarily one of reciprocal metabolism and mutual interpenetration? Is the projection of humanity as a form of supremacy among species really a "human" project?

For a Christian theology concerned with reimagining its mission in the face of this history of ongoing predation and devastation for which it has so often provided ideological legitimation, there is one question that cuts to heart of the issue. Can God be embraced as soteriologically incarnate in plant or animal in the way many indigenous cultures have in fact lived their spiritualities? Or is salvific otherness only imaginable as "human" (or now cyborg)? The anthropocentric privileging of the human species as supreme finds absolute theological sanction in virtually the entire corpus of written theology for two millennia. This chapter will propose resources for rethinking that assumption from within the tradition itself by giving Christological articulation to various facets of what might be called the "little tradition" of theology. Rather than focus on official orthodoxy, here we will ask what it might mean to take seriously the lived practices of indigenous cultures, "missionized," but not entirely "converted" out of their interweaving of human "being" with plant and animal being.

THE OTHER WORLD

An ethnographer in Indonesia in the 1980s sits in front of his hut in the morning, and receives a cup of tea from one of the women of the compound he is visiting (Abram 11–14). A moment later she passes by again, carrying a tray with tiny rice cones arranged on banana leaves. He is curious, interrupts her walk, and asks, "What are you doing?" "Making the morning spirit offerings," she says. The next day, he follows her, discovers the little cones being set out at each corner of the compound's various buildings, and upon checking again yet later in the day finds each cone attended by a long line of ants extending from whichever of numerous ant mounds was closest by, disassembling the rice a grain at a time and carting the kernels back to the mound. Ah, revelation! Simultaneous spirit propitiation and pest control!—by sharing the day's "bread." And he then is thunderstruck by a realization: for the indigenous, there is probably no distinction between the "spirit world" and the living tissue of other intelligences and life forms surrounding the human encampment like a nest. Spirit offering and ant offering are one and the same.

Contrary to Western phobias for all things organic and not yet marketed, for communities living close to the earth, the otherworld is not transcendent and elsewhere, but imminently and always incarnate. Flesh of animal and fiber of plant are irremediably the face of spirit— before (as an indigenous paraphrase of Philippians 2:5–8 might say) they give up "equality with God" as a thing not to be grasped, and empty themselves in the economy as a slave, taking the form of a commodity, being born in the likeness of the commercial. Christianity is late to the game in its claims of divinity "taking on flesh"; indigenous cultures have lived such for millennia. And it is miserly by comparison, when brooding over John's vision of the Word "tenting among us" in grace and truth—positing paucity where indigenous culture comprehends a voluptuous abundance.

Why such a parsimonious vision of incarnation, limiting it to what is only human? Especially when the human is *not* able so to limit itself, as we are now discovering, late in our brief day in the sun of evolutionary pride, thinking the table had been spread just for us? Today the blowback from creation is relentless—saying, in effect: "No, even *your* body is actually much bigger than just your own little body, composed, as it is, of other bodies large and small, bacterial bodies and antibodies, viral bodies and germs, corn cells and carrot fibers, fish eggs and cow muscle, rib of pig and leg of hen, supernoved star chemicals from way back in the ancestral story line, as well as (indeed!) sweet, sweet juice of the vine last Sunday—not just metaphorically, but in the most physical finding possible—blood of the Great Being we elevate as host." Our own physics *does* say that any one of us, breathing here and now in our own little rooms, wherever we are, is metabolizing molecules of nearly everything in the biosphere (as well as inhaling, in all statistical probability, atom of Caesar and nuclei of Hannibal, particulate of Cleopatra or late Mama Lucy, just breathed out into the atmosphere by the cemetery's waving blades of green, green grass or bone-dry *haboob* blowing up from Aethiop to circle a globe and land in our nose). If *we* are incarnations of everything else and everything else, in some sense, is an incarnation of us—why not God? Why the historic Christian stinginess, limiting *theos* to *anthropos* (and indeed, that to just one man)? To actually answer such a charge, not just flash its bristles like a rhetorical barb, a wide-angle lens must be opened.

LINGUISTIC INNOVATION

Hegel, more than any other modern thinker, set the tone for our contemporary fascinations with questions of identification. Likely such obsessions are the peculiar pathology of modernity, erected out of the dominant liberal mythology that a human being is primarily an "individual." (The notion of a great executive ego, operating through the boardroom of the mind, articulating intentions inside a body bounded off from all other bodies in a great existential solitariness that now finds social enshrinement most starkly in the homeless man sleeping under the bridge or the demented woman on deathwatch in the warehouse of decrepitude we call the "nursing home"!) Hegel caught onto the dialectic of the subject like none before him, and elaborated a dynamism of "self realizing itself through the other" that remains compellingly suggestive 200 years after the fact. Whether for Freud and the psyche or Marx and the economy, Lacan and the imaginary or Fanon and skintone, the idea that human beings constitute a workable (if distorted) sense of themselves by way of otherness and negation, again and again, surfaces as conundrum and paradox, galvanizing theory and leveraging revolt across landscapes mental and social, seemingly interminably.

Here I offer the insight as simple shibboleth to think with—an organizing device for wider inquiry. As hinted above, I want to posit the journey of our species through varied moments of self-consciousness as dialectically mirroring, for human action and reflection, our most radical moments of technological change. Language, within this ambit, is grasped as perhaps a kind of *Ur-techne*, a form of work with the sound envelope mediating relationship and meaning for human groups. It operates, epigenetically, as a kind of second body, enfolding and articulating the physical body that emerges out of the womb, buffering and bridging that body's experience of the "world" around, both blocking and constituting its "bodyness." Freud and Lacan, as indeed, Kristeva and Iriguaray (and many, many others), have much to say about such; here I am just working with the barest outline.

Written language emerges then as a yet another layer of technology (Zerzan, 1999, 31–44). Commensurate historically with the agro-urbanization whose violent concentration of surplus product alone secures the leisure time and patronage necessary to freeze words in or on an object (stone, papyri, etc.), writing is ideological from its very first tracery. It wraps the organic body in yet another layer of meaning and distortion—walling off more of its primal *sensorium* from im-mediate flesh-on-flesh contact, and filtering experience through a point of fixation so radical that bodily experience unmediated by such language constructs becomes "literally" unimaginable.

Historically, the layers accumulate—layer upon layer. Animal skin and plant fiber, oil-fat and tree branch, wood smoke, cobblestone and mud wattle, wool, bronze, iron, steel and cement, glass, plastic and polymer, hot and cold air, burnt coal and diesel, the entire architecture of the city itself, and now silicon and chip, digit and plasma, and soon-to-enter nanohybrids of virtually everything. So profoundly have these "supports" been engulfing human organic concourse with the rest of the biosphere, over the stretch of ten times ten centuries now, that children think food comes from a can and adults face death as a kind of "failure," rather than a form of fulfillment.

Humanity in our time has already emerged as Machine-Being. So dependent upon this artificial armature have we become that we no longer have either the imagination or the skill to live without it. The Human-as-Transformer is now at least *imago hominis* if not the new phantasm of Logos incarnate. Inevitably (dialectical theory would argue)—such annealments onto human flesh rebound into human experience and consciousness. Whether in the process the human species is giving rise to a successor organism on the evolutionary horizon is perhaps not a fully askable question, by definition (though savvy "cyborg-monster" theories like those of Donna Haraway and company certainly tempt cranial flights to the heights of Icarean danger. And popular culture, of course, has no qualms about dramatizing the question as a salvation-by-Schwarzenegger wet dream).

AGRO-IMPERIAL EXPANSIONISM

For our purposes however, I want merely to mark the passage at its moments of greatest shift. As already indicated, literate religions (such as Christianity) emerge in the centuries surrounding Jasper's axial period as creatures of agriculture. They articulate soteriologies dominated by agrarian experience, in which human relationship with the rest of the biosphere is mediated especially by grain. These are social orders organized around urban concentrations of power, controlled by ruling classes, stockpiling agricultural "surplus" under the duress of law codes demanding "fealty surrender" of somewhere between two- and four-fifths of peasant production to float elite lifestyles. The ultimate sanction in such a subsistence system is the violence organized by elites in the form of standing armies, employing state-of-the-art weaponry. The resistances regularly provoked in these hierarchical orders are, typically, just as regularly crushed. This mode of "civilized" order, driven to expansion by its own logic of increasing population by way of increasing production, has launched a "missionary ethic of conquest" across the face of the planet that has not ceased to ferret out new frontiers of exploitation for more than 5,000 years. Hunter-gatherer lifestyle in the mix has been almost entirely "disappeared," either reengineered into a new periphery of metropolitan control, or genocidally eliminated. Biocolonialism's effort to penetrate the last remaining undomesticated ecologies in the name of civilizational "advance" (the project of invading and isolating genetic code and re-splicing it in service of human consumption and control) is merely the most recent in a long line of historical takeovers.

And at the ideological heart of this 5,000-year-old social process lays the image of the "king." Royal machinations of domination and courtly prerequisites of pomposity have long served as the privileged storehouse for religious imagination of the Ultimate. Christology is merely a case in point. The evangelist Mark's polemical sideswiping of Roman imperial iconology and witness in creating his "gospel"[2] account of an upstart rabbi, criminalized and executed by Caesar in the first century, is loaded with two-way traffic. It finds its logical denouement eight centuries later in the recasting of that renegade rabbi as Teutonic warrior-king when Christianity is thoroughly Germanized in the Middle Ages (Markus, 1990, 88). Inevitably, dominant power imagery is borrowed by resistance movements to articulate their champions of alternative values and community. And just as inevitably, sooner or later, some of the latent assumptions of those dominant images reciprocally take over and recast those champions. For my argument here, the issue is the broad claim that soteriology inevitably speaks to and from the social iconography in which it is imbedded.

My point, however, is broader still. Settled agriculture has the human community as its focal concern. As a lifestyle centered in, controlled by, and servicing growing urbanization, it offers its inhabitants a way of living increasingly "encysted" in communal interaction. Human-to-human experience becomes ever more compelling as the primal reference point. In the same development, it is also other *human* beings who increasingly emerge as the primary archetype of untamed Power (e.g., of an Otherness that is potentially overwhelming and annihilating). They appear on the horizon as conquering invaders or oppressive leaders. And here I take Rudolph Otto's formulation of the experience of Ultimate Otherness as a kind of prerequisite: a mystery that is not only "fascinating," but also "terrible" (the *mysterium tremendum et fascinans*, in his famous phrase; 1950, 13 ff.).

At one level settled agriculture is a social form seeking to eliminate a certain kind of "terribleness" from human experience—at least from the experience of those elites controlling the social order. No longer, as in hunter-gatherer society, is awe primarily experienced in relationship to large animals or vast tracks of impenetrable forest or surging floodwaters or volcanic eruptions. Awe-full-ness is rather increasingly a feature of primarily human-on-human contact, in the mode of war (although for peasants, a certain more prosaic hardness and awfulness may also be experienced in having to labor land into domesticated form—but this is an experience that is increasingly "walled off" from elite experience in the city). It is the human "stranger" who begins to emerge archetypally, in this domain of experience, as the most intriguing and titillating and potentially terrifying appearance of otherness. It is not surprising then that for Christianity, the otherness of a divinity capable of reflecting a possibility of salvation or its (awful) inverse is primarily human. As with many other world religions that begin codifying their experience primarily in sacred texts, spiritual communication is more and more restricted to human mediation. Writing necessarily presupposes urban social formations in which the community at large has less and less interaction with the wild. Plants and animals begin to "disappear" as divine agents.

Here my argument is merely an outline, the positing of a possibility. Obviously, much more work would need to be done to substantiate or invalidate the generality of the claim. Judaism, for instance, emerged in part as a protest movement against the animal images of Baal and the plant potencies of Anat (common to Canaanite modes of worship) that (inevitably) imported part of what it protested against (the Spirit as Mother Eagle in Gen 1:2; the bush encounter of Moses in Ex 3:1–7; the day of YHWH as like meeting a bear in Amos 5:19; etc.). Hinduism makes use of the elephant Ganesh and the monkey-king Hanuman. Christianity speaks of Jesus as the "Lion of the Tribe of Judah" or the "true vine" in John 15. But I would understand these as nonetheless wild images that have been largely anthropomorphized. They are carried over in memory—perhaps from a time of more commonly experienced encounter with such flora and fauna in integral interaction with their host ecologies—as symbols. In the literate emergence of Judaism or Christianity at least, they are grafted onto urban existence and experience largely as metaphors for certain kinds of human strength or virtue. The point here is not the mere appearance of the image, but the question of the experience it references. Are the images of wholeness for most inhabitants of a given social order primarily found in interaction with other human beings . . . or other life forms? Are the encounters that are integral to existence—indeed, the vocabularies for bodies that mediate life to the human community—domesticated or wild? For settled agriculture, it is increasingly the case that for ever larger numbers of its denizens it is human interaction that matters most. It is uncertainties and possibilities in that interaction that are most dangerous or most vitalizing for the future.

TECHNO-DIGITAL MESSIANISM

Within this broad purview of human emergence on the planet, modernity comes into focus as a mere blip of time. It is an untested duration of experience, an evolutionary gamble whose returns are as yet unclear. The imposition of a globalizing economic metabolism that begins with 1492; the now exponentially increasing submission of "raw material" to a project of "reengineering for human use" in technological innovation; the adaptation of ecologies to an evermore homogenizing enculturation of the human animal (rather than the adaptation of human cultures to local ecologies that had been the case for all of our prior experience on the planet)—these all are, from one angle, merely continuation of the history conquest and control. They embody an "ethic" that first found purchase in the turn from hunter-gatherer lifestyle to settled agriculture. They find logical extension in the beginning of reengineering the human body in thrall to a machine image of durability and replaceable parts. That popular culture would begin to reimagine a "saving messiah" in terms of a "reality construct" like Neo in the sci-fi thriller *The Matrix,* is merely to be expected. Neo represents the new "other" in relationship to which human identity and destiny demands formulation in the information age. Teased out of the manufactured interface between programmed intentionality and unforeseen possibility, this is the great Cipher-Construct that begins to hover like a ghost at the edge of AI algorithms. Here the body is cyber, the capability hyper, the character human—a kind vernacular hypostatic union! And such fascination is de facto testament to the "transcendent power" we *actually* trust in on a daily basis to leverage our future! In life and history—as indeed today in our best understanding of neurobiology—practice precedes consciousness. Our confessions are generally late formulations of what we have already begun to live out at more inchoate levels. Measured in terms of resources, time, and energy applied, the "mediation" of salvation most vigorously attended to in our time is not a ritually confessed Jesus, but technology itself—the great salvific "cyborg-to-come."

In the shrine of late capitalist orthodoxy, instrumental capability begins to rise out of the flesh as the practical meaning of divinity. But this is largely the sequential outcome of the entire project of domestication of plants and animals begun 10,000 years ago. Yes, debates unfold at this juncture that wax sublime in fascination. Does evolutionary adaptation—the development of teeth as tool or brain as model—admit of any real line of distinction? Once the "tools" are no longer organically imbedded in the body, but implanted, put on, lived within, injected, interspliced, or driven—have we somehow stepped outside of "nature"? Where does the body stop and technology begin? But the logic of control and ultimately of avoidance of dissolution and demise remains a continuity from settled agriculture through industrialization and on into the information age.

HUNTER-GATHERER FORAGING

The only social ordering *not* structured around the drive to incarnate control that realizes its most totalizing form in Foucault's "biopolitics" is the lifeway that represents nearly the totality of our time on the planet: hunter-gatherer society. As noted in previous chapters, the recently emerging body of scholarship loosely known as "anarchoprimitivist" reads the warning signs of environmental collapse as a summons to question deeply our operative assumptions about the supposed *telos* of history. If sustainability is taken as a major criterion for evolutionary success, modernity and even "civilization" itself appear as relatively disastrous experiments. Certainly there is evidence that some hunter-gatherer societies foraged and hunted wantonly and fouled their nests. But there is also evidence that many did not. The same cannot so far be said of settled agricultural societies whose record is a nearly ubiquitously one of violent overreach of their resource base, fracture, decimation, war, and finally evacuation or at least dependency on another settlement elsewhere, re-initiating the same logic in a new environment. But now for the first time in our history, the "elsewheres" are all gone.

Anthropology since the 1960s has reevaluated the data on hunter-gatherer societies, itself gathered in service of epistemologies committed to colonization and Western expansion and anchored in normative assumptions about human "progress" that read foraging under one or another trope of backwardness.[3] The likes of a Marshall Sahlins and a John Gowdy, as indeed interdisciplinary thinkers like John Zerzan and Paul Shepard or novelist Daniel Quinn, for instance, will now argue that the hunter-gatherer social order in general represented "the original affluent society," keeping material needs simple, enjoying natural abundance, devoting only three to five hours to production per day on average, and thus majoring in "leisure time" pursuits like various forms of social intimacy, ritual activity, art-making, and play. Many such societies had no words for "crime" or "war" (some not even needing concepts for either "want" or "need")[4] and embodied levels of gender equality estimable even by modern standards. Violence, in many of these groups, was largely symbolic, directed to signaling boundaries and warning neighboring groups to keep away from encroachments. Far from the popular culture picture of a life lived in a constant struggle with hunger—in general such groups knew a diet far superior in variety and amount to the average peasant lifestyle under settled agriculture. Indeed, life expectancy for hunter-gatherers exceeded that of the 80 to 90 percent of settled agriculturalist populations devoted to actually producing the crops. And the history of contact between the two often enough gives evidence of hunter-gatherer awareness of the costs of "settling." Forager groups typically resisted incorporation by expanding monocrop social orders—until their lands were entirely taken over, their food sources cut off, and a choice for either annihilation or "conversion" brutally presented. Much of the history of European colonization of the Americas is replete with such stories.

Offering such a sketch is in no way intended to generalize all hunter-gatherers as pacific and altruistic or romanticize them as green and ecologically benign. It is rather to take issue with our own received wisdom about their "savagery" and open up a deep question about ancestral practices that may well embody profound insight or even "salvific" challenge for a species in the throes of self-annihilation. Quinn, for one, "historicizes" Genesis as encoding originally an indigenous memory of the violence that expansionist farming visited on a more nomadic lifestyle of pastoralism in southwestern Asia Minor. While focused on herder-farmer conflict rather than forager struggles, the dynamic on the agrarian side of things is the same: aggression bent on taking over land not yet under plow. Genesis names settled agriculture as "fall" and the urban pride and predation resulting as "murder" (grower Cain not only kills herder Abel, but subsequently founds the first city, as we elaborated in chapter 2; Quinn, 1992, 168–178).

CIVILIZATIONAL CRITICISM

As already remarked in previous chapters, two of the more radical visionaries to think in this vein are feminist globalization theorist Teresa Brennan and eco-philosopher Paul Shepard. The writing corpus of each is extensive; here I can only throw up a few more of the challenges they offer, behind each of which lies a profundity of theoretical orchestration and interdisciplinary synthesis. Brennan's work pulls together an integration of Marxist insight on the logic of capitalism and commodification with psychoanalytic probing of repression and narcissistic hallucination to articulate a sustained challenge to the idea of the "contained subjectivity" that anchors so much of Western thought and practice (1993, 9). At stake in her theorizing is the grandiosity of a primal hallucination projecting infant passivity and desire to destroy onto the body of the mother. In the grip of the technocratic imperatives of commodity culture, this primal fantasy has unleashed a globalized project of "objectifying and dismembering" now coming up against the very limits of planetary endurance (1993, 12, 18, 20). Interlinking the two bodies of theory (Marxism and psychoanalysis), and the phantasmagorical projects of dismemberment and consumption that they allow us to "see," however, is a shared failure. Neither is able to see past the fetish-fantasies they explore to the primordiality of nature as itself the ultimate foundation, generating value and meaning outside of the subject-object structure assumed in either dialectical materialism or Lacanian deconstruction. Neither the comprehension of nature as raw material found in Marxist elaborations of use-value nor the misprision of the self-presencing subject so piquantly deconstructed by either Lacan or Derrida manage to escape the false fixity into which subject-object dichotomizing leads (1993, 16–17, 18–19).

Brennan does not herself pretend to escape the dilemma of using fantasmatic metaphor to reference material reality. Rather, in confessing an inescapable "(con)fusion" between "generative natural chain" and "socially constructed overlay," she insists that we not stop our theorizing as if metaphor is the only reality, and nothing exists "outside the text" (1993, 21). In giving powerful critical articulation to the way Western egoic construction by way of repression finds global extension in capitalist interdictions of natural energy in the fantastic form of the commodity, Brennan offers an "alternative energics." She seeks to give more accurate account of the energy exchanges in fact constituting life at the level of both psyche and body, individual maturation and species survival. As global capital now presses on the natural order in ways that begin to threaten exhaustion—using its ability to mobilize its exploitative operations around the globe *spatially* to circumvent the *temporal* rhythms necessary for either human labor or living nature to reproduce themselves locally—the end game of such a technocratic fantasy of living "after nature" begins to appear. One way or another, the energy dependence of human productivity and life on natural rhythms and cycles of regeneration will claim its due recognition. Returning "living generativity"—"reproductive force" at both micro and macro levels—to its necessary place in critical theory is the task Brennan both engages and enjoins.

Shepard, on the other hand, begins with cross-disciplinary evidence on hunter-gatherer societies to throw down a challenge about human nature that offers up cynegetic society as more fully human than any of the agro-industrial developments we have witnessed with the advent of so-called civilization. His range is part of his argument, claiming a culling of biology, genetics, zoology, anthropology, psychology, ethology, history, theology, poetics, and myth as necessary to construct an adequate "ecology of humanity." His broadly interdisciplinary reprise tracks our travails from Pleistocene emergence into a certain genetic posture in the world up to the present planetary-wide crisis of destruction that begs the most rigorous questioning of human "nature" itself. Shepard will argue that beneath the layers of civilized stunting of human "epigenesis" lies a still vital and discernable possibility of maturation that may yet be capable of rescue. Here we will cull his first book (rather than the later *Nature and Madness* as we did in chapter 1).

Especially germane for the argument here is Shepard's thorough and provocative recasting of the 20 years of ontogeny necessary to bring the human animal to its full adult wholeness. At stake is the carefully attended process of construction and initiation that historically required plant and animal familiarity for its cosmological and religious "success." His argument essentially marks human linguistic development as biologically driven, but ecologically underwritten. Plants and animals encountered in a shared ecology formed the earliest vocabularies and living textures of childhood "literacy" and education (Shepard, 1973, 194, 202, 203). Codified in cultures adaptive to their niches, these "other" life forms were tracked, identified, differentiated, dissected, and organized in taxonomies every bit as complex as any urban dweller's computer-speak of today. During adolescence, they also become the totemic tutors and mythic signifiers for a process of "cosmic maturation," orchestrated in initiatory sequences of "reprogramming." These rites of passage ritually recapitulated the world itself as multileveled "pun," humanizing death and opening out the living community to both ancestry and future in a panorama of mystery and fulfillment (Shepard, 1973, 198, 201, 210).

Shepard's deep conviction is that the human genome remains "humane" only in its wildness and cannot be schooled to its deepest vocation except in concert with a wild natural world. Against the seeming impossibility of such in a technocratic world he points to the catastrophically escalating failure of the model of human nature we have adhered to for the duration of settled agriculture. As counterpoint, he sketches out possible practical reconfigurations of technological society that might enable a slow recovery of the demands of our Pleistocene genetic orientation. Here it has to suffice simply to say that much in history and science, experience and even cybernetics, would agree: human "nature" requires living wildness for its own sustenance and identity formation at risk of otherwise becoming merely a vacant adjunct of its own technological fetish.

At its core, Shepard's argument is animated not just by concern for the environment, but for the human. Human maturation demands plant and animal familiarity not only for material survival but for cosmic orientation and symbolic attunement to a continuity that crosses the threshold of death. What is now deformed in modern society is the necessary initiatory "breakdown" of humans in general and males in particular, that can recuperate infant terror in service of mature posture in the world. Adolescent anger today has no appropriate counterpoint to the Paleolithic hunt for large mammals (like elephants or bears) whose killing answered to both the physical need of the tribe for nutrients and to the mythic need of youth for encounter with death as the ultimate pedagogue (Shepard, 1973, 214–217). In the turn to settled agriculture, the deep fear of nonbeing has been transmuted into treating other humans as nonhuman. Genetically programmed as we are to require the "other" for our own coming into adulthood, if nature is literally and figuratively "walled away" from our experience, we will necessarily graft subordinated human "others" into the vacant role.

In Shepard's diagnoses of the condition of civilization, it is the animal body that is "missing in action." "The living world now faces," he says, "a massive failure of interspecies dynamics, signaled by the enormous destruction of life" whose psychological effects are equally devastating (Shepard, 1973, 233). We would simply add that the same is true of its spiritual mystifications. If Shepard's grasp of human development is roughly accurate, then the primordial and original "body of salvation" leveraging material survival and cosmic orientation alike is the living and dying flesh of large game, necessary for food, capable of killing, whose dying at human hands "schools" our species in the mysteries of metabolism and reciprocity that our own dying signals, but cannot assuage. And here the argument of this essay turns full circle.

Read from the vantage point opened by such a depth-critique of the history of civilization, Christianity's own theology of incarnation remains woefully docetic. It articulates an agro-industrial vision of salvation that has all relevant teaching and "transubstantiation" locked up inside the human species as a solipsistic creature capable of mediating its own ultimate meaning. Recast in light of hunter-gatherer ancestry and wisdom, the old saw would read, "man does not live by man alone," but by every animal and plant proceeding forth in our actual ecological reciprocity. Coded as creed, this latter symbiosis might be read as offering its own mantra of "flesh from flesh, true life from true life, of one being with each other" as the real image of wholeness adequate to and worthy of incarnational liturgy and discourse. And indeed, we find provocative testament to such emerging within the history of the tradition itself. Foundational moments of the tradition beg reading under indigenous rubrics and give suggestive slant to heterodox adaptations of Euro-normative Christianity in various colonial theaters post-1492.

"Christian" Indigeneity

Here I can only sketch in shorthand and in closing. The entire tradition of Jewish and Christian mission has its primal moment of emergence in Exodus accounts of the calling of outlaw Moses, wandering Sinai as bedouin herder. There he learns the desert ecology in an unwitting 40-year-long preparation for his role as liberator, in which he will guide a previously enslaved people through a harsh terrain, on the run from the imperial powers of the neighborhood. In the middle of that long escape saga, Moses's ability to know precisely where to strike crusted-up rock to release dammed-up rainwater (as many bedouin today can), will prove uncanny and legendary—a bit of local ecological savvy remembered as divine providence. Indeed, such environmental wisdom should occasion no surprise given the plant epiphany that launched this career (Ex 17:1–7). It is only over a long stretch of time and across multiple cultural chasms and much historical trauma that what began as an originally *vegetal* revelation eventually effloresces into the heights of Euro-Christian "metaphysical" speculation in a Thomas Aquinas, holed up in his Parisian room, wrestling with Moses's great apparition without an incarnational clue to the botanical materiality of such a "saving" desert disclosure. The ethereal and evanescent "I AM" was once a desert shrub "alight" with haunting Presence and terrifying Incandescence (Dt 33:16).

Fast-forwarding to the primal revelatory impetus of Christianity, we find the locust-eating, hide-wearing Baptist, submerging peasant Palestinians under Jordanian waves. He is not at all astonished when one of his water-purified ones emerges with third eye[5] open wide and staring, seeing through the torn veils of ideology and religiosity without apology, while a bird descends with coercion in its talons, driving the initiate into the desert on vision quest (Mk 1:1–14). The 40 days there incubate vocation, separate from all social input—naked skin absorbing sun and sweat, wind and dark, going down into the bowels of need and deprivation, listening only to crow cries, sand flies, and the whispers of ancestry inside the demons of history. We are told significantly, with all the economy of Markan expression, that Jesus was "with the wild beasts."

Of course the tradition, a scant three centuries into its outlaw struggle with the Roman imperial power, is suddenly in 313 CE co-opted into Constantinian service. It becomes imperial itself, nearly disappearing by the seventh century in the long, slow collapse of Roman social order. It survives only at the far western edge of Europe where its more radical impulses find reformulation in Iberno-Celtic vitalities and the shamanic-monastic zeal of Ireland.[6] Though having its local genius suppressed in favor of "orthodoxy" at the Whitby Synod in 664 CE, the "green" flavor that Irish Christianity embodies and carries back onto the continent gains emblematic memorialization in illuminated manuscripts giving us a tranced-out Christ encircled in a luxuriant tangle of natural bodies, all eating each other, infinitely. Ironically (we will be told by twentieth-century punditry), it is Irish Christianity, in effect, that "saved civilization" (Cahill, 1996, 1–5).

But by 1492, that salvation is clearly at the expense of any real rootage in an indigenous materiality. Christianity—except in the outback and among certain "heretical" sects of women—has gone entirely imperial in vision and consequence. Columbus and crew carry out its hubris, unrelentingly. But not totally! Again and again, around a globe evermore tightly drawn into the noose of capitalist commodification and orthodox indoctrination, local cultures living close to other creatures inflect the tradition in service of their indigenous wisdom.

Here there is only space to mention three, and those only in passing. A Gabayan Christian community in Cameroon will respond to twentieth-century evangelical mission by adapting Christ to its local herbal integration, recasting messiah Jesus as "my sore-cool-thing," as recounted by Lutheran-ethnographer Thomas Christensen (1990). This is a veritable plant-Christology, giving the Protestant savior new chops as leafy healer, bending the gospel toward a new dimension of incarnation. In the Amazon, a similar immersion takes place in the rain forest, giving rise to communities with names like Santo Daime, Uniao do Vegetal, and Barquinha (Madera, 2009, 68, 83, 85 ff; Wright, 2006, 183–184). All three center their practice in *ayahuasca* use, weaving their traditional hallucinogenic vision quests and healing rites into Christological accounts that radically rework the gospel into jungle terrain and terms and Jesus into the phylum of plant-teachers. And more closely related to the peculiarities of North American church experience itself, *vodou* in Haiti, under the veneer of an imposed Catholicism, transmutes and amalgamates west and central African traditional practices—kept alive in slave communities—into a survival religion capable of galvanizing and sustaining the planet's only successful national slave revolt (Perkinson, 2001, 566–567). Under its ready dismissal as merely "black magic," *vodou* codifies the gamut of human experience of duress and ecstasy, birth and demise, into a sensate extravaganza of collective experimentation with spiritual dynamism. Here local waters and falls, fish and flora, give choral counterpoint to the spirit-*loa* of ancestry, themselves emerging as patterned possessions provoking reflection and negotiation, translation and innovation, in the key of everyday experience and concern. Here the epitome of the residual memory might be *Damballa*, serpent-persona, taking flesh-of-human to crawl in concert with ancient rhythm and present need, dancing the human "horse" into a momentary visitation of the reptilian portion of our family phylum. Or it might be *Agwe* of the waters, drifting off to the deep with offerings and dreams or *Gede* of the graves, refusing to "go gently into that good night." And here again—all of this is for the sake of a gathered community, interpreting and submitting to a hidden wisdom, mediated in incarnate form whether from snake to human, water to community, or cemetery to grieving family.

All three alike yet await serious Christological attention under the rubric of anthropology's idea of the "little tradition"—a move that theology would do well to imitate (for a first attempt at such, see Perkinson, 2001; 2013). I have only tried to outline a basic frame for the questions they raise, and underscore the stakes in a world gone wildly overboard in its pretensions to control. While not exactly instances of the big game threat that Shepard thematizes, all three examples do nonetheless position their potency in the dialectic of life and death, offering physical intervention for bodily health, while encoding the possibility of working up their dangers into ritual embodiments. All of them open up the cosmos as a continuity of mystery, extending beyond the visible and durable. Their question yet remains extant for a globalizing Christianity, gone imperial in its neoliberal patronage: Just how incarnational is the human wholeness imagined in the gospel? Do we really take the *body* of the messianic flesh seriously? It extends as far as those living others who are the closest thing we will ever know this side of death to the "infinite qualitative difference" that a Kierkegaard or Barth so loved. In a first-century Palestinian voice—is not one of the primal saving words thus: "I am the vine" (Jh 15: 5)?

CHAPTER 5

CHRISTIAN SUPREMACY AND INDIGENOUS SAVVY: READING RACE AT THE CROSSROADS OF EUROPE AND THE AMERICAS

He had rejoined the old ways and was never the same again.

—*Gary Snyder talking about Alvar Núñez,*
The Practice of the Wild

The late August landing of a category-5 storm in 2005 marked a new moment in national consciousness in the United States. This natural catastrophe emerged as environmental counterpoint to the still raving fears of the 9/11 terrors unleashed four years earlier with such irrepressible power in dominant culture minds. Mainstream culture had suddenly been presented, in those earlier September airs, an unforgiving mirror and a searing taste of transnational rage serving heavy-gauge notice that the rest of the planet would not simply "knuckle under" to Western geopolitical pretensions to run the globe. Those two events constitute, I would submit, a double-barreled figure of "blowback." As signs of coming times, they served to ramify with profound effect the long-running racial subtext of the country. Here was violent force, in registers human and natural, exceeding every calculus of gated-community or gated-country bliss, registering the reality of vulnerability in psyche and body like few other events in the history of the land. But it is 9/11 that lodged with deepest political consequence, I would argue. Hurricane Katrina, in media (mis)representations of the fact, was indeed portrayed as having horrific effect.

But the terror of the portrayal was largely dependent upon those whose color had long before the storm's coming already marked them out as "monstrous" in national calculations of concern (and whose invented "savagery" eclipsed poor white and middle class suffering, in the mix). The advent and aftermath of Katrina was, at one level, simply more "TV drama" for much of the white middle class—fascinating to watch, with popcorn bowl in hand, but scarcely earth-shaking. The 9/11 attacks on the other hand, were seismic.

KATRINA AS TERROR

Nonetheless it is Katrina I wish to pause before in this writing, as posing the deeper sign of coming trouble. Whether itself related to global warming or not, certainly that particular Gulf Coast fury heralded a range of climate change danger even defense department planning comprehends—anticipating as it does, levels of cataclysmic upheaval whose resulting geopolitical struggles, it says, will make even the "War on Terror" seem tame by comparison. While the 2005 hurricane revealed more of the same in historic race relations and depictions, its emblematic punctuation of the interconnection between natural and social potency points to something new: a wildness of energy neither racial denigration nor wartime aggression can contain. That wildness is the subject of interest in what follows.

Most of us who inhabit the post-Katrina United States returned quite quickly to business as usual. The spectacle of a postmodern city of more than a million rendered uninhabitable in a single day of wind and water, and then tendered catastrophic by bureaucratic incompetence and financial commitments to war-making rather than care-taking, was just that. Spectacle. We tittered in titillation or boredom as New Orleans's poorest and blackest denizens descended into delirium or death on prime time live. All while we continued running our cars on the fumes of the oil we once thought as endless as the sea, running our mouths like words are reality, running our eyes across the kaleidoscope of trivial pursuits we have pulled around us like bedsheets against the anxieties of the coming night. But we who seemed so untraumatized by these fearful events are actually part of a long history of terror that is virtually the precondition of modern (so-called) progress and prosperity. This latter terror is the unnamed horror that Katrina's "headlined" terror dissembled. Its other name is supremacy. Its goal is control. Its practice is business as usual. Its sign is the commodity. Its color is whiteness—even when it allows tan- and yellow- and brown-hued bodies "honorary" occupancy of its well-policed domains of gated narcissism (whether called a suburb or a country). (An occupancy that is subject to revocation at any moment of frightened profiling, however.) But already I am betraying my own particular dis-ease in this peculiar world we share.

I am a poet by desire and an academic by vocation. I live and love by words. I am also white—but a white man, who in more than 25 years of living, working, organizing, and educating in black inner city Detroit, has been slowly (and irrevocably) educated, in psyche and body alike, about the difference skin tone makes. I am a white man who lives—as do all who look like me—in debt to the rest of the world. Other colors of appearance were made the excuse for my ancestors to raid, pillage, and plunder, degrade, enslave, and cut asunder—bodies from cultures, assets from ecologies, resources from the natural reservoirs producing them, to be mobilized on a global scale for my (typically) unthinking enjoyment and ready reduction, in short order, to mere garbage. But I get ahead of myself. There is an antihistory here that must be uncovered as the modern organization of terror that reproduces itself ruthlessly. Modernity *is* terror—but a terror with a color and with war as its preferred means and primal meaning of male being. The terror that Katrina signaled had its roots in this other horror.

THE HISTORY LEFT BEHIND

Premodern "Europe"[1] existed tenuously in 1492. As a restive domain of Christian supremacy, it was dwarfed (and surrounded) by the opulence and power of Islamic Mediterranean hegemony. It labored crudely as a small backwater of social and ecological devastation in the northwestern corner of a great east-west landmass known (today) as Eurasia. This latter vastness of steppe and mountain, sea and desert, shaped Europe profoundly over a considerable scale of time. Its longitudinal topography and trade routes bequeathed to that northwest corner most of her peoples and inventions, as well as her deep habits of reaction and restless hungers for freedom. This same axis of migration was also historic witness, in its Fertile Crescent navel, to the earliest domestication of plants and animals, the first genuflection to the tool of war, the most virulent incubation of the ideology of conquest, and the most relentless parade of imperial-paid warrior-mercenaries and their urban slave states on the face of the planet. Jared Diamond's *Guns, Germs and Steel* has poignantly and compactly outlined the development. The early "advance" and resulting advantage this peculiar combination of geography and ecology offered for the will-to-domesticate it birthed (and has suffered over the last 10,000 years) is otherwise touted as "civilization." The quite evident "superiority" of weaponry, technology, and cruelty that colonial historiography discloses as Europe's major calling card around the globe since 1492 is not a result of genetic predisposition, cultural predilection, or clairvoyant vision. It is rather, in the long view, an accident of ecology (Diamond, 1997, 25). More large mammals suitable for taming and controlled breeding, and more grains and legumes available for manipulation and controlled cultivation, existed in the temperate environments of the Crescent zone, and sites extending longitudinally both west and east, than anywhere else on the planet.

Innovations in technology fueled by these Mesopotamian possibilities of floral and faunal domestication readily found application in the similar ecological latitudes of China and the Mediterranean. In consequence, settled agriculture, urbanization, population increase, militant aggression and takeover of forager lands, and all the history of imperial expansion that followed quickly in its wake, took place *there* before showing their face elsewhere on the globe. Yes, Africa, Pacifica, and America have also undergone their own subjugation to the logic of hoarding and harrying. They too have ended up harassing plant and animal and human alike into pre-fixed ideas of purpose and price. But they have done so on a scale more circumscribed by the differences in topography and latitude that define their land masses and at a rate of diffusion and exchange slowed down by those north-south differences. The now nearly ubiquitous conquering and reengineering hubris that has never ceased to wreak havoc on the foraging gnosis and care-taking savvy of our ancestry around the globe had its root in near eastern routes into biblical lands. It had its first global champion in Europe. The modern move of this will-to-control into the hyperorganization and ruthless exploitation characteristic of globalizing capital after 1492 is not innocent of this longer history of advantage. That advantage is not explained by race or ethnicity, but primarily by geographic location and the accidents of biodiversity (Diamond, 15, 18–20, 28–32).

Race, however, has become the great inchoate apology and relentless ideology of the modern era for evident differences in so-called development and the technological initiatives of prediction and control that are the modern measure of such. Why did the West conquer the rest? It's in the genes, my boy! White ability is a God-given facility to commandeer the best, eliminate the pest, and rule the rest of life, like a Creator-become-incarnate-in-the-flesh-of George W. Bush, or now even the white mask over the black skin of Obama and his Wall

Street brood, invested and stewing in the House so aptly named. It is the burden of what I have to say in the rest of this chapter to unmask race as a modern form of fantasy gone ultimate in self-understanding and religious in effect. My words are careful here. When colonizing Europe went on march around the globe after the great accident of 1492—with Columbus and crew on quest for oriental silk and spices, bumping into the Bahamas and precipitating a crisis of commerce never yet resolved—that great sailboat venture was a quintessentially religious enterprise. And it has never ceased to leverage theology as the hidden modality of its presumed superiority. Even as its consciousness has become secular, white supremacy has remained a spiritual parody in all the places of its subsequent recreation of itself around the seven seas. Europe as both Catholic conquistador and Puritan settler did not have any room in its mental compass for spiritual intuitions that were not immediately and prescriptively "Christian" in confession and submissive and repressive in disposition.

Coming out of a 700-year-long struggle with Islam—most immediately in the hothouse tri-culture of medieval Spain where Muslim tolerance fostered tri-religious exchange with Jew and Christian—European colonizers quickly and preemptively "read" indigenous practices in terms of religious heresy and supralapsarian infidelity. That is to say—Native American dance, African trance, Indian *darshan* glances, Filipino prances in service of *anitos* and *agong*-chimed romances of the ancestors were all alike dismissed out of hand as heathen if not demonic. No one with pink-gray pallor bothered even to learn the code of those cultures on their own terms. Instead, all such gestures and meanings were instantly and peremptorily incarcerated in a Christian code that loaded the memory with shame and a fear of Adam's destiny. Indeed, both materially and theologically, the effect of Christian contact with indigenous practitioners was precisely a Cain-like "cleansing" of such "Abels" from the gardens and pastures of their respective ecologies and goodnesses. Even in places where some inhabitants (unlike African villagers or Georgia Cherokees) were allowed physically to remain on their ancestral domains as the new laboring class of Euro-profits, cultural genocide went bail for the physical version. Postmodern forms of globalizing pretension today have, as their inmost conviction of this economic right of preemption across the planet, a deep-going and denial-precipitating supremacy that is first of all a historic mode of religious chauvinism, buried in doctrine. White supremacy historically is the bastard son of a Christian supremacy that first raped, and then reified as demonized, the indigenous spiritualities it both pimped and decried.

Understand here that I am someone for whom Christianity has been focal and central most of my life. A born-again experience and Pentecostal spirit-baptism in 1970 led quickly to a rearrangement of educational priorities and lifestyle commitments leading to my leaving hometown Cincinnati for the northern Motown lair of auto company brownfields and ghetto despair in 1974. There I entered an intentional community of asset-sharing, communal-decision-making, poverty-level-dwelling fellow believers, black and white, married and single. Over the better part of two decades we struggled to translate "body-of-Christ" biblical language into urban activist initiatives of community development, cooperative housing conversion of slumlord apartments, neighborhood association crime watching, and community land-trust visioning for control of local geography and business enterprise. Christianity for me has not just been a Sunday morning activity with a Wednesday evening prayer meeting thrown in on the side. For much of my life it was the centerpiece of my pride, the determiner of my lifestyle, the arbiter of who I side with politically and live with socioeconomically. Its counsels helped decide who I partied with on the weekend, ate with in the morning, slept with at night, wept with in strife, and laughed with when life was good. Within its vision I found those with whom I would dream for the future and struggle alongside for the present. And its message of solidarity meant living in a core city neighborhood that was home for more than 20 years.

I do not say what I say about Christianity in history lightly. But my entire trajectory has been a long pilgrimage out of doctrinally leveraged terror of pre-Christian insight and into embodied struggle for indigenous people's rights to live and move and have their being. Among other things, this has entailed learning to discern the spirits of local places and honor the wisdom of traditional initiation rites and embrace ancestral lights in confessions not beholden to the control of a verse-shouting thumper of Pauline scripture. I recognize Christian convictions of the place of spirit in space and time as having their ultimate test in the scene of human depredation and exploitation.

At the center of that tradition is finally a man on an instrument of state torture—screaming his repudiation of any fusion of imperial delusions of grandeur with religious certainties of succor, not going into that good night quiet, but raging against the dying of the light, raging, indeed, against the political use of God as the guarantor of the violence of the king, raging against all the slow depravations of poverty, the silenced invasions of patriarchy, the slaughter of peasantry, the infanticides of Herod, the ecocides of Halliburton, the killing of a planet in the name of a stupid invocation of rapture, a God incarnate raging against a God disincarnate, bellowing without answer against every canker of despoliation!

I indeed embrace such—but realize that this vision of the deep meaning of Christianity is today actually anti-Christian, a raging of Jesus against the use to which Jesus has been put. Historically that appropriation of Jesus by imperial pretension has to be grasped in all of its real material depredation of actual cultures and peoples if it is to be grasped at all. Thus my demand that, in modern form, the relationship between Christian convention and white presumption has to be traced to the core and exposed! But also my conviction that indigenous witness must be re-entertained in all of its poly-vocal patience and recombinant practice underneath the Christian veneer to which it has been subjected. White supremacy will not be undone unless and until Christian supremacy is overcome.

THE WHITENESS ON TOP[2]

Colonializing Europe was a commercial venture undertaken as a spiritual crusade. It relied—for its organization of space and place and bodies—on the categories of Plato's Great Chain of Being, updated for modern meanings of ontology. On top, in this Euro-perception of reality, was God, followed in descending succession by angels, dead saints, living claimants to literate Christian belief, ignorant Euro-peasants, women tenants of male-controlled households, renegade heretics and mystics, Jewish (so-called) "Christ-killers," Muslim (said-to-be) "infidel worshippers of Satan," wild men denizens of the forests, monstrous hybrid creatures of the deserts, animals, fish and pheasants, vegetable residents of the ground, minerals, rocks and the entire round of the soils beneath the feet. The vision was hierarchical in the extreme, buttressed, especially in its Calvinist versions, by a double-predestination rigidity determining destiny for all, up front, with no recourse for change or conversion. Native peoples and practices around the globe were quickly inscribed into this system, assigning bestial position to the darkest skinned and reinforcing European male ascendancy as the very meaning of Christian vision. First Peoples here in the Americas, and African hosts enslaved on the coasts of Guinea, were judged animal and expendable, right next to the apes and chimpanzees. Filipinos, Hindus, and aboriginals, Maoris and Melanesians, Caribs and Mapuches, Mesquitos and Aleuts alike were objectified by the blue-blinking scientific eye as "other" and available for either labor or elimination, as the growing trade in land and commodities dictated.

Epistemologically, outer appearance became the theological short-hand for inner disposition. "Blackness" was birthed in the scheme as presumptive evidence of an obdurate heart—a supposedly dilatory spiritual condition given epidermal expression as the visual sign of a divine curse underwritten by the biblical story of Ham. That presumption and its theological underwriting anchored European comprehension of all other meanings and conditions of two-legged existence. This racialized apparatus constituted Euro-perception of physical difference and social distance. It quickly became what looked out from the white eyeball, impervious to all examinations in the mirror, the very light that sees darkness in the first place. Its half-life inside the Euro-American cranium is like a cesium of the soul. It operates as an imagined supremacy of white over dark, degrading constantly under assault from initiatives as disparate as the Civil Rights movement here and native rights agitation in Canada, anti-apartheid upheaval in South Africa and Gandhian struggle in India, but continuously irradiating into ever new subtleties of vision and euphemisms of expression, institutional practices of discrimination and foreign policy decisions to invade and "democratize."

Its payoff back behind the gates of affluence and inside the psyches of indifference is a certitude of superiority as unconscious as it is ubiquitous: a supremacy so thoroughgoing and unthought that it is now arguably the very basis of marketable "salvation." Make no mistake; Madison Avenue is profoundly apprised of the size of the prize whiteness figures: even when Victoria's Secret offers a cameo of tan allure in a bra, its profile and hue remains an augury of white. The latest marketing rage in the Pearl of the Orient, just to take one example, is a whole new raft of creams and liposuctions giving promise of becoming Barbie overnight to "benighted" dwellers of the 7,100 isles of the Philippines. Advertising as the new articulation of human wholeness—the secular version of salvific change towards bliss-bound personhood packaged in a commodity—is virtually irresistible in our day. Its discourse permeates the life-world even of the Borneo pidgin-speaker. And its 5,000 images per average day that assault First World minds and pelvises do so with singular virulence. Advertising—by any other name—is a theology of the popular, no matter its crassly material provenience! It no longer even pretends to hide its bid as ultimate: Buddhist chant as Christian proverb, Sufi swirl and Lakota eagle-bone whistle alike are fair game for its pabulum. Any one of us can easily resist the siren song of any given ad; what none of us can insist is that we are unaffected by mass marketing's subliminal pervasiveness. Its proffered destiny is a coveted wealth and purported well-being that remains overwhelmingly "white" in its cultural codes and violently Western in its geopolitical control. China is emerging as the ultimate rival in the game, the "first coming" of an off-color contender to the modern reign of white sameness, but even its culture is being tamed in the commercial, while its land is ringed with U.S. bases and bombs.

Whatever else it has been, the white supremacy birthed from the loins of coercive Christian self-certainty in early modernity has remained theologically germinal (and ultimate) even in its turn to technological visions of salvation. From its first mode as an overtly religious superiority, it morphed into a scientific conviction of racial ascendancy in its philosophical and biological assumptions in the eighteenth and nineteenth centuries. By the early twentieth century, it took shape as a color-blind fiction of "human being" normative for cultural achievement and moral progress. And by mid-century, it had become the patent motive of preemptive social architecture and organization of urban space by way of policy-assisted suburban and exurban movements, carving out their gated enclaves of affluence from the growing hordes of color here and abroad by way of state-of-the-art security systems and high-tech policing forces. (Part of the deep reason that New Orleans warranted only disinterested and languorous federal mobilization and light-hearted cackles about past drinking bouts on the part of W. when he did finally visit was almost certainly the interminable significations of race: after all, "those people" chose their impoverished and abandoned condition and only resisted evacuation because it interrupted their opportunity to loot.) Today white racial supremacy operates almost entirely by covert fiat. It has pushed so far under the surface of the smiling faces of our corporate technocrats and consumer-loving mall rats, as to be virtually unassailable, leaking out only under influences of alcohol ("I used the N-word last night at the party? I was just drunk, I don't really think that way!"), or in the protocols of ignorance (like the relative of mine who recently said of a church mate of hers, "Glenda is so nice you don't even notice she is black"). But the identity and entitlements leveraged in the presumption of white rights to global domination function very much like a this-worldly vision of salvation. The belonging that they buttress is virtually religious and ultimate. They are things for which, finally, we who are the beneficiaries are willing to get violent (even those of us whose whiteness is only off-color and provisional). The Iraq and Afghani wars and the vigilante and police killings of black males like Trayvon Martin or Michael Brown are merely some of the latest wrinkles in the historic bellicosity. Whiteness is to die—and kill—for, even if rarely today by that precise name. It remains itself even under a State Department smirk.

THE STORM AS TEACHER

But something else also remains unnamed under the imperial surface and the corporate glitter. There is an indigenity maimed and lame, but not dead. Its blood is red, its bone white, but its spirit is one of night and close-held intimacy with a ferocity much older and wilder than life lived vicariously through *Fear Factor*. We recognize the "blight" of cyber-control: it is no mistake that we now require extreme sports as partial remediation for our predictability and domestication. Those, like Gary Snyder, who still tramp the outback and listen by firelight to the language of what is yet able to bite a man (or woman) back into oblivion, write that humanity is not yet fully submerged into the vanity (Snyder, 1990, 13–16). Surprisingly, we have so far not manipulated ourselves into the genetic condition of "goofies" as Paul Shepard names our domesticated canine companions bred into docility for our petting hands and tiny yards (Shepard, 1998, 142–145). But we are at the near edge of such a turn to self-colonization in the cloning impulse; close to deeming ourselves capable of deciding what the optimal human is, over and above the complex attunements of our genetic origins in Pleistocene biodiversity. If we do opt to try to resplice the thousand-thousand years of DNA adaptation in service of a postmodern vision of efficiency and control, who will get to say what should be bred out of the mix? Do we think the average white man will vote to have children of color? The question is far beyond this brief exposition, but it sets the dilemma in stark relief. Do we believe in the evolutionary mystery of a biodiversity that includes the human animal in varied ecologies of reciprocity and obligation? Or place our bets on a cyber-eschaton of the universalized nano-machine, scene of zones of terminator drones policing the silicon palace of cloned beings, calculating existence in the algorithmic efficiencies of a Super-White House?

I am on the side of the stones and groans of million-year-old insects and animals (including my own species). And I am convinced our spirits have need of nurtures mythic and symbolic rooted in the soils and souls of primal cultures. Modernity is a huge and sustained effort at forgetting, a vaunted self-importance that is virtually pathological in its dismissal of what our ancestors knew. What if it is true that the entire project of civilized aggrandizement is a lockstep march off the evolutionary cliff of being? That is the historical record on

10,000 years of settled agriculture and the industrialization that has followed in its wake: it has virtually nowhere been sustainable. Why do we trust it? Its modern version has been a ceaseless promulgation of coercion across the entire planetscape. It has "disappeared" in rapid succession every trace of what small groups living in concert with their environments have based their vision of human "being" upon. It has unleashed a relentless parade of wars of conquest visited on every shade of human congress with natural process. And its calculus today is clear. White reserves the right to every place and resource for itself—underneath all the smoke and mirrors of an ideology of inclusion, freedom, and democracy for all. The image of the "all" deemed worthy of existence continues to be the norm represented in the halls of our Congress. Under any other shade and shape of appearance, it is that of the modern white man, the regnant ghost of the global machine. So in counterpoint, I want to invoke and hear the memory of a different vision, still extant underneath the revisions of neoliberal collisions and Christian conversions.

The example involves one of the earliest recorded experiences of a hurricane refugee along the coast of Louisiana. And stands in marked contrast to the likes of archetypal Euro-explorers such as Hernán Cortés—conqueror of Mexico, who ended up, in the words of Snyder, a "beaten, depressed beggar-to-the-throne." Or Nuño de Guzmán, crazed and sadistic governor of more than 25,000 Indians of the "New" World, who sold 10,000 as slaves, precipitating a mass exodus from otherwise peaceful villages, according to conquest historian Todorov (Snyder, 1990, 13). The Andaluzian pilgrim recruit Alvar Núñez Cabeza de Vaca came as treasurer with a 1526 expedition of conquistadores to Florida bent on gaining intelligence along the panhandle coastline and points west. But he was quickly stranded and abandoned among the First Peoples of the area following a terrifying killer storm in the fall of 1527. He spent the next eight years wandering the Louisiana, Texas, and New Mexico wilderness and being himself refashioned as "wild" under tutelage of various indigenous wisdoms and ecological exigencies (Archives of the West; Snyder, 1990, 13, 22–23).

At one point, while out gathering spring bittervetch with the Avavares Indians who were his hosts and saviors, Núñez lost his way and endured five nights alone, naked under a north wind in the Texas winter. He huddled in open pits he dug in a riverbank, covered only by picked grass. He reemerged from this terrifying ordeal as a reluctant healer, prevailed upon by native folk for cures he himself did not recognize or believe he could offer. Belief, however, was not the coin of this game, but rather indigenous confidence in experiential potency, activated by Núñez's condition of vulnerability and the poverty he shared with them, reinforced by his return from the winter landscape as from the dead. Indeed so unwilling was he initially that the Indians had to force his hand by withholding food until he performed the kind of rituals they demanded. He prayed Catholic, believed not at all, but breathed and gestured "shaman" in native rumor, transformed as he was by the loss of everything and re-born as himself "native" to the place. No native ever died in his presence thereafter.

Once back in Spanish mission headquarters in Mexico City eight years later, however, he found himself once again "lost," now among the "civilized," able neither to effect nor to will healing in the city. His subsequent account of his travels remains Euro-accented, but nonetheless instructive. In Snyder's words, he learned the "old ways" and was transformed into a person of the New World (Snyder, 1990, 13). And his experience points toward a general condition of the difference between modern Western Christians and the average indigene after European contact that has found one of its most prescient characterizations in the analysis of religious studies scholar Charles Long.

THE WILDNESS UNDERNEATH

In one sense, Long's vision represents the heart of what I wish to say here. Working out of the Chicago School of History of Religions, Long is renowned for having raided Euro-theory and adapted it to argue back against Euro-presumption of objectivity and superiority in studying indigenous religiosity. German Lutheran scholar Rudolph Otto, in particular, supplies Long a seminal schema for aphoristic summary of the religious result of Western conquest of native cultures. Otto's ideogram for cross-cultural examination of spiritual intuition around the globe—the *mysterium tremendum et fascinosum*, the Great Mystery that is simultaneously Terrifying and Fascinating—is taken up by Long and thrown down on the anvil of colonial encounter to articulate a profound difference of experience (Long, 9, 137-139). Where the colonized suffered not only physical violation but also epistemological dismemberment, the West merely enjoyed seeming confirmation of its own myth of superiority (Long, 123, 177, 193). Obviously Christianity was preeminent compared to native practice—after all, there was the dark body lying dead on the ground! For European Christians, the encounter with native others only provoked fascination and disgust: see how they dance with eyeballs staring, growling like bears, strutting like birds, seeing ghosts! What exorbitance and stupidity! Christian ritual, by comparison, is tame and secure, a predictable series of gestures invoking a stable deity, locked in a book, monopolized by an elite, who looks and acts remarkably like the king of Spain or the queen of England!

Indigenous practice, on the other hand, was forced back into its deepest recesses of memory, codified in myths of origins and regularly reactivated in ritual. These stories typically recalled a time when some minor human fault—peeling the banana the wrong way, stepping into the wrong puddle, eating the wrong fruit—resulted in the fracturing of the entire known world, a fault line appearing that forever after separated the human community from the divine world. This indigenous Ur-experience of a great pain and loss, mysteriously visited on the tribe for some tiny infraction in a golden age of origins, is revisited across the globe after 1492 in its new and terroristic epiphany as the Great White Colonial Cataclysm. Far from fascinatingly safe and forgiving, this colonial advent of Irresistible Force is ineluctable and terrible, a sudden apparition of power embodied in white skin and iron cannon, galloping horse and silent disease, that brooks no propitiation. It is a coming of violence that is entirely gratuitous, unresponsive to native notions of economic exchange or ritual amendment. It tears open native bodies and cosmologies alike. And the work it enjoins among those who would survive is virtual re-creation from the ground up, amalgamating what remains of indigenous myth with Christian verse, labored into livable texture in ritual forms of translating agony into vitality (Long, 170, 196–197).

Such, would argue Long, is what we have historically in Native Ghost Dance and Pacific cargo cult, Black Church shout and *vodou veve* stomp, Rasta vision and Filipino *Pasyon*—a vigorous recasting of the catastrophe of colonial arrival into a new hybrid survival mode (Long, 110, 166–167). This is initiation writ large, the experience of an engulfing and unexplainable terror that provokes something like ritual judo in response—colonial violence relativized in a refigured Absolute, encountered as *Tremendum*, embraced as the Great Mystery that finally eats everything and everyone irresistibly, that cannot be tamed in tautology, maimed in a holy meal, controlled by a robe and a prayer. No! This is God encountered as Wild. And the human being who does suffer and survive such is likewise confirmed in an undomesticated animation and an adamantine interiority. The examples of such are many—ranging from Malcolm to Martin, from Dorothy Day on the east coast to Caesar Chavez on the west, from Aun Sang Su Chi in Asia to Mandela in South Africa, Leonard Peltier in prison to Chico Mendes in the grave. Even more to the point, there are examples all around, anonymous to all but a handful of family and friends who comprehend their heroism and resilience, whose lives and breath yet remain a question addressed to the rest of us.

While there is much more to be said about this juxtaposition of relative experiences of the West and the rest in the colonial theater, suffice it here to summarize simply. The former emerge as a people of the book, for whom the Spirit is a fascinating Allurement, merely confirming an imagined refinement and supremacy of cult and culture of which they are already convinced, God as one more bauble of glitter hanging on a middle class lifestyle, a living license to steal on a global scale and war darker-hued others into submission or disappearance. The latter, on the other hand, know the Ultimate as Irreducible Other, as likely to appear as Sheer Terror as One who cozies me like a child in a cradle, who demands not abject trembling, but intense recognition and vital animation, even if death should come in response. And this conundrum of postcolonial difference—of tame sameness face to face with serpentine otherness coiled like a cobra within, coded in color and ritualized in quite alternative religious practices (even in those instances when they are both carried out in the name of Christian witness)—forms the new matrix of the entire globe.

THE POSSIBILITY OUT FRONT

The argument I am pressing in this chapter is that indigenous memory of an "other" way of being human not beholden to the seemingly omnipotent force of market calculus, the All-Hallowed Hidden Hand of Adam Smith's riff on reality, marks a hidden transcript of hope that may be the key spiritual resource in avoiding planetary catastrophe and species suicide. The shards of that memory remain extant all over the planet. They appear in practices as diverse as "getting happy" in inner city Baptist church hours of whooped text and hollered reflex, dancing delirious in Trinidadian Marti Gras or Ati-Atihan powers of blacking up and getting down in a January version of the Filipino tradition of *balik-bayan*, native vision quests beyond the gaze of New Age eagerness to try to buy salvation in a dream-catcher, or even the spin-fests of a DJ Qbert, cruising out to the edges of the known universe in ambient sound, scratched from a vinyl disc, trancing the consumer mind into a multiplex bind of hidden signs of infinity, for a brief time of respite (as we shall see later; see also Perkinson, 2013, 207–221).

The issue is not the precise form of an upstart claim of a different "human" design. It is rather, how we who have been cut off from our bigger being, "reduced," as the Spanish colonial initiative liked to put it, from feral wildness to civilized conformity, now "read" that *reducido* and resolve to live in consequence. Western Christianity historically is a vine bearing violent "white" fruit that yet in its root still harbors, and sometimes even nurtures, indigenous sap. The trap is to continue to buy into the upwardly mobile rape of the planet like it was a divine intention. The rap that counsels otherwise calls for a downsized revision of human decisions to enslave all other species and a turn away from growth as the god of the age. The time may soon be upon us when we have entirely lost the capacity to listen to this other history of our ancestry. But it remains, for now, alive as the primordial "groan" underneath our more trivialized complaints. It rumbles in the dark as the vague inkling of a journey lived courageously and raw—neither idyll nor nightmare—dreaming "at-home-ness" in the great concert of living beings, rather than continued haunting and insomnia inside a Disney bubble of deadened sensations. It remembers . . . But of course, such a task of reading is not easy, given the lightning quick capacity of global capital today to take over every least upwelling of vitality in whatever form, package it in plastic wrap, and sell it back to us for dollar. But we, indeed, have not been promised merely a garden of roses.

The demand is severe. How learn to hear all over again what remains kicking and clawing for attention inside our own genes? How renew our appreciation for the caterwauling cacophony and keening of not-yet-disappeared wildlife outside our doors and cars, as yet unsubdued in the code of the commercial, "pheening" merely for space to breathe and live? Our deepest vitality will not be satisfied with mere TV watching. Reduced to such, however, it will wage war in its silenced rapacity, its hunger for living meaning, and project all manner of "night" on those it deems different from itself. It has not ceased to do so for 500 years now, and screams "terror" at every voice, every counter-vision, that would call it back to itself. My own discipline in the mix, however, is to listen with the ear, not only of my head, but my entire body. Who I listen to are especially those dwelling in great poverty—pushed, by the great white-war-machine, the great global grab-fest, to the very edge of existence, where human efflorescence cannot control the future, cannot even control its own circumstance, but settles, instead, for defiant gestures loaded into recalcitrant postures, choreographed with humor and beauty, with a memory of polyphony, given a tongue and a toe, refusing to die before death actually does come.

The poor of this world often—not automatically, not infallibly, but often and very evidently—know the sheer gratuity of existence as a thing of unutterable eloquence. It is all they have left. Inside that memory, showing up inchoately in the words and grimaces of poverty, is an even deeper intuition of a life lived for long ages on this planet, indigenously native to places and local powers. Such a life is not lived in the conviction of human superiority to every other life form. It is not ready to launch itself on a millennia-long death-march to prove it so (and in the process prove itself an experiment in evolution gone awry). But it is rather the grateful and wise comprehension of the kinship of things and the limitation of all lives and beings, and the imponderable and astonishing dance that all creation engages in, anyway. Learning all over again, in the midst of war and death-incarnate-in-history, to give our bodies to such an ancient force, to such an irrepressible groaning of life for uninhibited living, is the task of all of us. It will not promise us escape from either death or pain. But the Great White Dream of the Suburb, in spite of its advertisements otherwise, does not do that either. Rather we will find ourselves summoned to dare follow our deepest intuition of adventure and justice and mobilize our best energies for a lifetime of battle and bold celebration, in spite of apparent failure and demise. The question remains as irresistible as it is bracing for all of us bought off by a tepid vision of destiny: For what are we willing, finally, to give our life?

PART III

THE QUESTION IN MODERNITY: COMMUNICATION AMONG THE SUBORDINATED

CHAPTER 6

UNDERNEATH GUADALUPE; INSIDE
EZILI: READING POSSESSION
AT THE CROSSROADS OF
PERFORMANCE AND TERROR

Cuix àmo nican nicà nimoNantzin?
(Am I, your mother, not here?)

—*La Virgen de Guadalupe to Juan Diego in Nahuatl,
in Harris,* Carnival and Other Christian Festivals

Harvard physician-anthropologist Paul Farmer, an activist doctor, underscored a significant dilemma in his 2004 work, *Pathologies of Power*. Laboring unremittingly to bring health-care treatment *to* some of the globe's poorest residents—and laboring, doubly thus, *against* the structural violence that so overwhelmingly adjudicates who has access to such care and who simply suffers—Farmer struggled with a contradiction. As one concerned with "unveil[ing] the pathologies of power" that so prodigiously cause and compound global pain, he often found himself torn between the responsibility to bear witness and the necessity to respect silence (Farmer, 2004, 26). In Haiti, in Chiapas, in Russian prisons, among HIV and tuberculosis sufferers destined to die early and often, Farmer faced a condition he wrestled into analysis with the aid of Graham Greene literature. "Dr. Plarr was a good listener," Farmer quoted from Greene's *The Honorary Consul*:

He had been trained to listen. Most of his middle-class patients were accustomed to spend at least ten minutes explaining a simple attack of flu. It was only in the barrio of the poor that he ever encountered suffering in silence, suffering which had no vocabulary to explain a degree of pain, its position or its nature. In those huts of mud or tin where the patient often lay without covering on the dirt floor he had to make his own interpretations from the shiver of the skin or a nervous shift of the eyes. (Greene, 1973, 59)

Farmer offers a chiding correction: the silence of the suffering sick-bays of Peru or Chiapas or inner city Boston is an *imposed* silence, "from above" (Farmer, 2004, 25). Had Plarr been a better listener, Farmer rejoins, "He might have heard the true cacophony of the barrio" (25). Subjugated people do not expect to be granted the pliant courtesy extended the privileged; they can indeed be reported as stoic in their pain. But underneath that mask of quietude lies a great and bitter eloquence. In his own practice, Farmer found himself sometimes enjoined to scratch at that surface silence, triggering an articulate eruption. Just as often, however, he decided not to scratch. And here lies the dilemma. In his discussion, Farmer notes a warning issued in the 1970s by Laura Nader: "Don't study the poor and powerless, because everything you say about them will be used against them" (Nader, 1972, 294). Going beyond mere voyeurism, beyond the temptation to a "lurid recounting," requires self-reflection and serious political compassion. Solidarity must be navigated between the possibilities of a first and a second silence: one imposed by the powerful; a second chosen by the researcher, astonished and chastened by the vocabulary and artistry and agony hidden beneath that (misperceived) first level, sometimes better left quietly respected than exuberantly explained. For the essay to follow here, this dilemma emerges as the deep question of the analysis: what finally is our responsibility in our work? Is it merely to know and exhibit? Or also to *be known*—in our privilege as academics—by what we come *to* know? And thus in quest for a better world—theorize and live a certain limit?

SUBALTERN SILENCE

How can we speak *to* what we dare not speak *for*? The immediate task at hand in this chapter is to probe the possibilities of inchoate political spiritualities encoded in three different emblems of Marian devotion. These include the Lucan tradition of an "original" renegade Mary mothering Jesus in Roman-occupied Palestine; a *Mexica-Azteca* counter-ritualization of the Madonna tradition imposed during Spanish colonial incursion; and a Haitian reworking of the Roman Catholic

Virgin Mother archetype in service of slave survival. But as backlight to this focus on covert forms of Marian resistance, it will be useful first to gloss a well-known modern intervention organized around the memory of an ambiguous act of political refusal on the part of a young female operative in the twentieth-century Indian independence movement.

In her (in)famous essay "Can the Subaltern Speak?" postcolonial scholar Gayatri Spivak labors to pose a question to intellectual responsibility regarding representation of those who have no access to the writing of their own history. After slabbing up dense layers of theory across more than 30 pages of text (ranging from Marxism, feminism, and psychoanalysis to deconstruction, colonial historiography, and discourse analysis), only in the last two pages does Spivak finally land her theorizing "on the ground." There she sketches, in tantalizing brevity, the example that dramatizes the dilemma she is bent on expositing (Spivak, 1988, 310–313). Spivak's focus is the 1926 North Calcutta suicide of guerilla activist Bhuvaneswari Bhaduri, who hanged herself in her father's apartment in apparent delirium at being unable to face carrying out the assassination assigned to her. Cryptic as her description is, Spivak is yet at pains to point out that "deliruim" here finds its own dilemma as a characterization. Bhuvaneswari had carefully waited until she was menstruating before killing herself, dispelling the idea of pregnancy outside of marriage as a precipitating factor. It is a delirium that bleeds across the page to engulf the reader. Strobe-lit as it is in the kaleidoscope of theory offered, the event eclipses itself in silence.

The postcolonial scholar herself supplies only the most tentative "speaking." Can Bhuvaneswari's act be read as a subaltern rewriting of the text of *sati*-suicide, she asks, in context and detail, displacing any way her body might be inscribed as captive to the passion of a single male (lover)? Or even more provocatively, can she be understood to have side-stepped interdiction by Brahmanical texts proscribing *sati* for menstruating widows (Spivak, 1988, 308)? *Sati*-sacrifice, historically in India, was a Brahmanically approved practice encouraging widows to leap into the cremation flames consuming their dead husbands' bodies in order to preserve their patriarchal legacy intact and to earn karmic merit for themselves (increasing their prospect of being born in a "higher form" in the next round of reincarnation). Spivak had only one page earlier already underscored that *Sati* is also a common proper name referencing the mythological sacrifice of the goddess Durga—archetypal "good wife" of Shiva—whose unwanted intervention in family matters as an "upstart" daughter defending her husband's honor to her own disparaging father, occasions abusive conflict and results in her choice to immolate herself. As recounted in the patriarchal Vedic account, Durga's dead body is then borne across the entire cosmos in Siva's resulting fury-dance, until her dismembered body parts are strewn over the earth, marking out the pilgrimage paths for which India is famous. *Sati* as ritual is thus grounded in the tragedy and dignity of divine struggle. Spivak pointedly juxtaposes Bhuvaneswari's own intra-family act of self-immolation alongside this well-documented mythic image of a "blazing, fighting Durga" regularly invoked by independence movement males as a popularly remembered icon of dissent. The conjoining is provocative. The meaning, however, remains indeterminate. Bhuvaneswari's timing cannot be assigned simple clarity. In concluding, Spivak affirms definitively, what she had previously only asked as question: "The subaltern as female cannot be heard or read" (308).

The reader is left with this quiet indicative, backed by a stare. . . . In the mix of patriarchy and mythology, archetypal hegemony and opaque agency of an unsung actor for autonomy, lies an unanswerable question of subaltern consciousness and resistance. But it is also a punctuated silence that demands a tentative speaking. In what follows, Spivak's insistence that intellectual advocacy must always foreground its own interdictory powers of representation forms the background for our own inquiry into a Marian-menagerie of fighting female figures hosting subaltern ironies *writ large*. In question ultimately, in such an enterprise, will be the politics of representation itself. How far down into subaltern silence dare we extend a tentative and uncertain voice? Spivak outlines the plausibility of a cryptic gender critique of independence politics, complicated by a Goddess-memory encoding indigenous agency before Euro-colonization. Neither is definitive nor simply clarifying for political resistance. But the complexity thus divined, among those deemed unworthy of history's speech, is itself both a "speaking" and a silence demanding respect.

And so shall we find among the sequence of Mary figures contemplated here. Like Bhuvaneswari, their witness will prove cryptic and polyvalent. As I will underscore, each of the three Marian icons negotiates histories of rape and abuse in the process of celebrating maternal agency and political dissent. For her part, Bhuvaneswari refuses patriarchal politics and romance altogether, even as her choice provokes consternation and "wondering." Just how much these respective emblems of female struggle inside colonial theaters of power are actually congruent and similar will have to remain part of their "subalterities." But certainly Spivak's writing of Bhuvaneswari under the rubric of "underclass silence" likewise comprehends something of the

Marian texts. As does her hint that the choice exhibited, both summons and questions popular mythology.

It also brings us to the edge of an even deeper abyss of "maternal silencing" and "mythic remembering." Inside and beyond the struggles of these archetypal Marian warrior-mothers lies the subalterity of the earth itself. Can this subaltern speak? Indigenous myth did presume to give voice to such. But it did so in a mode of "not knowing"—carefully disabling certainty within layers of polyphony and idiosyncrasy and simple honoring. Underfoot was an otherness so potent that it could not and should not be penetrated except with grave care and self-offering. For many indigenous, earth was both primal mother and ultimate destiny. Mythology was her muse—in a speaking so obviously storied and fantastic there could be no mistaking its humility and restraint. There, indeed earth *could* speak, because not spoken *for*.

But how about now? If the land could vent from under the blade of plow and roof of concrete, puncturing the deafness of our civilizational ears to the silences of soil and river, ocean and mountain, what might we hear? Certainly a report back on the rape and dismemberment that "is" agricultural clear-cutting and industrial explosion and urban paving over! And indeed also what today we *are* beginning to hear from the environment: a biosphere upending in revolt!

But here, we do not attempt such ventriloquism. The earlier allusion is simply caution. Human subalterity is still a kind of "speech" on top of an even more primal silencing. In what follows it will be enough to hint a renegade and promiscuous complexity exercising one strand of our own species' *mythos* of mothering and survival. The motherhood and erotics and rebellion of "mother" earth herself still lie largely unspoken in our time. "Historiography" is so far inadequate to her voice. That text is more likely sprout and hunt and volcano and tsunami. And now, climate change! Perhaps, however, learning to listen to the subaltern rebuff encoded in three popular Mary myths across time and geography can aid that more urgent task.

The Meaning of Murk

Scholars of communication tell us that somewhere between 65 and 92 percent of what is communicated between human beings is carried by nonverbal behavior. Other scholars in the field have begun to map the force and patterns of a rhythmic "entrainment" undergirding and enabling verbal exchanges of the tongue, whenever humans try to engage in meaningful interaction with each other (Leonard, 1978, 17–22). This essay builds on both of those orientations to probe the domain of a creative and corporeal "murk," generated through creolized forms of transmutation in situations of domination where subordinate peoples have had to invent necessarily subaltern identities to survive their captivity inside the taxonomy of exploitation.

In particular, this chapter will examine folk iconologies of female saint-deities in the traditions of early Palestinian Christianity, popular Catholicism in Mexico, and *vodou* in Haiti to explore the way cultural critique and political inquiry are often coded into hybrid public symbols in situations of colonial and postcolonial domination. James Scott's notion of the difference between hidden and public transcripts will supply the theoretical trope (Scott, 1990, xii–xiii, 1, 8–9, 37–39, etc.). Our particular interest is the double-valence by which these folk-figurings explore popular power as they are employed in fests and fiestas, carnivals and cavortings, in their respective geographies.

In each case, the claim will be that "what you see is not what you get." Rather, "what you see depends upon to whom you belong" (Albrecht, 1995, 162). Each of these "icons" will be analyzed as instances of a collective and creolized form of "inverse tricksterism." They will comport as folk-agency, gathering up the limitations domination imposes on subordination in public rituals and—in picaresque ribaldry encoding political savvy—parading and celebrating the "limitation of limitation" in full view of authority. Said another way, I will claim that these vernacular posturings exhibit and enact an oblique mastery *of* mastery by refusing the dichotomy between domination and subordination. They simultaneously mimic and subvert—and subvert precisely in mimicking—the forces that overwhelm. At the least, these performances stand forth as "inquiry," a material and embodied mode of thinking by means of mixing, investing colonial symbols with indigenous histories in such a way that the reciprocal and uneven interpenetration of traditions becomes not a problem to be solved, but an embodiment lived.

The analysis will proceed by juxtaposing these various versions of Mary—each taken up over time, by communities struggling with imperial domination—in ways that exhibit something of Scott's delineation of the transcripts of power, encoding a politics of struggle inside a public discourse of compliance. Ultimately the inquiry will question Scott's own claim that consciousness remains clear behind the veils of the code. We propose, instead, to query the possibilities of a resistance that is neither clear nor conscious, but for all that, not unresistive and creative.

The Palestinian Mary

The degree to which the gospel of Luke stands as a certain kind of *apologia*, before the bar of Roman power, for a first-century Palestinian resistance movement, remains an open question. Certainly this gospel writer is "translating," for a Greco-Roman sensibility, what had begun as a vernacular Jewish initiative. Launched by John and led by Jesus, it was a movement of both revitalization and confrontation. It challenged authority in a charged-up symbology of popular messianism and rural apocalypticism and championed the concerns of peasants and the poor. Luke's gospel in particular, clearly but cryptically invokes Jesus under the rubric of "Jubilee," casting him as a prophet who embodied the ancient message of debt-release and land-return that formed one of the early ideals of Israel. Such a message would have aimed radically at the very lynchpin of Roman imperial power that worked its colonial imposition through comprador elites. These latter were composed of "priests" (cultic authorities), "scribes" (media-intelligentsia), and "elders" (entrepreneurial landlords) using imminent domain and debt-extension to redistribute land and power toward those supportive of Roman control. This much seems patent. But it is also the case that this "gentile" gospel is written after the fact of Roman re-conquest of Palestine in response to the 64 CE Zealot revolt that had temporarily reinstalled Jewish autonomy. How then to read the subtext of prophetic critique that so thoroughly underwrites the Lukan text is uncertain: the intent could as well be "accommodationist assimilation" as "veiled dissent."

What is certain is that Luke, in a time of proliferating gospel tracts including at least one going by the name of "Mary," introduces the mother of Jesus as iconic figure, spitting rhymes of ancestors (Lk 1:26–56). In an account opening his gospel with the innuendo of revolt, Luke has a young female villager making a unilateral choice for motherhood absent any "male" input save that of the (supposedly male) deity-on-high, Yahweh. She then seeks comfort and confirmation in the company of elder-kinswoman Elizabeth, who had just conceived after menopause. This little coalition of "unusual" conception immediately erupts in political polemic once together. Elizabeth gives vent from her belly full of the kicking of cousin John. Mary goes ecstatic and bombastic in response—ventriloquizing her far-distant relation, Hannah, who had heralded Samuel's birth, a millennium before, with a proto-Magnificat diatribe of her own, likewise directed against the power-mongers of her day (I Sam 2:1–10). Though often celebrated in high-brow musical sophistication, the rant from Mary's lips is actually peasant jeremiad gone eloquent—singing the downfall of wealth and uplift of want in undisguised longing for inversion of the social order at hand (Lk 1:51–53).

What is amazing in hindsight is the degree to which the political edge of this eloquence has been effaced by its long career of spiritual inclusion in various imperial projects. Most Christians across two millennia of history would scarcely identify the Virgin with a sentiment of hot revolt, but the text is extant for all to read in unvarnished poignancy. Here we have—whether Luke had intentionally smuggled in the insurgent hint or not—the beginnings of a recombinant religious hegemony: sharp-tongued challenge gradually silenced in favor of the sweetness of obsequiousness, image overriding language once the Madonna-tradition has gained its ritual obeisance and patriarchal *hermeneusis*. In terms of Scott's trope of transcripts—this is an intimacy of conspiracy, hidden in the furthest outback of empire, slowly pulled into public service of the imperial palace and made iconically the inverse of its private counsels. Further down the road of imperial redeployment, Mary will end up crowned as patron-queen of the world-potentate. But it is also an adolescent female subalterity, given significance only in a male text, overwriting her voice. Whatever the actual mix of contestation and conformity cobbled together in the practical struggles of her own life—her witness as a woman and a mother is lost within the patriarchal silencing that shrouds her action. Mary, certainly, as Spivak might say, cannot speak.

What glimmers darkly *ir*-repressible, however, is an out-of-bounds pregnancy, troubling the memory coded into the patriarchal rewriting of a revolutionary chant. Some scholars will even intimate that behind the surrogate speaking is an incident of rape by one of the Roman occupying forces (a practice that was certainly part of the Roman razing of Sepphoris near Nazareth in 4 BCE according to Josephus). If so, it is a travesty quickly transvalued into divine uptake of the cause, making of victimage a beatific virginity, and of the resulting "bastardy" a messiah (Schaberg, 1987; Sawicki, 2000, 186–187, 192–193, 195–197). Whatever the historical truth of Mary's pregnancy, the impenetrability of the pre-text is also opportunity: the canon will ever after harbor a "subaltern oppugnancy" open to all manner of seizure and "possession." Rumor of Jesus' illegitimacy will cloud the tradition long afterwards. And the name "Mary" will come to harbor all manner of projection and beguilement—a people's haven for hopes and desires intolerable to official orthodoxy.

THE MEXICAN *GUADALUPE*

Fast forward an epoch to the "New World" theater of Euro-colonial rise from the shadows of feudal backwardness and self-loathing. Newly emerging nation-states are seeking to go "back door" on the 750-year hegemony of Islamic ascendancy over the Mediterranean basin, in order to gain Euro-access to Asian goods and enough gold and silver to launch a new crusade. Exactly what happens in the year 1531, in the Meso-American ruins of the former *Azteca* empire, also remains an open question. Gradually reorganized as New Spain under Cortez's genocidal policies and Catholic auspices of evangelism and forcible conversion, "Mexico-in-the-making" is host site to pandemic native hopelessness and recurrent suicide. On December 12, a peasant Indian christened "Juan Diego" reputedly encounters (apparently for the fourth time) a vestal virgin and vestigial goddess named "Maria," issuing commands and giving signs for episcopal building projects on the Tepayac hill-site of the formerly regnant Tolteca earth-mother, Tonantzin. As is often the case with dominant-culture significations gaining traction in popular-culture idioms, the exact provenance of each of the many meanings signified by the Virgin of Guadalupe is finally unrecoverable. What seems assignable, in scholarly investigations to date, is a gradual accretion. A sixteenth-century *culto* practiced on a quite local scale gains theological advocacy and exposition in the mid-seventeenth century in service of a growing *criollo*-consciousness of Mexican-born prelacy, eager to energize their movement to secede from Spain. Indeed, this Maria has her own four *evangelistas*, giving emblematic representation to her visage in four "gospels" of *guada-lupanismo* dating from Sanchez's work in 1648, through Lasso de la Vega's and Tanco's texts of 1649 and 1666, respectively, culminating in Florencia's 1688 *La estrella del norte de Mexico* (Taylor, 2003, 279–282).

While the "subaltern" beginnings of the 1531 Tepayac-apparitions remain as opaque as a Marian rant in first-century Palestine or a Bhuvaneswari *sati*-offering in 1926 Calcutta, what is clear in the textual tradition initiated in 1648 is an emerging utility. The cojoining of an originally sixteenth-century "Indian" devotional stream with a seventeenth-century Spanish urban concern to make a New World break from the old proves potent (Taylor, 2003, 293). The history of subsequent political struggles unleashed under the Guadalupe-image of *La Morena* ("the little brown woman") is estimable. It enrolls in its lists: the nineteenth-century independence initiative of Hildalgo, lifting Guadalupe banner against the Spanish Virgin of Remedies in a battle of Virgin against Virgin; the twentieth-century revolutionary rupture of Zapata ironically deploying this "little mother Tonantzin . . . even as he destroyed churches and seized temples"; and finally the contemporary United Farm Workers movement of Chavez and Huerta, organizing striking California grape pickers under the insignia of this most Mexican of Catholic Madonnas (Dussel, 1995, 126–127, 205). Dussel (among many others) unpacks the complexity of the trajectory and the symbology that the tradition brings into play. It is a story memorialized in the Nahuatl *Nican Mopohua* (of Lasso de la Vega), marking the "sixth sun" of *Aztecan* apocalyptic mythology, announcing the cataclysmic collapse of the *Mexica* world order. On a December Saturday, ten years after Cortez's decimation of the land, that same sun illuminates an unexpected hope for the Indian peasant Diego—coding in song and rose petals and bright rays, the signs of an *Azteca* sacred event (Dussel, 1995, 124–125, 204).

The image that appears on Juan Diego's coat—however it got there—interweaves Spanish Christian virgin and Indian earth-mother in a thematic Euro-*Indio* amalgam. Beckoning toward a post-*Azteca* future, the mix opens, in some retrospective thought, a new mode of existence for a crushed culture. But the blending is motivated. It positions the Virgin as champion, initially, of *criollo*-concern, even as that white patriarchal project is itself wrestled into service of more sharply *mestizo* sentiments among those caught in the deep contradictions of the Conquest ("mixed bloods" were hated by poor *indios* and *ladino* overlords alike, even as they were despised by Euro-elites for being off-color and anomalous, and they thus learned, in the pain of an impossible positioning, to repudiate each in turn).

The Nahuatl story, nonetheless, continues to carry other traces as well. It offers the open embrace of a hyphenated race mother, Guadalupe-Tonantzin, come expressly, as the tale goes, to hear the cries of the conquered. She herself graciously "waits," in not-so-veiled preference, on a poor *indigenous* passerby (Juan Diego), in subtle counterpoint to the marked refusal to do so, on the part the archbishop to whom she sends her lowly client (Harris, 2003, 50). And as some vernacular accounts have it, she initially addresses him in his own tongue, Nahuatl, gently asking, *Cuix àmo nican nicà nimoNantzin?* as highlighted in the epigraph to this chapter. The "Little Brown One" is Goddess-Mother not just of Jesus alone.

And this then is the emblem not so much of some definitive *persona* in history, but of a submerged archetype of earlier myth. But it is not the less real for being a mere image-effect. Indeed, it encodes the possibility of a rebirth from below in the mixture of its ritual murk, hiding, in the hinted transcripts of sunlight and roses and song, a *collective* subaltern subject. Indeed, Octavio Paz reads the deep code of the history as significant of a popular repudiation of patriarchal filiation *on either side* of the divide of conquest. Neither victorious Jesus nor conquered Quetzalcoatl is the featured focus here, but rather a turn among indigenous towards ancient intuitions of *earth matrons* (Dussel, 1995, 126). Unbridled imagination might even choose to "see" a double subalterity—an originally Palestinian provocateur, teenage rhyme-spitting mother, hidden in a patriarchal Christian text, gone underground in energy and insurgency for more than a millennium of imperial masquerade, resurfacing in cross-signifying insurgency under an earth sign—subaltern of the colonizer meeting subaltern of the colonized in a doubly eclipsed exposure.

But in any case, it is the postcolonial practice of the Virgin-Goddess in our own time that most intrigues for this writing. Max Harris's *Carnival and Other Christian Festivals: Folk Theology and Folk Performance* (2003) points the direction. Tracking contemporary Christian street enactments of vernacular pieties from Belgium to Bolivia, Puerto Rico to Peru, Spain to Trinidad and Mexico, Harris posits a Scottian principle of interpretation:

> I have learned to pay more heed to the dramatic action of a fiesta and to the casual remarks of performers and audience than to the standard explanations offered to (and by) clergy, government agents, anthropologists, and other outsiders. I have learned to look for those details of performance that are quietly at odds with the public transcript, for it is amid these dissonances—just because they are apt to be regarded as innocuous, garbled, or irrelevant by scholars and others in authority—that folk performers are most likely to insinuate their hidden transcripts into the public square. (p. 10).

Among the fests of saints days, Corpus Christi, Carnival, and Christmas, Harris finds a pagan trope on a Christian tack, festal mask itself coding a performative unmasking of history's official outcomes as partial and reversible. Here is a waltz of authority and its discontents, interrupted by slight stutter steps and comic leers, firecracker sneers and bombastic veering toward an "other" evaluation. "The hidden transcripts can be variously signaled," says Harris:

> The dancers' masks may be reversed so that the Christian warriors have dark skin and the heathen villains have beards and rosy cheeks; the victorious Christian troops may be identified as Aztecs by decorative emblems sewn into their costumes; or the marginal actions of the

"clowns" may undermine the scripted Spanish victory. While the public transcript may be safely recorded in a prescribed text, the hidden transcript generally finds expression only in signs visible in performance. (2003, 10)

In 1998, the writer joined six million other pilgrims at the basilica of Guadalupe in Mexico City for the Virgin's annual feast day celebration. There he encounters a multitiered tango of players and patrons. Dancers and devotees rub shoulders with travelers wearing Plains Indians emblazoned T-shirts; teenagers from neighboring towns cavort with troupes from the rural outback and urban enclave alike. The sensual "explosion" is a veritable menagerie of imagery in syncopated street-step with a syncretic congeries of instrumentation and sound! (But where also, not surprisingly, constructs of *indios* are more valued than the Indians themselves!) Here *Totonac quetzale* dancers frolic beside Nahua *inditos*. *Santiaguitos* compete with *danzas aztecas*. *Concheros* mix it up with *negritos* from Sierra de Pueblo. Whip-cracking *gracejos* parade in counterpoint to tight-rope-walking, cross-dressing *maromeros* from Acatlan. Harris's analysis is nuanced, teasing out from the mix of autochthonous memories and European rhapsodies entire histories in cameo: a middle-class mestizo nostalgia for noble savagery; a subtle Nahua reversal of the signs of *moros* and *cristianos*, in which "Christian" Indian Mexico surreptitiously defeats, in dance at least, "pagan" Spain; an Andean *negrito* parody of "monstrosity," conducting whip-battles in animal masks, battling wits in high-pitched whistles and hoots.

From this fantastic Guadalupe pageantry, Harris distills a trifold tradition of mothers sacred (Harris, 2003, 49, 52). The Christian Mary as the *Virgen de Guadalupe* is read back into her rootage in biblical hints of a feminine side of deity. The icon of *La Morena* beloved by the mestizo *"Raza"* ("Race") is referenced to the pre-contact Tonantzin-haunt of the heights of Tepayac. And a colonial Malinche-Maringuilla ("little Mary") figure—danced as consort of a messianically remodeled Moctezuma—is made both to display and contest, in that very association, the colonial father-line tracing back to Cortez and rape. Never mind that both Tonantzin and Malinche may well be postconquest Nahuatl reconstructions—on the one hand, projecting the colonial Maria back into the precontact past by reconfiguring the mestizo Virgin as the pre-Columbian goddess; and on the other, repositioning the tainted indigene-concubine reputedly used and abused by Cortez, as the powerful partner of the revived *Azteca* ruler, with whom she now cavorts as a spirit-figure (Harris, 2003, 60–61). This is history as living myth, not a science of the dead. The proliferation of names and stories mediates a complex politics of the street.

Harris tracks the resonances of this multifaceted Mary across the barriers of race, class, and gender articulating modern Mexico. In the celebration, the basilica wall-hanging of the Virgin Mother anchors orthodoxy and centers space for the dominant clergy and urban upper class. But from that inert wallflower slips a recalcitrant and recombinant double, indeed a ghostly multiple, raucously materializing themselves in the plaza, cavorting with the crowd. As Tonantzin, "partner of the sun," "Mary" camps out in the atrium among the mestizo middle class, who struggle for position between the excluding elites and the subordinated Indians. Here she crystallizes middle-class ancestor nostalgia in the *danzas aztecas,* venting *ressentiment* while enabling festal claims to indigenous names and values in a publicly negotiated transcript that privileges the "primitive" even as the dance itself marginalizes actual Indian presence (Harris, 2003, 63). The latter group, finally—though historically they are mere sweepers of the precincts in the person of Juan Diego—engages the battle of meanings by multiplying the names, diffusing the power, and inverting outcomes. In the living intimacies of Malinche-Maringuilla, the Guadalupan *Maria* does not merely watch the footwork below from a mobile banner bearing her image, but in the flesh of devotees herself dances with the soldier-*concheros,* dons the guise of a little angel to stop the war dance of Moors and Christians in favor of the indigenous Mexicans, sides with Moctemzuma at the *danza de la conquista,* and walks the tightrope in cross-dressed finery just above the marching *maromeros.* Acting against the fixations of dominant class interpretations, this is a Mary of the multitudes, who recenters sacred space in vernacular places, refuses mere nostalgia, and contests the constraints of purity and patience. Indeed, she will finally go home to the huts of the excluded in wanton embrace of an unchurched "station" of the double-crossed and downtrodden. But for all that, the Mexican *Maria* remains the subject of alterity—image of a consciousness unfathomed, even in its florid signage, grinning at the gullible.

Part of Harris's point is to assert a gnosis of the street—a performative parroting of positions public and intellectual that hides its surprise endings in the guise of naïve bendings and blendings of the obvious. "What is articulated in performance," he says, "may never be rendered explicitly in words even by the performer[s] [themselves]" (Harris, 2003, 18). Harris does claim some measure of accessibility for the transcripts hidden under the official repartee occupying verbal speech, but no guarantees. Careful scholarship, local legendry, and contextual knowledge all can help. But the *hermeneusis* is two-way and fluid, changing as tension and politics morph. It marshals silence against the scholarly conceit that typically privileges speaking, offering mere shape and gesture to sidestep danger, and bridges the hunger to understand and the desire to be understood with a festive "body-burst" of meanings that have no final author or arbiter. Harris seemingly retains some hope of discerning intentionality inside the hidden-ness, even if the grammar is grin and gesture. Postcolonial subalterity, however, may be even more grounded in the groin of inarticulation than even he allows.

THE HAITIAN *EZILI*

It is when we turn to the Haitian version of a creolization of Mary that, arguably, we hit the deepest murk of our inquiry. Here we find an Afro-diaspora reworking of the colonial representation—a refiguring under the duress of slavery's down-pressing that makes the Madonna herself into a possession-spirit. For a people plunged into the great abomination of enslavement—ripped from their "mother" continent, packaged as property in the Middle Passage, "seasoned" like meat in spirit-breaking "finishing plants" in the Caribbean in order to be auctioned as "goods" on the market—Mary-as-Ezili embodies the extremes of colonial history (Dayan, 2003, 48). This is a Mary arrived late on the scene of creolization, a missionary-mix conjoined to a diasporan "fix" making meaning out of a fracture so deep its bones speak defeat and defiance in the same tongue. The surface is the Virgin who is also a Venus, the "Tragic Mistress" of multiple liaisons, a "Love Goddess" of coercive lust, marking the radical depth of slave-master delusion, where white males had intercourse with their "objects" (Dayan, 2003, 40, 48). The extremity is a subalterity of irreducible concatenation—anonymous concubinage in a regime of rape, mastery dreaming romance (48). The Mulatto Mater emerging on the underside of slave practice is necessarily a judo-queen, breaking the body violation into a river of water spirits, still drowning in African forests of memory.

What appears at this nadir of possession is sheer liquidity. Oshun of Nigeria and Ezili of Whydah (Benin) mount the head with a vengeance of the sacral wild—a Yoruba-Fon cross-fertilization receiving the thrust of missionary-positioned mastery, converting Catholic lust into a New World myth of Mami Water (Desmangles, 1992, 143–145)! The conversion is two-way and recombinant. "Mary-tokens" like blue robes, glimmering halos, shimmering crowns, and jewels and rings of gold enable the short leap to African models where the same symbols invoke already-intact meanings peculiar to Oshun and Ezili. Here, in leaping cultures, the same signifiers call up different signifieds. But when we come to tokens like the Madonna-symbols of the heart and the letter M, on the other hand, the work is improvisation, syncopating the African model into a creole hybrid, signifying not virginal love and Marian devotion, but macrocosmic fecundity and lithe promiscuity. Mary-*Ezili* is a multiple—ever proliferating in both her persona and her paramours, manifesting now as *Mater Salvatoris-Ezili Danto*, now as *Virgen de los dolores-Metres Ezili*, once again as *Maria dolorosa del Monte Calvario-Ezili Freda*. The fracturing "calves" continuously into promiscuous personalities, rich with ancestry, subsuming the trauma of slave coercions and post-slavery exorcisms into a deep memory of living elsewhere and desiring otherwise. Where humans were held as property and beloved illicitly, the body is crossed with ecstasy and terror—ghosts of decorum and sorrow, lust and lacey elegance, race and romance tangled with rage and dread and abandon in the same impossible longing.

Domination here meets its damage in a living ceremony—the ruins of history like a cemetery of flowers disgorging irrepressible perfumes. The image of the black Virgin, cheek-scarred and heart-stabbed, allows loneliness and anguish over the crucifixion to be overwritten with the emblem of *Petro* anger, *Vodou*-Mama-Fury erupting against slave-holding violence or devotee-dalliance alike. The child on the lap is not Jesus of the Immaculate Conception, but the issue of one of her many liaisons, needing defense and protection. *Ezili* as *La Sirene,* on the other hand, is water-waif, pulling the world back down into its womb-dream, silent and gone as a lost childhood. As *Ge-Rouge* she sobs in cosmic tantrum, fists clenched against all such losses; while as the *Mulatresse,* she wafts sublime and absorbed, enchantress of wealth and refinement, unattainable in each of her successive scandals. She can come on as *Gran Ezili*, broken grandmother, crawling along with cane and arthritis, or equally as the limp *Maitresse,* when her weeping empties into paralysis, pain become perpetual and cosmic, pinioned at the crossroads of lack and eternity (Deren, 1953, 137–145).

And almost inevitably—as was the case with Guadalupe—here too, we have appearances in out-of-the-way places challenging church orthodoxy in favor of vernacular accessibility. The Haiti pilgrimage site in this case is associated with two waterfalls and a tree in which a Blessed Virgin apparition surprised a crowd who thereby invited the white Catholic vicar of the nearby parish to join them in witness and prayer. Unable to see what the people saw (!), the vicar declared the appearance "blasphemy," closed the site, and ordered the local police captain to shoot the apparition. She proved elusive however, leaping to new branches at each shot until the exasperated priest ordered the tree cut down. In vernacular tradition, the site was immediately engulfed in a suffusion of *Ezili Danto* "mother-anger," resulting soon after in the death of the vicar by paralysis, temporary insanity and vagabondage for the police captain (until he came to his senses and sought pardon from the Virgin), and the burning of the priest's church. Today the event is memorialized annually in a split medium— subdued Catholic service in the village church under the protection of Mary-*Ezili,* followed by loud singing and violent possession at the waterfalls, where *Ezili* mounts "Mary" in the actual bodies of her devotees, with desire and healing in her wings (Desmangles, 1992, 135–138). This is a veneration of virginity on the terms of the indigent: a purity not of chastity, but of beauty; in circulation; promiscuous in materiality and spirit alike; a figure of transcendence available precisely in the mingling of sex and life, and quite literally in the mudbathing possession rite common to the site. And here is the rub for our rubric of subaltern rhetoric.

This is not a virgin-portrait, but a flesh-and-blood enactment, returning even the original Mary of Palestine to her own "subtextual" ritual enshrinement in pre-Christian cults of "willful goddesses and harlot saints" (Dayan, 2003, 48). No pious compromise this, but a passion-story of slavery and its discontents, arising from the grave of mastery and denial with possession on her mind, riding women and men equally in cross-gendered augury of the full range of female hungers and repression. The *Ezili*-displays are body trances offering history in the grammar of gesture and desire, unreadable in mere verbiage, undecipherable from the outside, a language of exposé signaling a subalterity internal to the psyche but also mapped onto the local ecology, giving the memory of impossible intimacies—between slave masters and their "objects"—a cubist vocabulary of improvised ritual, a syntax of insurgent rupture, a body of rage and longing, elaborated ever-anew across time and fresh breakages (of relation). "Consciousness" of the transcript is here suspect—a presumed "mastery" perhaps even more derelict than the desultory meanings enacted in this living text of domination and its fantasies. This is the embodied cult of a creole analytic of power, necessarily erasing every binary line of clarity in learning to survive a coercion of agency more radical even than death. Here is Hegel's master-slave dialectic "possessed" and rendered "polythetic" in the real flesh of women—a subalterity that asks whether anyone can speak when love and rape intermingle in offspring and flood an entire island with inchoate groaning and come-uppance (partially realized in 1791).

KNOWING THE NOT-KNOWING

English professor Joan Dayan's analysis provokes the final irony. The cult queried, in her estimation, is not by any means an abolition of domination, but its displacement into a context of proliferation. The *peristil* space of ritual, crosscut with *veve* lines of summons to the spirits of the day, overcomes the imperial line of "dichotomy between master and slave, victimizer and victimized, colonizer and colonized," by opening its positions to the same person, whether human or divine (Dayan, 2003, 47). In thus materializing an alternative history of *vodou*, mastery is itself made subject to a regime of articulation serving the subordinate community. Identity is here ramified in slavery's strange non sequitur—a physical flesh, pirated as "property" in the 1685 *Code Noir*, with its will/consciousness/soul (*ti bon anj*) legally vacated as belonging to another (even while sometimes "loved" as if more than mere "object"). The vacuity is trumped in the ritual of the people, where the stealing of that "little angel" is now stolen back in a living vocabulary of African deities (*lwa*), who enact in the bodies of their devotees a simultaneous mastery and abjection, speaking from the head and the hand at once, commandeering even Christian saints into the work of "haints" and "horses" (Patrick mounted by serpent-queen-become-python-king Danbala, Mary by Mama Erzili).

This is indeed flesh remade as paradox—but caught now not in the bind of slavery and its impossible romances, but of spirit-possession and its remonstrances—a physicality yet distended and "exercised," harboring an *axis mundi,* within its palpable limitations, upon which the spirits climb and the passions divine for meaning and sweat, a compound of heaven and funk, tethered to the vernacular, rooted in trees and water, yielding pleasure in spite of the pain, and insight only on the outside of the subject's own consciousness (in the community gathered for the possession-appearance).

Indeed, we might say: this is the hidden transcript of divinity itself, speaking in the arbor of the body, split between its figure and its meaning, a subalterity at its nadir point of opacity, where the speaking is *by definition* not one's own. Is the subject of this text Mary? Or Ezili? Or perhaps the anonymous "spirit/ghost" of all the raped slave women of an unrequited history? Or their impossibly placed mulatto daughters? Or something even more broadly unknowable underneath their historic intercourse—the serpent-goddess-power of the "under-earth" itself, also enduring "colonial" violation and dismemberment, rising up in interminable thirst to drink the world's waters . . . and all the losses they contain (as we might riff on Dayan's hints about Danbala of old in Dahomey [2003, 46])? Maybe the "or" should be "and."

And whence and whereto the work of representation in the mix, attempting to track in linear discourse a polyvalent embodiment? It is perhaps the entire claim in a nutshell that some of the most poignant studies of this most ravaged of colonies have issued from the pens of scholars whose final disposition was to have been overcome by that which they examined. Whether Zora Neal lying in her initiation hut "crossing over" into the other world (Hurston, 1990, 166ff), Maya Deren possessed in dance without the usual *lave tèt* (washing of the head) preparation for such (Deren, 1953, 258–260), Karen McCarthy Brown out of the detritus of a broken relationship marrying her anger in the form of *Ogou* (Brown, 133–139), or Katherine Dunham importing Danbala's *yanvalo* into her modern dance performances (Dunham, 1969, 62, 92, 128, 132–133)—the density of an entire body incarnating a sign of divinity is a subalterity finally irresolvable. Here what is knowable is negotiable only in the collective ensemble where the gnosis is a lightning strike forking between unconscious performance and an observance (and observer) put in question by the suddenly appearing *lwa*. Unless "you" are possessed, you cannot know (Deren, 1953, 249; Murphy, 1994, 27, 41–42). But if you are—it is not you who "knows." Indeed, who is the Subject under this mask of silence?

PRAYING WITH THE CORN/PLAYING ON THE HORN: READING JAZZ AT THE CROSSROADS OF THE COUNTRY AND THE CITY

Did John's music kill him?

—*A. B. Spellman*, Four Lives in the Bebop Business

We move from the subalterity of chapter 6 to a focus on myth in this one and bridge from rural ritual to urban conjuration by way of Euro-instrumentation. The question of this chapter is that of the codification of myth as memory for life when one lives under a death sentence. Juxtaposing *vodou veve* drawing in the ritual place of the *peristils* (shrines) of Haiti and saxophone or trumpet playing in the after-hours space of the clubs of New Orleans or Chicago may not seem to represent likely linkage for mythic enquiry. Myth, after all, is normally thought as narrative, a trick and talent of the tongue. Corn-meal incantation and bent-brass improvisation are titillations of the hand, serving talents of the feet (to the degree both function to energize and direct dance). Why explore myth in the key of sonic beat and visual beacon when the subject is story? But then myth is not mere story, but the organization of contradiction into the flow of representation. Myth closes the gap of existence with a hypothesis about living. It imagines a living of meaning over the void of absurdity. Charles Long's long-standing styling of myth as mode of making-do in the face of mortality issues especially in a consideration of the human capacity to codify rupture into resilience. It is the category of

the "break"—between worlds, between persons, between human and
humus, between now and then—that pushes this inquiry towards its
evident fascinations.

THE MYTH OF MODERNITY

And what is that fascination in the focus here? The idea that jazz is
myth. A feeling—arising out of my own late-in-life encounter with a
Miles Davis excavation of silence with the soliloquy of his horn, a The-
lonius Monk materialization of earthquake in poke of finger on piece
of ivory, a John Coltrane search for a different kind of supremacy
in carefully orchestrated screech-ometry. This chapter will posit the
possibility of a god emerging from a saxophone, even as, in the older
forum of colonial Haiti, gods climbed up the world axis from the forgotten depths of Africa into the fraught lights of slavery in response to
a masterful mesmerization of cornmeal drawing on mud floor. Thus
bebop concatenation will be read alongside *veve* conjuration in search
of verbal articulation of a certain "Something" that has forced itself
on twentieth-century America[1] with all the thick indeterminacy of
deep memory.

    In brief resume of the terrain to be traversed—I want to take up
Charles Long's delineation of the historical apparition of religion and
"think with" it in the direction of what is most immediately before
and just behind us. The sound-text that first emerges in New Orleans
after the 1894 Jim Crow laws force Creole downtowners into concert
(figuratively and literally) with dusky-skinned uptowners, that issues
in the bright light trumpet of Louis Armstrong's Bach-like advent
as America's first impresario of the kingdom of sound, that whispers
inside the mind of an elegant Ellington as proud Duke and subtle
rebuke of all previous indigenous American composition, that goes
soft in swing, grows hard in bop, becomes cool blue in the cruel fifties, freelances into furious flight like an atonal air raid on the head of
John Cage in avant-garde or goes abstract across the bar in an Ornette
Coleman caterwaul—all of this effervescent entrainment of the metals
and minerals of modernity into syncopated two-step with the silence
under the surface of frenzied Americanity is not mere ritual. It is the
anti–myth making war on the myth that is America. Or so I want to
argue.

    But that part of the argument is not new. Wynton Marsalis in a
1990s *Callaloo* interview argued, for instance, that in Ellington,
jazz had waxed classical and mythic, putting cultural pressure on the
nation to address the music seriously and in so doing deal with itself

and its racism (Thomas, 2002, 296). Beat wordsmith Bob Kaufman imagined a jazz instrumental takeover of the city in his 1965 poem "Battle Report"—a thousand saxophone cases like a Trojan horse of sound suddenly disgorging militant destruction in a guerilla action of rhythmic violation that takes the audience by surprise in its naiveté and sleepwalking (Kaufman, 1965, 8). The audience thought it was hearing entertainment (Kohli, 2002, 175)! At core here is the question whether jazz is merely "rivulets of trickling ecstasy" as Kaufman would indeed argue it was for African Americans under duress, or also the "historical tears" and "smothered rage" that it was his concerted effort to agitate into expression in his poems ("Jazz Chick," "Second April," and "Walking Parker Home"; see also, Kohli, 2002, 166). Perhaps it is in the desperate response of a white auditor/imitator like Bix Beiderbecke that we meet the answer—a shy Iowa boy rendered helpless and haunted, ripped from family and farm by the seriousness of the demand that confronted him in Louis Armstrong's horn. Poverty, perfidy, and powerlessness before the bottle were not enough to pull him back from the siren that plunged him into a life lived forever after, up to its tragic end, inside a coronet. Jazz could indeed kill. And not just whites. The litany of lives lacerated by an impossible dream of experience, by a love that leapt off the edge of the universe in its call to clairvoyance, is long: Buddy Bolden, Jelly Roll Morton, Parker and Coltrane and Billie Holiday . . . The seriousness of this possible end of myth was not mere mythology.

And such seriousness illuminates the tack taken here. What if jazz is read as myth not merely by way of metaphor, but in the rigor of a history of religions meaning? The text then twists like a gyroscope in hand, revealing as much about the intention of the lector as about the universe. But such is the case of all myth. What if jazz, in fact, augured "America" in a very particular, very peculiar meaning of its hidden history? And what if this mythic uniqueness of a jazz-summoned America is arranged alongside the *long dureé* of human figurements of divine advents? These latter—as Long tracks—range across the big scale of our species time on the planet: nomadic-pastoralist sky gods, breaking into agricultural innovations of Earth Mothers and chthonic numinosities, rejoined by World-Parent joinings-at-the-hip (and subsequent god- and goddess-ling war efforts to rupture the millennial-long embrace of such Parents), finally culminating (?) in the subsequent return of the Sky King now jealously gathering all god powers to himself in a lonely domain of demand called monotheism. What comes after the late-agricultural ascension of this monotheistic patriarchy to domination? Is there a god-birth for the epoch of industrialization that has yet to be announced in the ears of us so close to the birth stool, so drenched in the blood-mess and placental after-arrivals that we can scarcely hear? What if jazz is allowed to speak, for a moment, at this latest lathering point in the sweat chamber of history, where indistinct powers and forces shift and shape our fantasies into stuttering approximations of meaning? Is a new god rumbling under the finger of a Charlie Parker? And how might we know such?

We might listen with an ear open like a third eye when Robert Kaufman cuts loose with a pen played like a 'bone:

> Hawk joins in with his comrades and as he puts the horn to his lips out comes:
>
> Numbers, notes, song, battle cries, laments, jazzy psalms, tribal histories in cubist and surrealist patterns, and an unmistakable call to arms, to jazz, to him, as others put down their horns in silent thanks that he had come, as the drums had promised he would come, come to lead into the unpromised land, littered with pains, odored of death, come to lead, with his pumping, grinning throat. (1961, 227–228)

The advent augured is not merely human. If not a god of the age, here we have at least a Hadean psychopomp, relishing an unredeemed visitation. And the far shore hosts losses without name, awaiting a search party.

For me the search begins not immediately with jazz, but with its prefigurements in the cocoon that incubated such a sound. Congo Square in New Orleans orchestrates in space and time, the cojoining of consideration I propose to improvise by swinging *vodou veve* into syncopated dance-step with jazz jubilation. But before turning to that particular locale of "second-line" parade-lyricism, we need first to spend a moment with Long's argument in his book *Alpha* (1963) to gain some history of religions footing.

THE RELIGION OF ROCKS

In his introduction to *Alpha*, Long offers an argument for a *sui generis* approach to religion that privileges mythic rationality as the modality of comprehension of the sacred. In the "new hermeneutic situation" first adumbrated by the likes of Rudolph Otto and further elaborated by Mircea Eliade, Joachim Wach, and Gerardus van der Leeuw, religious experience is embraced as irreducible to other experiences, other discourses. It makes its mystery manifest in the concrete. Its quality is numinous, but a numinosity appearing, suddenly, unaccountably, in relationship to the ordinary. Its apprehension and communication among humans is necessarily symbolic, perhaps even the basic meaning of the "symbol." It cannot thereby be flattened out in merely linear thought; it is not the solution to a syllogism. For Otto, the experience is fundamentally synthetic, a mixture of fear and fascination, of horror and allure (1950, 13).

The stone by the path to the river is just there, a part of the natural surround until the moment—remembered afterwards only in the myth in which the surplus of meaning first shimmers forth communally—it suddenly "speaks" divinity. It ceases to be merely ordinary but—strangely, compellingly, repulsively even—discloses an uncanny "more." Long will clarify that the stone is not confused by the people worshipping its disclosure as being a "god." Nor is it merely an adventitious "occasion" for a god's appearing that bears no intrinsic relationship with the lithic-ness of that particular piece of granite or basalt. Rather, says Long, "the 'natural' structure of the stone gives qualitative specificity to the deity and the stone becomes a sacred reality because it is a mode of revelation" (Long, 1963, 8). And the complex subtlety of these relations is only capable of representation by way of symbol.

Long is careful to delineate this appearing as a certain kind of non-human "difference": "what is revealed in the stone is a reality which is other than [the hu]man" (1963, 8). It is an otherness that the symbol, however, renders open for human "participation and communion" (ibid.). Citing anthropologist Redford's designation of the strangeness of the revelation as the "Not-Man," Long also asserts that this other world of animals, plants, and sky phenomenon was historically revealed as a manifestation of power and sacredness, and indeed, as a "generic aspect of human life." Thus for Long, the "manifestation of the sacred" is simultaneously a "manifestation of ultimate reality-as-being" (ibid., 8–9). The equation points up a temporal quality of sacral manifestation: it emerges as a modality of crisis. Only when people are in transition from one mode of being to another—at birth, puberty, death, and during certain kinds of historical ruptures in communal life—does the revelation constitute itself. It responds to the threat of nonbeing and gathers momentum within human experience as a quality of intensity. An edge of otherness is heightened in the experience of oneself and of life. The crisis periods of cultural history identified by Western nomenclature as "technical advances"—discoveries of new tools or of agriculture, for example—are comprehended inside the cultures doing the discovery in the mode of religious language shadowing the innovation with religious aura (ibid., 11).

Myth, then, for Long, is a mode of apprehending a world. It is a type of thinking, about an encounter with power, seeking to leverage an existence. It precedes rationality and relativizes literality. And it is discarded whenever new revelations of being and sacredness emerge and propagate new myths. Cosmogonic myths in particular, in both archaic and civilized societies, memorialize that moment of the destructive/creative emergence of the new. Against our current popular notions of both "myths" and "beginnings," all the myths to which we have access presuppose history, says Long (1963, 19). They presume an existent community, emerge against the previous story, and reveal the sacrality of a discovery, whether such novelty is plant or animal or a new technique of metal-working, fire-making, or maize-growing. In securing the new, they express it as what is most essential in human life and orient it toward the act of foundation that it is the very purpose of myth to remember. In the process they weld together human psyche and historical particularity as a reciprocity in which "power" and "being" co-produce each other.

THE COSMOGONY OF CORN

When we turn back to the novelty that emerges as "America" with this understanding in hand, it is the newness of the place called "Orleans" that focuses our thesis. Called by some the least American of cities, the Big Easy offers a history that has often materialized prophecy for the rest of the country. LeRoi Jones (aka Amiri Baraka) notes that New Orleans existed in late nineteenth-century America as a kind of microcosm, exhibiting the "co-existing complex of social, cultural, and racial influences" that in many ways "predated the modern post-World-War-I Northern city" that would result from the mass exodus of blacks in search of work and release from Jim Crow segregation (Jones, 1999, 138). Here flourished the French, Spanish, English, African, and Caribbean cultures in a volatile and creative mix that would produce "primitive jazz" and anticipate the "later merging of the Southern blues tradition with the musical traditions of the Northern Negro" (ibid., 139). That later mix found its antecedents in Congo Square slave gatherings that began as early as 1819 according to Jones's genealogy. Though surveilled by the authorities, such gatherings were sites of celebration that combined not only African chants with French quadrilles and patois ditties shouted above the "great drum" base-lines, but "songs that were supposedly banned by whites for being part of the *vodoun* or voodoo rites" that less than 30 years before had leveraged revolution in French Saint Domingue (Jones,

1999, 72). Albert Raboteau (among other scholars) makes us aware of the degree to which the hybrid cult of Haiti had been catalyzed in its New Orleans growth as "hoodoo" by the emigration of slaves and free blacks during the Revolution (Raboteau, 1978, 75). The genealogy of jazz passes through blues by way of *gris-gris* as we shall see.

There is much here that cannot be pursued with rigor in a mere essay, but rather must only be allowed to signify suggestively across the gap of causality in good African American fashion of indirection. *Vodou* shows its contemporary face as deep as an African river—whatever its past dismissals as merely a "primitive" form of "whistling in the dark." Part of its ritual thickness in service of the trick of survival in impossible circumstances is the practice of *veve* invocation mobilized as ancestral conjuration. A skilled *houngan*-priest takes up pinches of cornmeal (or brick-dust or powered bark, ashes or even coffee grounds) and spills them around the ritual space through thumb and forefinger in rapid-fire drawing of geometric emblems associated with various *lwa* or spirit-energies coded as archetypal figures in West African myth. The drawing is itself initiatory prayer, "put[ting] pressure," says French scholar Alfred Metraux, "on the lwa and compelling them to appear" through possessing their devotees (Metraux, 1972, 165). Arranged symmetrically around the *poteau-mitan* or "world-axis" pole of wood that centers the worship area, the *veve* can be multiplied to cover several yards of ground with the symbolic invocations of the spirits. A well-honed *houngan*-hand can filigree the space with the lace-like emblems in perfect symmetry in less than half an hour—without need for a single correction (Metraux, 1972, 166). But the hand that thus orchestrates these spirit-summons does so animated by the accompaniment of song and drum, and, at the same time, the drawings so executed themselves invoke the drum rhythms that percussively embody the *lwa* being summoned (Murphy, 1994, 29). *Veve* then visually materialize a sonic memory that requires the human-body-in-motion for its complete arrival.

But here also lie heavy layers of mythic palavers. On top of each *veve* are sprinkled consecrating foodstuffs and libations—grilled maize, kola, rum, or other drink concoctions. Rattles are shaken and ritual formula spoken and finally water is thrown over the images as a salutation (Metraux, 1972, 165). On top of the *veve* are then laid the bodies of sacrificial animals and other "objects" sacred to whichever *lwa* are being pictorially piqued. The emblems thus energized in offering become the "pictorial face," a mouth on the ground, "through which the *lwa* may eat" (Murphy, 1994, 30; Deren, 1953, 205, 316, n5). But this is only the most obvious overlay. Mythologically, the materialization marches out to the perimeters of the known world, constructing in the microcosmic space of the *seremoni* (ceremony) the macrocosmic structure of the universe, mobilizing *peristil* as cosmic center, *poteau-mitan* as spirit-pole, connecting the *Vilokan*-underworld that is the subtelleric origin of the *lwa* themselves and the Ginen-abode of the ancestral-dead to the over-world of the living (Desmangles, 1992, 105).

This vertical crossover point, also rooting the four cardinal points horizontally, is thus made immediate site of the "crossroads," where spirits climb from midnight to noon, take over bodies, mirror human foibles and prodigalities in dramatically enacted sodalities comingling this world and the other one, and leave on physical deposit in the social body of the gathered community the memory of divinity (Metraux, 1972, 166; Brown, 74). In the process, the human bodies of the possessed devotees that "manifest"—momentarily, for the rest of the community—the gods incarnate, are themselves made ambulant *axis mundi*, linking sky, earth, and underworld, towering, in the mythic theatrics of that space, like somatic mimes of the great Tree of Time, rooted in the waters of Africa, drawing the past up into the present (Desmangles, 1992, 107; Murphy, 1994, 28).

But this sign-economy of crossover worlds and cruciform meanings is also horizontally etched as a history of place. French grillwork is amalgamated to Angolan alphabet, Masonic mystery with Dahomean intricacy, Mater Dolorosas entwine with Kongo serpentine sky gods (Thompson, 188, 191). The testament here is not merely metaphysical, joining day and night worlds in interpenetration of living humans and collective dead. The abstract emblematic is rather also historic, gathering universes cosmic and prosaic into abutted relations, signaling complex cross-fertility in cruciform simplicity. For Thompson, the *veve* constitute "the quintessential form of Afro-Haitian art"—before they are danced into oblivion by the possessed circulators of the *poteau-mitan* (ibid.). Then the figures are redrawn in living flesh.

When we turn from such an island tour to the Congo Square of early antebellum days, the musical forays and dance choreographies we meet there must be imagined as not innocent of the *veve*-shuffles of Haiti's revolutionary heyday. Certainly refugees reworking the eroding memory of *vodou* into its simplified Louisiana riff as "hoodoo" did not lose all mythic sense in their syncopated sensuousness. But the argument here is not one of direct influence or retention, but rather of somatic signification and rhythmic reinvention. What *veve* invoked and kept alive at least at the level of the feet was

"Africa"—not so much in synaptic vision as in stylistic convention and anatomical lamentation. The body was made the ground-plate for mythic re-creation inside the crucible of slavery. Not only had the waters of the Atlantic harbored an African ancestral world of losses and dreams, but so had the waters between Saint Domingue and New Orleans. In praise-hymning black Haiti as the *rara* school of the universe, for instance, Thompson will footnote the reference of the latter term as "Kongo-influenced pre-Lenten street orchestras" (Thompson, 293, n47). Among multiple other things, New Orleans jazz parades will constitute a mythic memory most fully embodied nationally as slavery-free "Haiti."

The Genealogy of Jazz

When we jump to jazz as the subject of inquiry, New Orleans remains the place of premium thought. What gathers in living bodies in Congo Square throughout the nineteenth century, what materializes as motor-memory in second-line funeral processions or Marti Gras carnival parades as the new century approaches, is thick with ancestry, but also may be thick with apparition. Early twentieth-century jazz virtuoso Sidney Bechet offers commentary that cojoins the possibilities. Writing about his grandfather Omar, who died a slave in early adulthood, Bechet (1960) reflects that his own music "had to know" the things that were "all the time happening to" his folk (103; also, Floyd, 1995, 8):

> Inside him [Bechet's grandfather] got the memory of all the wrong that's been done to my people. That's what the memory is . . . When a blues is good, that kind of memory just grows up inside it. (Bechet, 1960, 108)

Blues, as will be briefly indicated below, is central to jazz. Continuing the thought, Bechet remarks that the music taught him a great deal about Omar's trouble "in a way I couldn't have known about until I'd had some trouble of my own" (104). "If you're a good musicianer," he says, "its Omar's song you're singing" (202). Commenting on this commentary, Samuel Floyd (1995) pinpoints the point: "For Bechet, although he did not see or experience it, slavery was a 'memory'" (9). "What" was remembered was everything from Omar's Congo Square performances as a musician himself to slave intrigue; from Omar and his generation's anger, sadness, happiness and love, to the jazz funerals, picnics, parades and performances Bechet himself participated in both in and outside of New Orleans. Elaborating on his grasp of such music, Bechet continues,

> I met many a musicianer in many a place after I struck out from New Orleans, but it was always the same: If they was any good, it was Omar's song they were singing. It was the long song, and the good musicianers, they all heard it behind them. They all had an Omar, somebody like an Omar, somebody that was *their* Omar. It didn't need just recollecting somebody like that: it was the feeling of someone back there— hearing the song like it was coming up from somewhere.
>
> A musicianer could be playing it in New Orleans, or Chicago, or New York; he could be playing it in London, in Tunis, in Paris, in Germany. I heard it played in all those places and many a more. But no matter where it's played, you gotta hear it starting way behind you. There's the drum beating from Congo Square and there's the song starting in a field just over the trees. The good musicianer, he's playing *with* it, and he's playing *after* it. He's finishing something. No matter what he's playing, it's the long song that started back there in the South.
>
> It's the remembering song. There's so much to remember. (1960, 202)

Floyd employs the commentary in apology for his own idea of "cultural memory" through which he builds up an elaborate and sophisticated analysis of "the power of black music" (which is the title of his book; 1995, 8). For him, cultural memory explains the evident potency of African-American musics to preserve the "mysteries of myth and the trappings of ritual long after they are no longer functional," and accounts for the "vaguely 'known' musical and cultural processes and procedures" that cohere into the "spiritual quality of the musical and aesthetic behaviors of a culture" (ibid., 9). The category itself references the "subjective knowledge of a people." This is "kept alive in nonfactual and nonreferential motives, actions, and beliefs," often enough unconsciously understood and transferred, but capable of being brought to consciousness in practice and perception (ibid., 8).[2] And indeed, much of what we are tracking in this essay partakes of such memorial richness.

Floyd traces a genealogy of African American cultural memory through the paradigm/reality of the ring shout as a primary form. It is recapitulated in jazz, itself building on an inheritance of blues as the *Urtrope* of the tradition—immediate successor to the (sacred) spirituals and the (secular) rags—that all together bring forward into the Western Hemisphere the musics, myths, and hermeneutics of Africa (Floyd, 1995, 4–5, 81, 84). While Floyd himself focuses on what he calls "Drum and Song," he does so only after acknowledging and characterizing "Dance" as the privileged carrier of memory in the ring shout paradigm (ibid., 6, 19, 21, 26).[3] Like African proverbs of the past, condensing the wisdom and wit of the generations in aphoristic form, dance ritual served to condense memory in human motion, making the body itself a living proverb (ibid., 12).[4]

The deep structure of such an African culture-in-action was percussion: the intensification of energy by means of enlivened contrast and its regular resolution. The modality of memory here is motor-control: muscle in polymorphic mime of some vaguely apprehended vitality communally produced in gesture, sound, song and rhyme (Floyd, 1995, 57, 229). In reference to possession-cult celebrations, we could perhaps even say that ancestral visitation is codified and unfolded in the muscular tension of a quite nuanced and precise percussive structure. In a word, the beat, somatically, *is* the ancestor. African-based musics—in service of dancing human bodies—crystallize the experience of possession by the spirits of dead ancestry and living ecology into a mnemonic code, stored in a staccato chord, that is capable of unleashing that formally distilled history in the peculiar stylistics of a given rhythmic performance. The bravado of the forgotten survival struggles of a "hell-bent-on-living" Yoruba grandmother or the enslavement-resisting antics of a freedom-loving Fon grandfather (Floyd, 1995, 225)—mythically coded in the bravado-tales of the West-African trickster, Eshu (ibid., 48)—may well find ritual re-incarnation in the brief "bravado" played at the end of a line by a Bechet-finessed horn. Here is archetypal African cunning in a dime of time peeking slyly out of hollow metal!

But however we may want to evaluate such a willful elision of the various modalities of bravery, it is the blues that emerges, in scholarly consensus, as the incubation-chamber of African-American survival-memory later popularized by jazz. Floyd traces the efflorescence of ring-shout polyphonics through the mimetics of spirituals and ragtime, Holiness flutters and deep-night hollers, cornfield cries and Baptist stutters, to arrive at a claim that the post-Emancipation jook-joint hosted a reconstituted "African" party-for-the-gods that refused every distinction between sacred and secular and prefigured both early blues and nascent jazz.[5] Blues was the ring gone solo, giving virtuoso expression in deep growls and gravely moans to the cathartic and restorative powers of the older shout tradition and resituating the celebration in the post-Emancipation possibility of mobility made real by the railroad. Blues was also semantic code, giving euphemistic expression to the newly won possibility of exploring sexuality on one's own terms, free of the coercions of either stud-employment or rape by the master. Understood fully only by insiders, it emerged as the quintessential code of an indigenous communication system, grappling with the changed world of Reconstruction and its later compromise. It was an improvisatory rural proclivity that would soon enough issue in urban and urbane reconfiguration as "jazz."

THE HIEROPHANY OF HORN

But in this essay we are ultimately interested in Floydian figurings for two influences he did not follow up. In casting black musics as carriers of mythic memory, Floyd invests his theory with inquiry based on the thinking of history of religions' mentors, Sir James Frazer and Joseph Campbell. Campbell (1990) supplies an idea of myth as metaphorically "enzymic"—functioning as a product of the social body in which it works much like an enzyme does in the human body—cultivated and employed as spiritual catalyst by the poets and seers capable of recognizing its valence (6). And Frazer (1992) heralds myth as *hypothesis*, erecting tentative assumptions about reality as projections to be tested by successive generations. In the former we are directed to the present and by the latter to the future. Neither characterization is focused primarily on memory, as Floyd is. And here is suggestion for a new set of questions for the idea of jazz as myth.

Reverting back briefly to Long's example of the meaning of a lithic revelation of sacrality, we should ask: is myth, in such a community, only the memory of a past flash of stone? Or is it also the apprehension of a contemporary possibility? In narrative form, myth is perhaps irrevocably oriented towards what has already (in the past) emerged as clear: in Long's example, the story line fixes the aura around the stone "like a rock." But in sonic-augury and motor-memory, such as we encounter in Afro-diaspora mythologies of dance and music, the thing grasped may well be more immediate—myth mobilized to meet memory in a present manifestation as the first "sounding" of a *new* modality of divinity. Bechet's commentary, quoted earlier, points to the possibility of a potency of song not only begun "way back," but demanding to be "played with" and "played after" (Bechet, 1960, 202). The intuition invokes a present-tense "future."

What if the possibility of jazz as myth is situated in the ambit of a question about a contemporary revelation? Looking back across grave stretches of time, we can formulate a succession of gods and goddesses, focused in myths, charting a significance of crisis and change. The line runs, as previously re-counted, from Sky Gods to Earth

Mothers to World Parents and their Adolescent Disruptors to Sky Monarchs. But the account stops with an advent Lording it over the ground of medieval agriculture. Is there an Industrial Revelation? A god of the grinding funk of machine? A cyber Borg, a silicon Devil, a Revelator of the meaning of modern Metal? Asking such is not to propose a sanctification of the ideal of steel, an apotheosizing of Promethean hubris reincarnate as a Lexus. It is rather to take seriously the reading of history as provoking—in its breaks and bumps, its discoveries and desperations, its ruptures towards change—a continuous feeding of mythology. Myth does not purport to hallow a god, strange as it may seem, but only to outline its sacral otherness for the human senses. Myth divines, not consecrates, reveals without kneeling. Often as not, it highlights foible and violence. But it does "halo" with significance—or at least, "remember" such a moment. And here is the wrinkle: we may be too close to the advent I am asking after to see the outline. But I deem it worth the effort to try.

If the advent of modernity indeed marks a moment of monumental historical crisis—as most credentialed seers would agree—what is it that is showing itself as sacral? Certainly the work of Long breaks the old medieval ground here in a way few other religionists have dared, in reading the European colonial advent on indigenous cosmos as itself quintessentially "religious" (in a way quite different for the colonized than for the colonizers, as Long ingeniously shows). My own contribution is merely to work the "break thus brokered into theory" into a new fantasy of possibility. Long has insisted it is *myth* that comprehends the human meaning of such a mess more adequately than merely rational calculus. In so doing, he has required modern theory to greet its storied other as equal. He has also offered testament on the recuperative process among indigenous survivors of such a terrifying advent as one of "mythic re-creation," forging hybrid new modalities of being from the shards of their own dismembered cosmograms and the ransacked diagrams of the West (where useful). "Religions of the oppressed" are the result—Ghost-Dancing, Dread-locking, Call-Responsing, Cargo-Culting the Western myth of supremacy into service of an indigenous conviction of parity. In the process of divining meaning in such an indigenous refining of violence into vitality, Long renders Rudolph Otto's formula (the *mysterium tremendum et fascinans*) revelatory of a certain tack: Ultimate Reality is complexly engaged in such religious re-invention as not only "fascinating" but "tremendous" (Long, 123, 137–139, 142, 167, 170, 196–197). Indigenous judo performed on colonial jive rejuvenates the rejection as "revelation." The trickster is tricked. And the move is classic blues, singing the hardness of a rock-like-reality into the gladness of a rolling belly.

But I am now after the sacral motility of the ordinary in *secular* modernity, when it first begins to show a hint of hallow. And I am not inventing here, but only wanting to take seriously the tally that it is the *blues,* even more than the spirituals, that points towards that indefinable "Something"[6] that haunts America under its surface like a haint never faced in the space of its own nightmare. Obviously it is a nightmare America has forced its dark-skinned denizens to bear in desperate attempt to spare itself its own fate. Just as obviously, it will not work. But when and how and where that "facing" *will* occur *is*, in some sense, up to fate. Here, I am only tracking the more recent traces of its eventual unveiling. And the blues (again by consensus among many who know such from the inside) only goes fully "American"— and thus begins to tickle and trouble the white American surface of the culture—in the modality of jazz (Jones, 1999, 139–141, 148, 166).

Thus the question: what is being revealed when a Louis Armstrong blue note takes up an ordinary and clear European tone and loads it with resonances of "more"—working it before, and over, and after— embroidering, onto its pristine singularity, a polymorphic polarity of contrasting possibilities? (Floyd, 1995, 117). Can such be embraced as the beginning blush of a new god of modernity, not yet emerged in full identity, but already ghosting the horn with both fascination and dread? Or what shall we say of the foray revealed when Art Tatum first sits at piano in Harlem, and convenes a multiplicity of hands in his own two flashing sets of fingers, rumbling so ribaldly with his left and beating so steady with the right, that his auditors swear he is a trinity of beings and Fats Waller simply sits and sweats (Floyd, 1995, 112)?

I am here only taking Long at his word in suggesting that a new form of crisis such as modernity would occasion a new religious apprehension of mythology that builds on both the myth-shards of previous apprehensions and the specificities of the new situation to reveal another Other. I am not pretending to read the stories of a succeeded culture, but rather the practices of a ruptured one that a myth-story could be built upon (if story-building is even possible any more given the ever-increasing rate of social change). These would be practices that nonetheless exhibit something of the nature of theophany: a mundane object suddenly disclosing a more, an eternity flashing from the ordinary, a sacrality hidden inside simplicity. This is what happens when John Coltrane takes up "These Are a Few of My Favorite Things" and suddenly a simple ditty discloses complex profundity.

But I do not think the divine quality being thus revealed is "favorite-ness." The ditty is the shard, not the *structure of deity* being revealed. What this latter might be is the subject of four possibilities I offer in the following experimental probing.

POSSIBILITY ONE: THE SOUNDING OF THE CITY

That jazz historically is said to first emerge, recognizably, in late nineteenth-century New Orleans funeral practices, gives an origin out-of-doors and streetwise. The military marching band of earlier times is re-timed into syncopated street-stomp still spewing its spectacle across Lenten moroseness today, throughout the hotter climes of the New World. It begins as African-influenced, polyglot parade, refiguring burial as two-beat bombast, beginning low and slow toward the grave, but returning in up-tempo, second-line choreography of street-chaos into carnival-conquest of police surveillance and bourgeois order (Floyd, 1995, 21, 43, 81–83). But it does not stay there. By the 1920s, the sound has gone north and New York, where it times its tones to the night of ghetto-rightness, teasing terror and delight out of Harlem bricks and street tricks and all the styling wiles of black middle class Negro-philes of the New Renaissance (Jones, 1999, 232, 148). And becomes the darling of bored whites.

Chicago also witnesses a flowering, a sound growing from Delta blues and Big Easy blows, southern cooking and rural sipping, brought up the big water to Chi-town cold, where it burrows into deep midnight in a segregated club, but after-hours, in the time of cemeteries, gathers its black troubadours and white truants against the law, and, in sheer love of its own never-completed parturition, makes "base-line" concrete yield melodic cacophony. The fit is uneasy—like the departure from African ancestry in borrowing the two-beat bar from hymn and polka and military march, forcing 4/4 time to carry the design of another conception of life, having to doodle the space between the bars with spice of a different kind—black jazz struggles in the opposition between the container and the thing contained (Jones, 1999, 192: Floyd, 97). The northern city is not a hospitable mold for the country mode, and even high-stepping New Orleans style has to hunker down into a blast pit of smoldering peat, full of orange beat, and forge heat and repeated defeats in the struggle to accommodate (Jones, 1999, 192; Floyd, 1995, 119). The fate of discrimination, enghettoization and alienation from community places its own stamp on the sound. The blues of Jim Crow oppression is compressed into a more staccato syncopation.

Through Great Depression blues, bent to ribald purposes and sent "swinging" in big band stands of night-time forgetting, the sound goes small-combo secret in the early forties, returns to ring-shout beats and unprecedented feats of melodic angularity, bopping the outrage of night-stick on knappy head into a hotbed thread of running changes and rhythmic momentum—a new language of code, unintelligible to the uninitiated, but emerging as the primary dialect of the music from the fifties to the seventies. The bebop cauldron of the forties city reflected the riotous return from World War II bases to the place of race in an unrelenting America—jagged edge of attack-drumming, free-lancing piano, and atom-splitting sax, pulling the diluted dream of swing back to the basic hardness of the street. In the move, melody was invaded by base, making melody itself a rhythmic mode, mirroring the mood of the modern from the side of the down-trodden and blackened.

By the 1950s, House Un-American Activities Committee fear and integration hopes inspire a brief urban turn from the blues boldness of bop to the hip trope of cool, evoking a crossroads exploration of Euro-composition and African rhythm on the part of Miles and Co. By mid-decade, however, gospel and R&B influences invoke a return to blues funk, bop now going middlebrow "hard" with the forceful edge of (Art) Blakey phrasings, ("Cannonball") Adderly eruptions, and Monkish ironic dissonance (Floyd, 1995, 180–182; Jones, 1999, 222). Then the sixties city goes code red, as white flight marks the apocalyptic end of black migration towards the Dream, and nationalist ire and Pan-African fire boil over into the Carmichael cry of "beauty, now—in your eye!" (Floyd, 1995, 183–185). The democratization of rhythm with melody, the repudiation of a European hegemony of harmony, the adoption of Coltrane's riotous tongue and mysterious flair as torch-bearer for the fist-in-the-air movement, the emergence of AACM (Association for the Advancement of Creative Music) and AECO (Art Ensemble of Chicago) menageries of the whole history, from beeps to blasts, bops to whispers, knocking even hubcaps into pointillist postmodern raps on the African ring theme—all of it comes to represent the ventriloquism of the city in the polytonality of a jazz philosophy, thinking through life in serial signification of a remembered "Africa," with Europe, literally, on its mind (Floyd, 1995, 190–193).

And over the course of all this history in the North, it is arguable that jazz renders the city numinous and dark with allure, invoking night as the palpable body of the god of growl, giving blues a new groove of concrete indigo, on the streets of grime. Whether in guise

of Armstrong's horn or Ellington's orchestra, Parker's palaver of pop-
ping infinities or Davis's definition of cobalt abstraction, Coltrane's
"kinetic splinters of melody" or Coleman's atonal terrorizing of freedom, it is the archetype of the underground cemetery of desire—a
whole metropolis smoking the herb of ancestral incantation, harrow-
ing the hell of ghetto in bent-note burp of celebration, or tattooing
train-whistle-longings onto winter winds like the languorous disappearance of time itself, inside a brass mute. Jazz is the city in love with
itself, in spite of itself, fondling street-lights with the dissonance of
dense thirst, a subterranean cosmos of hunger, "hainting" the human
body with howl, blowing fat lips through hot reed tips across the
entire range of stars, like the kiss of eternity on the thigh of now.

Possibility Two: The Funking of the Factory

Whether the mythic "text" here being worried in my writing is actually
to be understood as the jazz sound itself, the jam session in after-hours
club, or more expansively, the entire chain of signifying improvisation
carried from artist to artist across the twentieth-century landscape,
is not fully clear and, indeed, in the theorizing of such a "heteroge-
neous sound ideal" as any of these three possibilities represent, is better *not* resolved in the argument (Floyd, 1995, 27, 66, 84, 114). But
the possible mythic "object" offered in this section—the industrial-
ized organization of metals and minerals and muscles and minds into
an ensemble of run-away production materialized as the factory—is
patent. It finds very concrete objectification in the bent brass or re-
worked wood of jazz instrumentation. This particular imagination of
the object mythicized as sacred obviously skips over jazz's beginnings
in the South and turns to the post–World War I migrations of black
folk northwards into the workforce of factory cities as its favored site.
   But it is an interesting thought-experiment to grant the horn itself
(like Long's stone) an aura of *orisha,* perhaps long-ago mounting the
leg of the ring-shout-shuffler, jumping to the lip of the blues-singing
boaster or a Bessie Smith toasting of trifling suitors, slipping back off
the tongue of an Armstrong *rubato* or a Dizzy Gillespie *bravado* and
locking itself inside the instrument itself. Or perhaps it is better imagined as emerging as a "new" revelation of forged metal or assembly-
line technique that is not so much a matter of mythic remembering
of the past as of mythic clairvoyance in the present. In any case, the
new squalors of trumpet or blowers of clarinet, the keyboard cavort-
ers and base-string thumpers of jazz fame find new resonances in the
old instruments; they make all manner of sonic creatures and deities

appear where mere compositions and single-note purities were want to abide in European playing (Floyd, 1995, 98). Of particular mention here is the propensity to render the instrument human-like in its *vibrato* or growl, to make it "talk," "squawk," "whinny," "whine" or "pine"; to make it moan for water or groan like sex (Floyd, 1995, 28, 80, 115, 117; Jones, 1999, 227).

This technique—humanizing technology itself—was not lost on more recent imaginations of the wild efflorescence of our postmodern technocracy careening towards a posthuman world when cyberpunk science fiction writer, William Gibson, wrote the African *orisha* Ogu into the pixel of the virtual. The archetypal energy of blacksmithing and hunting, of political order and political rebellion, Ogou is the quintessential Yoruban deity of modernity as the god of all things iron and metal—the likely find of an intuition of the divine inside the web of silicon and steel. That Gibson invokes an African *orisha* rather than some other religion's icon to climb the spine of computer and "mount the virtual mind" itself speaks "right on time." Jazz began this rhyme of factory and funk in the 1920s. But it built on a long "work-song" tradition of singing the hit of axe on wood, or hammer on iron—syncopated by human grunt—into a musical "metabolizing" of mere work into a much expanded vision of "workin' it," de-centering industrial labor as the core meaning of being a body and appending it to the night-time center of the dance floor or the bed (Floyd, 1995, 50, 230; Gilroy, 1987, 198–199, 202–203; 1993, 203). Here also is re-vision of Marx's derision of factory labor as a simultaneous atrophying of the worker body and hypertrophy of the worker hand into a monstrous caricature of human being (Marx, 1967, 360). The god/ghost of the factory is indeed a monster.

POSSIBILITY THREE: THE APPARITION OF AMERICA

Thinking through the idea of the country itself as the mythic object obviously departs somewhat from the notion that myth monitors sacrality as it emerges from some tangible object or technique rooted in local ecology. The country as "object' is indeed imaginary, but met in the moment of a world war (as it would have been in black migration north in the teens or the forties), the revelation would abound on all sides, in every institutionalization of matter as human.[7] The "native son or daughter," in alienated struggle to survive in a ghetto on Chicago's south side or in Detroit below Eight Mile Road, would have encountered the surreality of militant Amercanity at every turn as an unavoidable "revelation of rock"—a "lithic impenetrability" in

Long's words (Long, 1986, 178, 197). This would be "America" as invisible surround of death for the person of color, revealed in the eye of the white other as granite hard and gray.

And here we might say the myth-text of jazz goes cosmogonic, groping for the beginning in the face of the end, partaking of Hegel's master-slave dialectic as a kind of "myth of new origins," in which black struggle for recognition by white society becomes emblematic of the entire modern situation of people of color around the globe.[8] "America" is a myth-object apprehended by the black subject through the gaze of the white. It is an apparition of "being seen" in a particular way as Du Bois so poignantly played out in his double-consciousness theme (Du Bois, 1961, 16–17). In the Jazz Age, it is the encounter—no longer mediated by the tangible separations of the Jim Crown south, but in the mobile and intangible voids opened by the northern white presence—that was given its metaphysical voice in Ralph Ellison's *Invisible Man* as "what does not see me" even as it looks on in pity or contempt. "America"—as the eyeball of quiet or riotous indifference, seeing only "animal." Jazz is the revelation and recodification of the strange sacrality of that void in the pupil of an entire country looking at the Negro on every side in the kitchens and cabarets, over the lunch counters and pay windows, on the street cars and in the court chambers, the prisons, of the North. Here the unnamed "Something" borders on the demonic, is experienced, as Long has so presciently proffered, as itself "lithic," a mode of *Tremendum*. But the actual mediation of this "stone wall of unscalable night" (as Du Bois calls it) in the eye of white people might also be found, in a different form, in black-on-black struggles to gain recognition, as well.

This points to the Hegelian significance of the jazz "cutting contest"—sax against sax, trumpet on trumpet, invoking the struggle-to-the-death with the rival, carried over into life itself, shooting drugs, talking shit, boasting and toasting and roasting large, projecting a lion's stare and a regal dare in one's own bearing—no matter the actual share of the goods one is missing. And in jazz, it claimed more than Buddy Bolden as its victim. Here, indeed, is the dozens-playing of Tatum on Waller, the Armstrong signifying flair, the "I don't care," back-to-the-crowd, hard cool air of the Davis horn, the svelte seamless sheen of the Ellington orchestra, willing to include anyone in its "jungle" celebration, but demanding everything in return for its sweet swing. This is the sound of "America" as being of "ultimate concern," in the eye of the other, and in the era of jazz it was primarily, but not only, the black man's burden. Bessie Smith at the height of her blues-singing fame, bared a soul similarly laboring for a straining share of recognition. And Billie Holiday lived there.

The cutting contest rivalry indeed has its roots in West African gaming rules and love of trickster-spiels and all manner of energy-intensifying competition. But the ante is infinitely upped in post-slavery America, where the game is ended at the point of a gun or in a noose, and the withheld acknowledgement is a death-sentence inside a living body. Even as late as 1968 or 1992 or 2014, black youth have played craps with fate in burning up streets for the stake—as told in 1965 to a Martin King on a smoldering sidewalk in Watts—of being recognized.

POSSIBILITY FOUR: THE RECOGNITION OF THE RACE

But it is actually the revelation of the human race itself that remains in eclipse in this quaking hard epiphany of America. Cutting sessions cut multiple ways, culturally. They sometimes involved white musicians in epic struggle with black. Saxophonist Art Pepper recalled to writer Neil Leonard a night when Sonny Stitt challenged Pepper to gladiatorial combat and proceeded to "do everything on a saxophone a person could do" for about an hour, then stopped and gave Pepper "one of those looks," implying, "All right, your turn" (Floyd, 1995, 138–139; Leonard, 1987, 79–80). Pepper was shaking in his boots, hooked, drunk, strung out, about to lose his wife, fearful of arrest by narcs and faced with having to play one of the hardest numbers possible, just played impeccably, with breakneck speed and inimitable virtuosity. Pepper was tempted just to walk away and quit jazz, but took a deep breath, "forgot everything and [let] everything come out" (Leonard, 1987, 79–80). His description afterwards was that he played "way over his head," finding a different kind of thread into the piece that slowly opened into the kingdom of feeling and out to the screaming people, and then blew and blew until he finished in a lather of sweat and shivers, hardly aware of where he was. The account is evocative of being mounted like a horse of the gods in West African possession—an enhancement of performance by way of trance, built of drug and drum, base-line thump and throbbing buzz of crowd. Ironically, says writer Floyd in recapping that "scene of carving," Pepper was "a white musician who was thriving on African-American cultural memory and tradition" (140). In exchanging a glance with Stitt as the people roared their approval, Pepper was given in return a simple, "'All right.' And that was it. [But] that's what it is all about" (Leonard, 1987, 80). Here was the rare about-face, a white musician eschewing the minstrel-seduction of a previous century, hooked not only on drugs, but the music itself, hocking his entire life for the sake a brief nod of acknowledgement. There is an Ottoian *mysterium* at work here, fascinating and fearful at once, demanding everything, much as it did of a Biederbecke, but in the name of . . . what?

I would argue jazz has materialized a different revelation for whites, different because it opens out in the context of the heavy-duty socialization of white power and privilege. This revelation is one of the sacrality of humanity in the code of black. It emerges, profoundly, but not as a novelty, in the African-American community as well. The black community had long experience of knowing itself human and finding its paragon figures and collective flair flashing mythic mystery. But for whites, the suddenly epiphany of black as harboring a compelling vision of being, was unprecedented and, for those who dared look with vulnerability, irresistible. The statement I realize is dangerously fraught, easily made to fold into the fetishism of dark skin color by people of pallor that is really just the flip side of denigration. The stereotype always signifies two ways at once—into a caricature and untruth of traits both negative *and* positive. I am after a deeper question. Charles Mills is only the latest in a long line of scholars to bend their minds on the fact of light supremacy as an organizing shorthand of history modern and ancient. Certainly the regime of white power that has materialized as the logic of Euro-colonization and neo-liberal globalization is unique in its 500-year-old career since Columbus. But Edward Bynum among others has marshaled evidence even of a Greco-Roman color scheme oriented towards an apex of brightness. And certainly South Indian caste wove chromatics into its organization of occupation as *dharma*.

The base-beat heat of thought here is that, in modernity at least, for the species to emerge in full human expression any place on the face of the planet, the place of its appearing necessarily must transvalue the reigning racial code to be recognized as such. In a word, until "dark" can be embraced as revelatory of divinity to the same degree as light, white imagination of itself as human is warped. There is no reason the human subject should not be included in the repertoire of "mythic objects" that in specific situations suddenly disclose from within their ordinariness, a flash of the divine. In the specificity of a now global white supremacy, however, that mythic appearing begins in color. The revelation of the one race of humanity as a potency of sacrality itself flashes with different force in white and nonwhite communities. Jazz represents a beginning moment when a few white people in America began to perceive, dimly but deeply, that here was something of genius, of largesse, of profound and unspeakable compulsion, rising up in a mode of musicality that defied the social code loading blackness with indifference or worse. And that revelation continues to work defiantly under the surface of the continuing supremacy.

The argument itself requires at least a book to sustain, but in sum, builds on LeRoi Jones's contention that the blues is the thick code of vibrancy in African-Americanity that carries in its rhythmic density the core culture of black survival in defiance of slavery and its continuing aftermath, and encodes that vibrancy as irreducibly "American" (Jones, 1999, 50, 59, 63–66, 79–80, 136, 142, 148). And jazz for Jones is the modality that has historically pulled blues out of its subcultural inaccessibility, combined it with multiple other expressive tendencies and offered it in an ever-changing morphology that grants participation to whites, and middle-class blacks, and other folks of all kinds who otherwise would have no point of communion with its incorrigible opacity. Thought about in such a compass, jazz marks the modality in which black blues mythology first begins to agitate the surface of America. It is the first time some number of whites adopt blacks as teachers and inspirers of an impulse that is so large it cannot be simply spoken or played, but will demand the whole of a life to be displayed. Jones remarks, in his discussion of Biederbecke, that Bix represented the first white musician who brought to the jazz he created any of the *ultimate concern* Negro musicians brought to it as a casual attitude of their culture. To be sure, Biederbecke will play, in Jones's mind, not black but "white jazz," but will do so in response to an ultimacy demanding of him the totality of his life.

Such a moment represents one of the earliest of a white person embracing not merely black suffering as demanding uncompromising redress, but black culture as compelling myth and source of revelation. Some 75 years later, another white man, Yale art historian Robert Farris Thompson, in a talk in Detroit, would say "one of the unintended results of slavery is that now the entire Western world rocks to an African beat." What Ishmael Reed fantasizes in his novel, *Mumbo Jumbo,* as the irresistible "'Jes Grew," a dance frenzy wildly infecting the entire country, undoing supremacy "from below" by converting white racists to uncontrollably pleasurable movements that interrupt their apparatuses of control, in Thompson's view, is not just fantasy. Certainly, supremacy shows little sign of abatement, but it is also true that the beat Thompson detects has now gone global in hip-hop. Rap is ricocheting around the planet like a postmodern fetish. But it was jazz that first gathered some whites into a nascent recognition of blackness as more than "black."

I am not here trying to pin any easy hope on such a development. Dismantling white supremacy will likely take lifetimes of struggle and unswerving risk. But I do want to offer a perspective. R&B took the baton mid-century from blues and gospel and country-and-western cross-currents, pushed the edge of the multicultural mix and the splice of Euro-Afro-Creole riffs to the point of rocking Elvis's pelvis inside the entire culture of the country. Now a scant few years of soul-, funk-, reggae-, techno-, and rock-and-roll-playing later, rap rhythm has an entire world rhyming. But jazz was the decisive crossroads through which blues passed on the way to becoming rap. Whatever the ultimate outcome, jazz marked an indelible moment in the process: the cross-cultural realization of an insurgent mythic beat in the unrepentant feet of white America that augurs an unthought modern possibility: the full appearance of the entire race as bearing the trace of Africa. This memory is cosmogonic: black mythology reveals the beginning of all of us.

PART IV

THE QUESTION IN POST-MODERNITY:
COMMUNICATION AND
GLOBALIZATION

DJ Qbert as Cyber-Maniac Shaman: Reading DJ-ing at the Crossroads of Tradition and Information

The colonial enterprise was indeed a ravenous maw. Yet, the babaylan *tradition never really died; it remained alive inside the colonial religious infrastructure.*

—*S. Lily Mendoza,* Between the Homeland and the Diaspora

POETIC INTROIT

Filipino-American DJ Qbert emerged in the early 1990s as hip-hop's premier turntablist—someone not merely playing backup to an MC send-up of significance, but grabbing the ozone by way of scratch-tones, and beat-loans, and digitalized, mixer-synthesized, cyber-moans, that pulled the bones of history from the loam of urban ecology like a warrior drone of sonic insanity signaling the arrival of a new incarnation of rhyme-spitting dexterity in a cyborg-mode of selectivity transforming calamity into levity and depravity into beauty and new vision.

Thus far, the chapters already offered have tracked a kind of creative genealogy, improvising on various ecologies of empire. This chapter[1] will not be different. What empire elaborates as tool and trope of its control also harbors the possibility of resistance and counter-deployment. In chapters 2 and 3 we looked at the way land scarred by agri-business murder (farmer Cain killing pastoralist Abel) and seed "owned" by urban elites (in first-century Galilee) are taken up in traditions of Sabbath/Jubilee and Jesus parables respectively and thereby given the capacity "to speak" otherwise.[2] In chapters 4 and 5, the focus turned "panoptic," tracing the historical development of expansionist agriculture into imperialized projects of religious and racial superiority. There we examined the way the "Christological doctrine of incarnation" and the "colonial doctrine of white supremacy" effectively promoted the human species and European Christians as the divinely privileged life forms on the planet—and the way those supremacist logics of species and skin have been challenged both in academic theory and in indigenous practice on the ground. Chapters 6 and 7 concentrated their gaze more exclusively on the colonized. In these explorations, we elaborated complex examples of gendered and racialized "push-back" on "missionary Mariology" and "classical European music" respectively, in practices as diverse as Latin American Guadalupe fests and Haitian voudou possession cults, on the one hand, and jazz innovation, on the other. This chapter continues that tack; but here the modality goes postmodern. In what follows we read the cyber-coded sound conjuration of contemporary hip-hop DJs in the Filipino diaspora in California by way of a precontact Filipino tradition of shamanic healing called "babaylan"—amplified by insight from Amazonian *ayahuasca* practice.

GLOBAL SITUATION

And of course, the desperate situation of the planet continues to form the background. Especially in a chapter in one sense lionizing a new techno-sophistication with electronic sound production as a potential force of healing, it is important once again to foreground our global crisis. Technology is not simply a neutral "tool," but a dangerous Power in its own right. The planet is upending before our eyes and our fetishism of technological "fixes" are part of what drives the devastation. U.S. Defense Department planning for massive waves of climate-refugees as a national security assault ups the ante on the search for new capacities for surveillance and conducting war at a distance by remote control. Living as "one globe under the drone," subject to termination at any second, increasingly looks to be the future of most of us. Peaking oil—despite the frenetic hype about new shale extraction and fracking substitution (in say, North

Dakota)—signals the imminent end of our car culture addiction and oil-driven food production and packaging. It also pushes us into ever more radical intervention into the Mother-Earth body and the bodies of all of her offspring. Extinction rates of other species have so catastrophically increased as to render uncertain our own species' survival (Einstein gives our species about a year once the bees go). Bee colony collapse (among many, many other "disappearances") now stands as a "sign of the times." The many tens of thousands of synthetic chemicals being released, untested, into the environment are altering everything from the viability of these winged "laborers" who pollinate a large percent of our staple crops to phytoplankton composition and density in the oceans—organisms producing 50 percent of all the oxygen on the planet that have themselves disappeared by as much as 40 percent since 1970. Particulate plastic waste is emerging as a kind of indestructible "zombie force" disrupting endocrine function across much of the biosphere (including humans and sperm whales), as well as "colonizing" broad stretches of ocean, with who knows what consequences. And what can be euphemistically called "population overshoot" is turning increasing sectors of the globe into ever-burning garbage heaps hosting the new ecology of slum cities that will soon "house" nearly one-half of the world's urban population—a cadre of shared desperation whose primary vision is reduced simply to securing the next meal (Davis, 2006, 151).

As earlier argued, these four "horsemen of the apocalypse" drive to the fore the fundamental uncertainty that frames every spiritual consideration I entertain. It entails a suite of questions that calls *in* question our most cherished assumptions about what we are doing here on the planet. What really is a human being? A human society? A sustainable way of living? So basic a querying of fundamental assumptions is of course the lodestone of this entire collection of chapters. But it nowhere becomes harder to keep in focus than when championing a recent techno-artistic development like hip-hop. In a time when "history" and "ancestry" are themselves eclipsed by the rate of technological change, and capitalism relentlessly reorganizes time in service of the present moment of commodification and consumption, the focus on presuppositions is crucial. If we are going to think healing in the key of an older tradition like *babaylan* feeling and vision, entertained as exhibiting some kind of "half-life" viability inside a new allurement like turntablism (as we will in what follows), in service of what kind of future are we doing such? Is the fascination of this dialogue simply a matter of giving a bit of indigenous flavor to an otherwise upwardly mobile–aspiring lifestyle? Do we merely want to spice up a middle-class-dreaming, contentedly consumerist-buying, iPhone-scheming participation in contemporary globalization, hoping the War on Terror and the foreclosure bailiff stay out of the front yards of those of us well-resourced enough to buy the equipment and listen to the sound?

The challenge for me that arises out of any consideration of indigenous practice is profoundly polemical. Whatever else I take away from the engagement, I take it for granted that the basic issue at stake is lifestyle itself—an entire belief and practice system that I have been socialized into in this country. It is a system that relentlessly privileges growth and technology, consumer goods and Hollywood, accumulation of gadgets and rights to comfort, flush toilets and private closets full of Saks labels or Target imitations, police forces keeping the criminalized poor away from my door and a military, operating on my tax dollars, invading other "places" on average of once every six months to secure the resources that I am trained by corporate advertising to covet, by "patriotic" discourses to be willing to kill for (through defense department and mercenary surrogates), and finally by peer pressure and lifestyle choices to consume and so feel like "I am somebody"!

The issue in examining a revivified *babaylan* concern for healing inside a novel phenomenon like turntablism is, for me, a question about an entire way of life, not just what passes today for "spirituality." And finally it is about ecology—about my life as a human in relationship to all of the other human beings and life-forms I am utterly dependent upon, but have no knowledge about or appreciation of. I now live inside a gated country protected by war-on-terror legality and encased inside cement and silicon, wood and steel and plastic to such a degree I no longer even recognize the kinship and living vitality of the interdependence that I have lost track of. Underneath my postmodern urbanist sense of entitlement lie human beings and life-forms upon which I prey like the most rapacious and callous of slave masters or development engineers that ever lived! I live as beneficiary of a global system of utter pillage and depredation. I am content to have chickens live their entire lives bent over in a mesh cage so crammed with other chickens none of them ever get to raise their heads entirely—so long as I get my "healthy choice" chicken Caesar salad! And content, as well, to let darker-toned Third World "others" of my own species extract the raw materials and pick the fruit and stitch the clothing and process the garbage that leverages my own air-conditioned comfort.

Personal Confession

So just what is it that we are doing in reading a contemporary inno-vation like hip-hop scratching through older shamanic forms of "re-balancing" like *babaylan* healing or *ayahuasca* visioning? The "voices" that these older traditions channel, I would argue, in one way or another participate in the kind of remembering signified by the story of archetypal Abel, as we have already examined (the out-back bedouin of biblical infamy whose blood cries from the ground on which he was slain by agribusiness-city-builder Cain according to the Genesis text that remembers him: Gen. 4:1–17). This is a force of re-presentation and re-collection echoing through a cold colonial history of 5,000 years that has always had economic plunder as its rationale and that has never ceased its predatory conquest up to the present—even if today it goes by the name of "free trade." The subaltern voices of the crushed and disappeared indigenous—whether blood-soaked bedouin in the desert of the ancient Middle East, *babaylan* "indios" impaled alive by Spanish friars as "croco-dile food" on river banks in the beautiful archipelago of the South China Sea in the early days of colonialism, or beleaguered rain-forest dwellers in the burning jungles of today—demand full hearing if they are to be countenanced at all. And the full demand of that hearing will not merely celebrate its latest sounding under the flying fingers of turntable wizards plumbing the possibilities of vinyl to channel vigor. It will rather cut harshly against the very consumerist habits and commercialized desires that form the market substrate of our ability to "hear" today.

I speak to the topic by way of sufferance—a white male North American, unwitting beneficiary of the entire history of colonial rela-tions between, among others, my ancestors and the Philippine Islands since 1898. That history granted my people access to Asian markets at the expense of (at least) a half-million Filipino lives lost in resist-ing the invasion. That history has positioned me as social beneficiary of a century of Filipino labor never paid its full due over lifetimes of working these shores as farm hands or domestics, nurses or clerks, or of Filipino effort in World War II granting my family protection and safe prospect despite the fact that those soldiers were never honored as such nor given pensions or health care. Or more lately (if more distantly) conferring convenience as call center "help" imitating my region's dialect from across an ocean when I need assistance with my credit card, or masseuses for my tired bones, when I visit "the home-land" in company of my *Kapampangan* wife.

And whatever insights I bring to the table derive from my peculiar history of a quarter-century lived in the inner city. An eastside Detroit community of activist Christians, pooling assets and making life decisions together on a poverty-level budget, provided the base from which to engage a hard-rocking urban tract of African American struggle up against the fate race and class decreed as their state of existence. Gradually over a first decade in that "underclass" neighborhood, I unlearned some of my privilege, had scales fall from "color blind" eyes to see the deep effects of white supremacy on a dark-toned community. But just as provocatively, I also learned the subtleties of the cultural judo that this community performed on its incarceration inside a depraved stereotype (when not behind actual steel bars). Over time, debrided by black humor and anger, schooled in call-response antiphony and the polyphony of a jazz sensibility—crosscut with hip-hop antipathy toward all things "unreal"—I emerged in a new sense of identity and possibility, the joy and task of being more than simply "white." As a spoken-word poet, earning a living as adjunct professor of things spiritual in an urban college, I took in the angular pulse of rhythm with which my students of color and co-residents on the block probed life choices and broke down opposition. The ability regularly to refigure reality under the beat of syncopation, making desperation yield beauty in spite of itself, hipped me to what I would later come to call the gift of shamanic percussivity (detailed in my book *Shamanism, Racism, and Hip-Hop Culture: Essays on White Supremacy and Black Subversion*).

Black culture—in West and Central African origins, on slave plantations and southern reincarnations of the community after slavery, and in northern cities after the two wars and despite more recent postindustrial deprivation—has innovated consistently and thoroughly with rhythmic patterns of creativity. It has done so in dance, in music, in humor like Richard Pryor's and talk like Tupac's and thought like Toni Morrison's, in sartorial combat with the skin stereotype, in all manner of political organizing and cultural struggle to survive an impossible circumstance. The ability to take in energy from the environment, run it through a breeder-reactor core of the culture, giving out even more than was taken it, in a "stepped down" fashion—thus conserving anguish as an incubator of vitality—became a cipher for me for how an entire community elaborated pain into power in a shamanistic vein of visionary transformation. Part of that skill is a matter of bending words into new vibratory potency, stringing together an impossible riff of sound that elaborates the angst of rejection into an eloquence of off-timed[3] celebration, creating an alternative "body" of sonic freedom for the compacted life locked down by white society inside the oppressed black body. All of that became a schoolhouse for me—teaching me beyond the import of mere words, of the living possibilities of renegade energies, once they are given a new communal texture of expression. It is out of that experience that I offer my comments on a new mode of sonic improvisation going by the name of "scratching." Emerging in the last quarter-century as shamanistic probe of the hard surface of postindustrial urban life, the work of someone such as DJ Qbert, may even warrant examination as a diasporic echo of an older and peculiarly Filipino force of *babaylan* power.

FILIPINO RESILIENCE

But just what does the term *babaylan* invoke and why re-root a postmodern practice like DJ-ing in an indigenous orientation going back behind Euro-colonialism? My response to the latter question is what is teased out in the rest of the chapter. It is part of my broader academic work, laboring to reconnect postcolonial novelties with antecedent trajectories. Pushing back on modern "reductions" of human experience and identity to "life inside a commercial" has meant suggesting the durability of past innovations. Whether imagining Tupac Shakur as channeling Ogou Achade or modern race discourse as a mode of European witchcraft practice, black preaching as shamanic healing or Christian scripture as encoding much older pastoral nomad rebellion, as I have in previous publications, the project is not one of claiming some kind of essentialized retention (Perkinson, 2009, 2004, 2002, 2013). It is rather a matter of conviction that we do not create afresh, but out of the residue of the past, no matter how altered our present circumstance. As Marx once said,

> [Humans] make their own history, but they do not make it as they please; they do not make it under self-selected circumstances, but under circumstances existing already, given and transmitted from the past. The tradition of all dead generations weighs like a nightmare on the brains of the living. And just as they seem to be occupied with revolutionizing themselves and things, creating something that did not exist before, precisely in such epochs of revolutionary crisis they anxiously conjure up the spirits of the past to their service, borrowing from them names, battle slogans, and costumes in order to present this new scene in world history in time-honored disguise and borrowed language. (1963)

His thinking has been given fresh nuance in work like that of Avery Gordon's *Ghostly Matters: Haunting and the Sociological Imagination* as well as Mark Lewis Taylor's *The Theological and the Political: On the Weight of the World.* As Gordon and Taylor spell out, it is not only "costume disguise" and socially structured "circumstance" that get imported from the past, but energy. The issue is not just a matter of social forms of the past being used "to clothe" new scenes, but of the DNA of past generativity animating new bodies. Substance as well as shape may show up with the force of a kind of inchoate mission. What goes by the name of creativity in the present is not merely "the new" gussied up in older borrowings, but can also manifest ghostly hauntings and seething memories of unresolved histories (i.e., unrequited victims) (Gordon, 1997, 175–177; Taylor, 2011, 14). The "nightmare" Marx mentions can reemerge in good art, taken up by social movements reinvigorating past pain in projects to alter present structures (Taylor, 2011, xii, Perkinson, 2013, xxi–xxii, 26–27). And indeed (as argued at length in *Messianism Against Christology*), this notion of nightmares and ghosts arising from the forgotten agonies of ungrieved ancestors is profoundly "indigenous"—an intuition about the un-gone dead that appears around the globe in older cultures (Prechtel, 2001; Perkinson, 2013, 26–27, 215 n 4). Thus the power of persuasive art can be discerned as the "sigh of the oppressed creature" given texture and purchase in continuing history. Rupturing imposed silences and closures in the name of a quest for a more comprehensive healing and resolution, this "artful groan" stitches the present onto the past. And such is the tack taken here.

"*Babaylan*" is a Visayan term referencing a shamanic healing tradition shared across much of the Philippine archipelago under other ethnolinguistic designations such as *mumbaki, dawac, balyan, katalonan, ma-arm, mangngallag, beliyan,* and so on (Mendoza and Strobel, 2013, 13). It references both function and person. Cariapa, Bolandungan, Cabacungan, Estela BangotBanwa, Medung Sengal are proper names of actual babaylans that "ring down the corridor of history like a gong," among indigenous communities in the Philippines. But it is no longer just history and the homeland that resonates to that sounding. As part of an ongoing process of decolonization, two sisters in the Filipino diaspora—S. Lily Mendoza (my wife) and Leny Strobel—have recently made common cause in their careers in championing and extending (here in the United States) the work of a pioneer scholar whose initiative has influenced an entire movement in the Philippine Academy to recover indigenous Filipino understandings of the culture. Against the pejorative grain of Euro-colonizer interpretations of Filipino practices through half a millennium of Spanish and U.S. domination of the islands, Ver Enriquez devoted a lifetime to articulating what became known as *Sikolohiyang Pili-pino* (Filipino "liberation psychology"). The broad-based movement of scholars that carries his memory is known as the Indigenization Movement. It has devoted its efforts to enfranchising Tagalog (the indigenous tongue of the Manila area) as an archipelago-wide *koine*, used in both media and education, and to a thorough-going program of reinterpreting the culture from within and below by native speakers. And such it has done. But while subsequent research carried out in multiple fields over recent decades has influenced Filipino historiography and psychology alike, much of the theorizing has presumed the politics of nation-state-building as its primary mission. It has not questioned the way that counter-colonial effort has itself often become colonial toward indigenous hunter-gatherer or subsistence agriculture groups in the islands like the Manobo and the Aeta. Nation-building carried on in the name of "indigenizing" Western development has often come at the expense of actual indigenous peoples.

More recent theorizing and political activism—in concert with United Nations recognition of the precarity of indigenous peoples globally, enshrined in initiatives like the UN Declaration on the Rights of Indigenous Peoples and UN Permanent Forum on Indigenous Issues—has begun seeking to secure ancestral land claims and some measure of political or cultural autonomy for actual indigenous groups. In the Filipino diaspora, recognition of the complexity of the struggle against colonialism has given birth, among other things, to a concern to recover a more thorough-going indigenous sensibility. In 2009, under the leadership of Strobel in particular, a Sonoma State University–hosted conference gave public expression to an informal network of collaboration that formalized itself as The Center for Babaylan Studies (CfBS) in the same year. Organized as "an incubator and launching pad for scholarly research, culture-bearing creative expression, and political advocacy for indigenous peoples' rights," the center has hosted ongoing workshops, retreats, healing concerts, and festivals. These have aimed at animating a deeper possibility of integration between body-mind-spirit and local ecosystem (Mendoza & Strobel 14). The project is particularly centered on a recovery and extension of what in Tagalog is called "kapwa"[4]—an observable, island-wide cultural propensity to live life in a mode of "shared being," where the wellsprings of thriving are quite evidently profoundly social and exquisitely relational, rather than individual and self-aggrandizing. Diaspora dwelling for the better part of a century has not dimmed the orientation. The fluid dance of delicately nuanced communication remains definitive of Filipino style and pleasure even among those long ago exiled from the motherland. *Kapwa* feeling and connection identifies the kind of wholeness and integration *babaylan* healing seeks to re-invigorate.

BABAYLAN BALANCE

And it is this durability of a cultural trait that is recognizable in its signature behaviors that exercises imagination here. A recent anthology co-edited by the two sisters exactly specifies the resurgent history and capacity. Subtitled *Philippine Babaylan Studies and the Struggle for Indigenous Memory*, the book offers a selection of papers and performances from the 2009 conference. Its cover has an open-mouthed leviathan poised under the roots of a glowing and fecund tree. Within the coiled tail of the beast is a native woman with flying hair gesturing under a blazing sun and a cloud-boiling volcano. Headlining the depiction is the title inscription: *Back from the Crocodile's Belly*, hinting both trauma and its overcoming. A story from the 1663 *babaylan* uprising in Tapar, Iloilo, fills out the image. Spanish missionaries, terrified of *babaylan* potency and power, impaled the corpses of rebel leader Tapar and the group's "holy mother," shamaness Maria Santisima, on stakes along the bank of the Laglag River to be eaten by crocodiles (cf. Diaz, C. [1890] Conquistas de las Islas Filipinas, covering 1616–1694 as cited in Blair and Robertson, 1998). Given the aura surrounding such shamanic adepts, the friars wanted to ensure total annihilation. In its signal brutality, the incident captures a broader truth: "colonial violence did consume indigenous culture (the 2001 account of religious historian Carolyn Brewer details the systemic demonization of *babaylans* and their ostracism and social "dismemberment" as *brujas* or witches)" (Mendoza and Strobel, 2013 13). Colonization was indeed a metabolic force—a maw of consumption.

But the Spanish stepped into a mythic conundrum at the same time: the crocodile was revered across the islands. As in so many indigenous perceptions around the globe, telluric and aquatic powers of regeneration were epitomized in the mysteries of serpentine potency. Mythically, this was a beast that both devoured and rebirthed. *Babaylan* energy was not entirely disappeared within the creature's belly. Colonization might eat culture—and bodies—alive. But indigenous shapeshifting and pliability meant a likely return from the dead—in one form or another. (Perhaps even as the crocodile itself!). Here the logic of a historical linearity meets the spiraling durability of an older idea of life. *Babaylan* proclivity marks something not yet eliminated from either memory or desire. Still practiced under various names in more out-of-the-way places in the homeland, it is also showing its face across an ocean. Much like the biblical figure of prophecy rumbling inside the fish that ate Jonah, *babaylan* shamanism seems to have survived deep water transport, tumbled out onto a new shore, and begun speaking afresh.

"What" it speaks remains to be decided by those gravitating to its allurements. As a mode of indigenous healing peculiar to the islands, its rhizome must be sought in history, retrievable only in the fraught work of rereading the Spanish colonial archive with a different eye and with considerable imagination (as detailed by Brewer, 2001, 356–357, among others). But some of those roots might also by glimpsed in ferreting out contemporary practices in both the homeland and the diaspora—habits of thought, gestures of humor, dance-forms and food preferences, rhythms of speech, cadence of feasting, habits of reciprocation, uses of silence as message, and so on—that conserve body memory of a different grasp of wholeness than modernity typically installs. Of course, there is no essence of culture that perseveres no matter the setting or geography. But neither do long-standing traditions typically disappear without a trace. "Healing" as an activity is always at least partially recursive; it seeks to recover a prior health, to overcome a wound that by its very existence as "wound" implies a pre-existing possibility of integrity.

Babaylan healing is a catch-all term indigenous to the islands for what more generally might be glossed as "shamanism"—itself somewhat loosely adopted (and perhaps thereby illegitimately pirated—though the anthropological debate about this is beyond what can be engaged here) from Central Asian Tungusic culture for a style of interacting with the spirit-world and the local ecology and the human community that shares features across cultures. Those features include: a tripartite cosmology of underworld, this world, and overworld; a perception of affliction that often speaks in terms of "soul loss" to describe a depletion of vitality or relational entropy; the consequent need to divine causes, move across boundaries, do battle, and retrieve energy from wherever it is inappropriately sequestered or riveted; the use of trance to gain access to one of these "other world" domains of action; ritual gathering that employs dance, song, herbal intervention, and so on; animal or plant familiars that "teach" or communicate information vital to the healing process; familiarity with the local ecology and all of its various communities and their patterns of interaction (plants, animals, waters, weather patterns, soils, topographic features, etc.); and extensive ethnobotanical savvy (herbal lore) (Eliade, 1964).

Of course, particularly Filipino versions of shamanic healing would have emerged historically in modalities peculiar to each of their given local ecologies. The list of equivalent terms offered earlier hints at the diversity. Indeed, even the Spanish colonial archive in its effort to suppress the practices reflects a struggle to name. In her work on the "holy confrontation" between female shamanesses and Spanish *missionarios* that took place from 1521 to 1685, feminist religious studies scholar Carolyn Brewer tracks the centuries-long battle to contain and marginalize indigenous healers under a shifting repertoire of pejorative labels such as *bruja* (witch), *hechicera* (sorceress), *anitera maldita* (cursed priestess), and the like (Brewer, 155, 166). That suppression was finally only accomplished when coupled with a malign social strategy of using impressionable young boys to do surveillance on older female shamanesses and turn them in to the authorities (Brewer, 2001, 161, 165, 356). But it is the frontier of differential contact between local versions of *babaylan* healing centered in the leadership of older women (and cross-dressing men) and a universalizing Hispanic Catholicism that homogenized the various ethnic practices in the process of suppressing them that (obviously) proved most radical. In those places where encounter was continuous, Spanish inquisitorial prosecution resulted in a virtual "holocaust" of native social, cultural and religious particularity (Brewer, 2001, 159).

However, away from the lowland centers of colonial administration (which as targets of development have become densely urbanized, networked with highways and saturated with Western media) local versions of *babaylan* practice continue in hybrid forms. In the highland *cordilleras* or remote islands or inaccessible marshes, shamanic healing shows up under many guises. Some of these are now the subject of field study by CfBS-affliated researchers (among others) seeking to document, celebrate, and learn from the practitioners before they are entirely eclipsed by modern pressure and corporate takeover. In the face of neoliberal globalization and continuing Christian evangelization, these varied practitioners exhibit a common trajectory and increasingly find support from each other in a shared struggle to survive. They also may be able to recognize something like diasporic "offspring—or at least a fragment of kindred "orientation"—even in so wildly different a mode of seeking coherence and integration as hip-hop innovation.

Sampled Spirits

Filipino-American DJ Qbert emerged in the early 1990s as hip-hop's premier turntablist—someone not merely playing backup to an MC send-up of significance, but grabbing the mike with a cyborg strike of vocabulary coming straight from the future. With his posse of *Invisibl Skratch Piklz*, Qbert blazed a sonic trail into the inner ether by melding human hand and vinyl disc into a mestizo mix of tricks, doing judo on the diasporic clash of cultures defining California's coast at the millennial crossover. Today, he is both ancestor and cipher for an entire posse of wobble-fingered masters, whose demographic profile is disproportionately populated by vinyl wonks of Filipino descent, ranging in DJ name from Babu (Chris Oroc) to Eddie Edul, Marlino to Manila Ice, Geometrix to Jester the Filipino Fist, Kuttin Kandi to the Icey Ice man of LA's 93.5 FM—among others! DJ-ing in the manner of Qbert and company embodies a different ethic than the "beef culture" resulting from MC battles and "diss" rap. In a subtle divergence from the "playa" impulse to get over at all costs, reproducing capitalist competition in vernacular form, turntablists regularly share techniques, and make new scratch products available to each other in a constant search for elevating the practice collectively. They more typically embody a communal ethic of reciprocity. Qbert himself is vegan, careful about keeping his body in balance, and aware that limitation is a necessary part of vitality: he will voice in interviews, for instance, that overlaboring the tables is unhealthy. The issue is rather using the new vocabularies of sound to create a rhythmic probe of silence—to suggest, to quest, to open the world to an emergent form of intelligence that does not immediately submit to old conventions or expressive logics controlled by the status quo.

Scratch is here a technique of conjure, divining below the surface of machine culture, probing the possibilities of sensation released when substances newly minted by industrial design are brought aggressively together in rhythmic incantation. Vinyl grooves meeting steel needles under a beat yield an ecological significance not yet decipherable in conventional human language. Strangely, the result is rather visionary—a "seeing," by way of sound, through a portal without a tongue to convey the import. Like Amazonian *yagé*-drinking shamans silently orchestrating the undulating landscapes of color experienced by their "*yagé*-tripping" clients, as we shall see below, sight and sound are here pulled apart and put together outside grammatical structure, letting the world be reassembled as if in genesis again. This is perhaps the essence of healing, unlocking energies of meaning from entropic logics of pain and repetitive modes of self-destruction and rendering them available for re-creation.

Here the artistic and the shamanic join hands. Indigenous healing is nothing if not an orchestration of prodigious imagination. Its work is animate ecstasy; its dream, an alchemy of the elementary; its journey, an inquiry of existence. Traversing unseen underworld and overworld potencies of both spirit and matter, shamanism might even be said to craft a performative probe of the strange and fantastic grammar of serpentine information embedded in all life forms: the primal coiling and uncoiling of ever-proliferating DNA—common to vine and humankind, jaguar spots and clots of bacterial colonization in the colon—dancing in ceaseless antiphonies of the body like a micro-frequency of the galaxy, living imitation of the interstellar overtones and undertones of pulsating space, heard by Pythagoras, or the dark matter and dark energy of modern physics, whose mysterious absence grants to light its very possibility of speed and fecundity. Scholars today are reinvestigating the shamanic imagination with a vengeance. In a late epiphany, some are even recognizing remarkable "ecocentric epistemologies" of both botany and biology encoded in shamanic logics of metaphor and vision, song and rhythm, that may hold keys to our species' ability to survive the catastrophe we seem rapidly to be precipitating.

It is no accident that the term has also been drafted to describe the effects—if not the intent—of hip-hop wizardry working rhymes and beats into an epiphany of postindustrial delirium (Spencer, 1991, 7, 11; Dyson, 1991, 22; Royster, 1991, 61–63, 65, 67). In using fractal methods of sound creation opportunistically to seize a product designed by a corporation for consumption and profit (the vinyl record) and use it against its intended use to release levity and vision from within the electronic interior of deindustrialized ecology, scratching could be said to be articulating a new sonic vocabulary for the boiling up[5] of human enlightenment. At least such will be the tack taken here. I am not so much interested in lionizing Qbert as camping out on the creativity he signals and reading it shaman-istically. Transcoded across lines of gender and age for a changed historical situation, we might even say scratch innovation channels a fractured mode of postcolonial *babaylan* eloquence. Rightly grasping the nature of that fractured impulse, however, requires asking the deepest possible question about the intention of the pre-colonial practice. And as already emphasized, at core that question is, "What really is a 'human'"?

Shamanic "Humanism"

I do not pretend to be more than a distant learner in relationship to the deep impulses of historic *babaylan* healing, as indeed in relationship to indigeneity in various forms around the globe. I do think today, in the face of the crisis whose physiognomy I outlined above, sitting down before indigenous vision and struggling to learn its wisdom and challenge to a supposedly "civilized" world fast careening off the cliff edge of self-destruction, is an imperative of the species. If we hope to survive this century in any form other than that of a Mad Max movie or a Cormack McCarthy road walker, laboring across a postapocalyptic landscape of horrors, we would do well to listen to our ancestry. But rather than focus again on *babaylan* vision here, I want briefly to visit another culture's mode of shamanic healing to open perspective on the scratching virtuosity just enumerated. I have already alluded to its eloquence in the reference to rainforest dwellers using a plant extract known as *yagé* (or *ayahuasca*) to galvanize healing.

The particular culture whose skills and tradition throw interesting light on turntablist practice are the Shipibo of the Peruvian Amazon, one of some 72 *ayahuasca*-using cultures in Western Amazonia (Luna, 1986, 57; Narby, 1998, 41). The psychotropic tea that for millennia has animated shamanic ritual explorations of affliction in the rain forest is a carefully brewed mix of plants combining the alkaloid properties of the hallucinogenic *di-methyl-tryptomine* (which is also produced inside the human brain) and a *monoamine oxidase* inhibitor that inactivates the human stomach enzyme that would otherwise render the hallucinogen ineffective (Narby, 1998, 10–11). After centuries of European colonial suppression of the practices, recent medical analyzes of *ayahuasca* have clarified its long-term harmlessness and its therapeutic benefits, legalizing its use, even in Westernized urban centers such as Rio de Janero, in Brazil. But it is not primarily the empirically validated effects of the combinatory brew that are of interest here, but rather the ecological understanding of the practice when it is pursued in a shamanically supervised gathering, in its natural environs of the rain forest.

The indigenous comprehension of the kaleidoscopic visions that result from drinking the tea emphasize the experience as one of being "taught by the plants." The idea that plants might communicate has been a great stumbling block for Western scientific, and now commercial, interests, whose attentions have been provoked in recent decades by *yagé*'s verified benefits and well-studied efficacy. But as anthropologist Jeremy Narby (1998) has detailed in his own years-long initiation into its use, and the gradual disabuse of his own disbelief, the sophistication of the plant combination necessary for the tea to work belies discovery by merely trial and error. The natives' own explanation—that the plants themselves have taught their own use—can so far not be easily gainsaid (42–43, 51, 109–110, 127–131, 177). But it is not just that the plants "teach" through the brewing up of their own bodies, but what and how they teach that gives pause for my project. They invariably work their holistic potency in a multimedia ensemble of song and vision.

Indeed, among the Shipibo, seeing and hearing represent a synesthetic reciprocity that may well be a shared cultural trait. At the heart of Shipibo spirituality lays responsiveness to a non-manifest and ineffable world rooted in the rainforest that is evoked and invoked in the human world by way of creative design-patterns constituted simultaneously of sound and sight (Charing, 2008, 2). Their weave is patterned into textiles, embroidery, and artisan craft, for instance, by women initiated into the practice when Piripi berry juice was squeezed into their eyes as young girls. The seeing supposedly lasts a lifetime and is understood to represent the vibratory potency of the Cosmic Serpent, *Ronin Kene,* the great Anaconda of Being, Mother-Creator of all that exists, whose skin radiates in an electric reverb of color, generating all possible patterns—past, present, and future—in ever-new, inimitable fusions that permeate the world with form, light, and sound. These patterns can be invoked in songs that immediately generate corresponding visions, or grasped in a geometric gestalt of seeing that issues in song. What artistic production materializes before the eye is just as readily invoked through sound. The undulating iridescent snake-hallucinations that shamanic ritual regularly provokes in its clientele by way of *ayahuasca*-induced trance is accompanied by shamanic singing that itself generates, intensifies and moves the visions.

In either case—the geometrics caught in the art form or the mental apparition induced hallucinogenically are understood to be coextensive with the entire universe, not bound inside their respective "media" (whether textile, painting, chant, or visual field of imagination). For shamans, reportedly, the filaments of the *ayahuasca*-vision "drift" toward the shaman's lips and assemble in the mouth as an *icaro* or chant form that when sung, penetrates the patient's body and harmonizes the energies there with the larger canvas of creation (Gebhart-Sayer, 1986, 196; Charing, 2008, 3). Bodies—sonic, aural, visual, liquid, and solid—resonate in a precise vibrational harmony visible to the shamanic eye when the patient's physical and psychospiritual energies have "unknotted" over multiple sessions into a restored consonance and become clearly embedded in the body as a durable *Arkana* or pattern of protection for the spirit. The reported experience is one of being "saturated by design," a kind of cosmic tune-up in the key of interpenetrating frequencies, presided over by someone prescient in the operative synesthesia (ibid., 3). Here lies a living "visual music," as one scholar intones, that refuses the Western scientific modality of disclosure by way of autopsy or its epistemology of "the rational gaze, that separates before thinking" (Gebhart-Sayer, 1986, 196; Narby, 1998, 67–68, 179). And it is just here that this rain-forest modality of shamanic inquiry and healing offers silently suggestive commentary on the likes of a DJ Qbert and company.

KOSMIC SKRATCHING

DJ Qbert, in this essay, stands in for the entire enterprise of improvising a new sonic vocabulary in crosscutting the established technologies of sound with a syncopated rip of hard stuttered melody going by the name of "scratch." In industrial music production and popular culture consumption up to the 1970s, turntables dutifully spun discs of vinyl under phonographic needles to generate prerecorded "legitimacies" of hearing pleasure—jazz, chamber, pop— from the spiraling grooves. When Grand Wizard Theodore accidentally bumped a needle across the face of a still-turning record in his room as a young teenaged DJ in New York in the 1970s, however, his "hip-hop-headed" mind-set heard something more than "noise." Why had no one else ever caught this drift? Undoubtedly, millions of needles had scratched millions of records under countless errant hands in the previous half-century. But Theodore's ear framed the sound as cipher and meaning. And quickly the emergent DJ movement of the blighted Bronx of the 1970s "imbricated" the vibe with its necessary surround. Scratching became the aural invocation of urban desolation, giving a metalico-harsh tongue to a mode of experience rendered absurd by the postindustrial politics of abandonment. Burps of dissonance, purposely tattooed across heavily structured rhythmic intervals, established a whole new sonic currency.

In turntablism's growing finesse with the result, a new electrodigitalized cyber-language emerges. Throbs of earth-groan ground into the body by way of drums and base are suddenly irradiated with a meteoric burst of galactic laughter. The effect is ineffable. A crossroads of cyber-possession. Techno-riffs of trance mounting the beat like an *orisha* climbing into the head of a devotee of Santeria when the *babalawo* starts singing. Are spirits limited to bodies of blood? Can a machine matrix be mounted by an astral energy? A whole zone of new questions opens here.

In West African traditions of trance possession, the *orisha-lwa* known as *Ogou* presides over the entirety of modernity and all of its postmodern, postindustrial, postcolonial temporal offspring (Cosentino, 1997, 290–314; Barnes, 1997, xiii–xxi). *Ogou* in situ is patron of blacksmithing, at work anywhere human and planetary energies manage to pull hot minerals from their underworld forges of molten manufacture onto the earth's surface for new possibilities of hard-edged employment (Armstrong, 1993, 29). *Ogou*, in this understanding, is also simultaneously guarantor of political authority and animator of political rebellion—cutting open the community with explosions of uncontainable vitality when order waxes brutal and locks down creativity or puts the poor in early graves—such as in the 1791 Haitian Revolution of slaves or the LA Uprising of 1992 responding to the Rodney King verdict and generalized oppression in South Central (Brown, 1997, 70–82; Cosentino, 1997, 293, Baker, 1993, 45). These are understood by aficionados of the tradition as "*Ogou* events." While in-depth analysis of this particular coding of human perception and experience is beyond what can be pursued in this writing, suffice it here to note that, for initiates of this complex of practices (*Santeria, Candomblé, Vodou*, Yoruba, etc., in all of their African and diasporic expressions), *Ogou* hovers surly and insurgent over all innovations of metallic provenience—railroads, cars, planes, radio wires, computer chips, steel girders, fiber-optic cables, and indeed, turntables—the entire menagerie of mineral cacophony that goes by the name of modern technology. For the eye thus trained to see, Qbert and crew host a visitation characteristic of an entire age, spirit ghosting metal, boasting rage, toasting technique with a brown patina of organic warning, threatening to roast every gesture of high-tech repression in the fires of a rebellious explosion of flesh and earth.[6] Scratch riffs beg hearing under this code as prophetic omen—a language of the telluric womb singing ecstasy and foreboding in the key of a shamanic cyborgism.

But Qbert's emergence offers food for thought along another line of inquiry as well. Graham Townsley notes, in his treatment of Amazonian shamanism, not only the interweaving of song and vision, but the arcane strangeness of shamanic verbalization, seeking in human tongue to emulate the spirits of nature (Narby, 1998, 97–98; Townsley, 1993, 459–460). Rather than direct address, shamans speak in the "abstrusest metaphoric circumlocutions." Night becomes, for instance, "swift tapirs"; the forest itself is designated as "cultivated peanuts;" jaguars are "baskets" and anacondas "hammocks," and so on. In shamanic parlance, such wild indirection is *tsai yoshto-yoshto*, or "language-twisting-twisting" (Narby, 1998 98; Townsley, 1993, 453). As one practitioner told the anthropologist Jeremy Narby:

> With my *koshuiti* [spirit-songs] I want to see—singing, I carefully examine things—twisted language brings me close but not too close—with normal words I would crash into things—with twisted ones I circle around them—I can see them clearly. (98–99)

Townsley extrapolates to say that all shamanic relations with the spirits are "deliberately constructed in an elliptical and multi-referential fashion so as to mirror the refractory nature of the beings who are their objects"—beings both "'like and not like' the things they animate" (Townsley, 1993, 465). Metaphor then is not merely a manner of speaking *about* spirits, it *is* the mode of relationship with them.

Juxtapose with this the arcane vocabulary of witty-fingered record-warpers at the heart of turntablism's emergent tradition: *beat juggling* whose moves now include chirps and transforms, scribbles and tears, military scratches and flares, and all manner of cutting going by the name of uzis and tweaks, lasers and crabs, chops and skronks and squalls and strobes (DJ QBert, 2000). But the words are mere circumlocutions for the sounds, which themselves erupt in the head of a DJ like Qbert as "chopped up shapes" he cannot define. Mistakes and accidents continue to birth the ambient squiggles that become slight rips in the fabric of silence through which pops a glimpse of infinity. The DJs regularly reflect that they "see" far beyond what they can produce. We might easily ad lib that these are sounds simultaneously "like and unlike the technology they animate." Again, the issue here is whether mineral artifact can be made to host spirit animation. But for the artists in question this is undoubtedly a postmodern equation of access to other dimensions of reality, a bending or breaking into alternative planes of being through a "neuromancing"[7] of the machine, synching up nerve passages with cosmic frequencies and optic auras of digitized ineffability. The sounds thus found indeed circle round a resonance that can't be named without being crashed and distorted. But here is nonetheless a need to read the development in its historical traces for a time of mounting apocalypse.

SOILED BODIES

So far so good in my own burst of scratch-work, you might say, but what does this have to do with the *babaylan* tradition? To the degree that *babaylan* practice can be grasped as an upwelling of animate energy, particular to the island ecologies of the Philippines, ventrilo-quizing spirit-divinity through a human body and sensibility for the purposes of maturing the species and keeping it in balance, some of the intersection with what I have laid out should be suggestive and obvious. Qbert, as icon of a broadly shared capacity, could be embraced as Filipino-American ventriloquist of island currents of vital memory—channeling ancestral wisdom and *babaylan* vision in the key of a diasporic logic of "mixture," combining a *kapwa* sensibility with a cyborg propensity to make turntables and synthesizers yield healing and community in an impossible circumstance (of capitalist accumula-tion, American delusions of world-mastery, and neoliberal commodi-fication of everything everywhere).

But if so, the channeling must be recognized as partial and the ven-triloquism fractured, as already noted. The issue is not only celebra-tion of what has survived the ocean-crossing, but even more crucially right reading of the creative upsurge. To what does it point? And here the various local shamanisms already solicited converge. What-ever their particular means of practice—whether plant ingestion or danced possession, *anting-anting*[8] invocation or *agong*[9] percussion—they point toward a vital economy of reciprocal exchange with their local ecologies. And this is the hard truth of our time. The question already underscored of whether machine can be ghosted with spirit belies a deeper and more radical urgency. Indigenous shamanisms are quintessentially rooted in communicative intercourse with indigenous species of flourishing biota (and soils and waters and winds and rock) and function as a schoolhouse for the human spirit in the necessities of sustainable relations with life-forms far older, and (evermore con-spicuously evident today) wiser, in long-term survival than our own yet admits of being.

Taking diaspora fascinations with spirit animation seriously—whether in the form of more traditional modes of *babaylan* prac-tice or in the techno-trance version I have been exploring in scratch creativity—demands asking what life is ultimately about. The energies of invocation of ancestral spirits or postmodern circuits of sonic vital-ity require for their realization, healthy "bodies" of practice. Imagined with full shamanistic integrity, those bodies must be asserted as not merely human and individual, but as locally existing *eco-communities* of co-constituting plants and animals and minerals that nowhere today are surviving inside the market pretensions of globalizing capital. Everywhere the basic material conditions for a *babaylan* visioning of spiritual life are being ruthlessly dismembered. The litmus test for that vision of life, even in the Philippines today, must be the few remaining communities of indigenous—invaded and "uprooted" and under assault even as we speak, like the *Aeta* of Pinatubo—whose memory of how to live in symbiotic concert with their native ecology is being shredded as pitilessly as the ecology itself. Reading the impulse in the core *babaylan* message in actual historical context means giving up a dream of attaching the practice like an ethereal appendage to an otherwise upwardly mobile lifestyle committed to pillaging the planet in search of consumerist bliss and walling off humanity in gated-community supremacy from all other kindred beings. *Babaylan* singing and scratch-riffing alike point toward recovery of a bigger body of human being than that found inside a Gucci suit or an SUV. The songs and vibes cry for exiting commodity culture, and relearning the language of nurture and correction from the python and parrot, the squirrel and ferret, the coyote and salmon and ant, the cactus and banyan and *caapi* vine plant, the riverine flow, the glow of granite under the moon, the cloud-boil over the mountain-toil to raise its crest out of its nest of lava and pressure which is the womb of all. And from the few remaining members of our own species who yet know the names of the spirit-shrines and cosmic-designs capable of initiating us into our own true vocation in this world.

Reading Filipino fast-fingered scratching requires a tricky flipping of the script: we might say,

> this is scratch finesse as channeling
> a faint haint of the *babaylan* colonial fate of
> being fed to crocodiles by missionaries
> afraid of shamanic wiles resurrected now
> inside diaspora communities as a form of
> *kapwa*-immunity to the harsh insanity of
> consumerist inanity and capitalist criminality
> in seeking to put the entire planet up for sale!

It is we well-fed Westerners who are "read" by the probe of sound Qbert and crew spew and it is *babaylan* history that stands forth in *Aeta*-faced mystery as trickster-healer of the calamity modern humanity is precipitating in insisting on its specious superiority. And it is indigenous notions and animal motions and plant potions and ocean spray that offer the living script that requires our response of translation and transfiguration. Will we learn to dance like an *Igorot* echo of the gecko crawling up hauntingly inside all of our dreams? Or simply ensure the coming of the impending collapse by eagerly returning to our shopping once we've finished consuming the script?

CHAPTER 9

GRAMMAR OF SPIRIT INSIDE
DE-INDUSTRIAL FERMENT: READING
HIP-HOP BEATS AT THE CROSSROADS
OF BLIGHT AND ORDER

Hip-hop saved my life!

—Quote from a young teen at a Denver Freestyle in 2005

Early on in the 2012 Kanye West and Jay Z video release "No Church in the Wild," a growling Molotov-thrower faces off with a snarling German shepherd—point protagonists for the street mob and riot squad respectively depicted—while the police restraining the latter remain coldly occulted behind visors and shields and ready to batter, an impersonal force of imperial repression whose uniform is uniformity indeed. The hook cooks up the scene in a sight whose revelatory implosion is a heavy thud on church excitement over gospel indictments of sin and crime. While Frank Ocean throws down the heavy potion. (The reader is encouraged to go online to sample the lyric eloquence in its layered evocation of a raw situation.)

The word goes straight to the jugular of what we face today. Hip-hop in its deep heart is a bomb drop on our current condition. The reality is dire and the street a missionary enterprise of stone cold survival. "Church" for near on seventeen centuries has become an enterprise of empire in its mainstream mentality—apologist for Caesar, missioner for Columbus, acolyte for capital flight to the domain of things white and hoarded. And most immediately, prayer-partner to drone-powers dropping deep judgment on all them "Muslim demons," from ages 5 to 95, whether armed with AKs or merely burqa-eyed and chanting. Yep, straight up! "Ain't no church in the wild!" But soon enough— there won't be any "wild" up in there either! And that is *the* harsh question of the hour.

HIP-HOP ON THE GROUND

One of the more recent places of accountability for me in living life in inner-city Detroit is an ongoing huddle with an ex-vet, dread-headed, former Panther brother and his wife from the neighborhood, renting a falling-down house on the far east side. They live within sight of the Grosse Pointes, historic district of auto company execs that have all but seceded from Motown commerce, even as they continue to pull the strings on Motown finance and cheer Emergency Manager takeover of the city. (As I write, more than half of Michigan's African American population is under imposed governance, in a bloodless coup of draconian proportions.) On their broken down ghetto street just blocks from that rapacious turf of privilege, Wayne Curtis and Myrtle Thompson have seen the proverbial wall bearing handwriting. Allying themselves with other hard-scrapping, hard-cracking Detroit survivalists, they have concluded that the only revival worth preaching is apostasy from big corporation or big government dependencies, and a "fight-to-the-death" struggle to reinvent the city from the ground up, outside either political sycophancy or fatuous hope for no-strings-attached dollars from foundations like Lilly.

A half-decade ago Wayne and Myrtle "returned to the land." They began farming the vacant plot next to their rental and invited young folk from the block and the city at large to dirty hands and fill bellies with the result. The effort birthed "Feedom Freedom," a serious coterie of teenaged energy, relearning, alongside the adults, the "gardening angels" skills of growing beans and sprouts, greens and gout-reducing produce of every kind. Here, down-south elders and hip-hop youngsters mix motives and work on the same plot of earth. The labor is hard, the fruits without lard or sugar, with few takers on the block for Swiss chard over colas and candy, and obesity growing like an Industrial Age monstrosity. But up against the pomposity of the two-party inanities of the day—a first step toward a new way. Whether hip-hop in the hood can be brought into collaboration with a new ethic around food—despite the heavy way memory of King Cotton haunts all such urban efforts today—is one of the more compelling questions of the hour for underclass survival on the hot concrete. Wayne, in any case, dreams revolution on the block, liberated territory in a Panther frame, knows the clock is ticking toward collapse, and that the future requires updating the past with respect. Detroit is now notorious in a global stock-taking for its loss of population and business, its wide-open visage, one-third of its 139-square-mile land base vacant and rocking with revamping ecologies. Indeed: "Ain't no church in the wild," but the wild *is* now opening its *own* church in Detroit. And there lies the conundrum for me.

Hip-hop opened in the 1970s South Bronx with a "wild style" turn toward Afrika Bambaataa-notions of a livable community. The profiled wiles of this ex-banger/hip-hop-founder went bombastic in visuality as well as beats, giving artistic teeth to the existential truth that life is largely a riff on top of death. A truth gangs know particularly well! Bam left the bullets behind, but not the conviction. Looking demise straight in the eye and refusing to shy or stutter is the very heart of any spirituality worthy of the name. And hip-hop channeled a coiled snake of energy even in its early party flavors. The cobra ready to strike had its tail in the grave even when its flared hoodie shouted mad vigor and signs. Of course here I am mixing motifs and species, but the point is in the bite. Life *is* finally 'wild." Even if this thing called civilization is a pathological demonstration trying to convince us otherwise. The deep current that Rock Steady[1] and Zulu[2] Universality, Flash[3] finger-warps-on-the-vinyl or Basquiat[4] grit-on-the-brick, flipped into the "on" position and zapped the boroughs with, came from a subterranean vein of ancestry. The game Lupe and Jay, Kanye and Common, Immortal Technique or even Chief Keef in Chicago, are zooming today is an "old thing on the face of the planet."[5] Its primal interrogation, even when its takes a years-long vacation from intelligence, is the unanswerable question that never can*not* be left unanswered: what is this thing called life? What are we doing here? Or at least so I hear it.

The body doesn't lie and the hip-hop body is a refried bean of explosive possibilities, conjured by the street ghosts of a nation that has never been toasted on anything other than genocide. Roasted in slavery, hallucinating witchery, putting multimillions of bodies in the ground over the course of centuries, long before their trumpet ever sounded—the country of hip-hop's birth remains a trip. And its history remains a trip largely not taken. As sociologist Avery Gordon's *Ghostly Matters* argues, we inhabit an entire landscape now of unfinished business and unprocessed secrets—a psychic cemetery of haunts and haints and saints and devils, climbing the spines of suburbanites and farmers, socialites and Hollywood charmers, blue-collared factory boys and Barbie-blushing girls just wanting to be somebody's toy, with nary a tongue to wag. The unfaced truth of this past is an unground menagerie of early death whose most profound "achieve-ment" of "American exceptionalism" on the face of the planet today is our country's primacy in leading everybody else in addiction (con-suming 65 percent of the world's psychotropic drugs: Gordon, 1997, xvi, xix, 8, 16–19, 25, 27–28; Wolff, 2012). Of course we've got to drown ourselves in drugs and Budweiser, binge on TV trances and pulp romances! If we didn't we might have to look in the mirror and see someone else looking out through our eyes who has climbed up our bones from a zone of deep night who has never been given time to speak or a community to mourn—much less something called "justice." The black community in general in this country has been forced, like no other in U.S. history, to hover and live on the thresh-old between[6] our feverish attempts to escape our ghosts . . . and the ghosts themselves. It is no wonder its very survival has been a mode of channeling the unrelieved agony and brilliant ecstasy of so much unrequited life that has had no enduring body to live in. Because so much of its experience has been pushed into that very reality! But the black community is *not* a ghost! It just knows a lot about them.

When I look at hip-hop, I am not concerned to discern its sur-face appearance. Instead I want to probe its stutter-step groping after something way beyond its ken that it nonetheless taps into and gets jiggered by. What *is* up inside the grimace and howl of that fire-throwing guy in the video clip referenced to start this piece? And even more to the point, what appears in the bared tooth of the canine crew held on leash by the police, waiting to crush bone and lace faces with gashes of gushing red? Wildness. A shared wildness. An exchange in the heat of a street battle that suddenly recognizes *itself* in the snarls and growls on either side of the fabricated conflict! And does so, in spite of a hyperdeformed condition of supposed "civilization" where wolves have been coercively domesticated into "genetic goofies" called "dogs" (Shepard, 1998, 142–145) and trained into a *human*-like—*not* animalistic—ferocity to tear bodies apart for sport and not hunger. And humans have been reduced by colonial histories and post-industrial absurdities into "hunger-threatened herds of unem-ployed redundancies" by the policies of rapacious CEOs (backed by a horde of couch-sitting, channel-changer-button-pushing wannabes, imagining the meaning of life as an unending sitcom and the golden years as an unending round of swatting little white balls across fake landscapes into stationary holes in a great big nursing home called "Florida") What really *does* it mean to be *alive*?

Today we are being stripped down by our disaster capital-ist, drone-bomb-dropping hubris, stretched out on the rack of a prison-industrial-complex whose torture will not much longer halt short of the border called white skin, shot up by Big Pharma and Big Ag and Big Oil with multiple-thousands of untested chemicals and multiple-more hundreds of well-tested toxins, forced to face naked and alone on rooftops or in flood-filled, blacked-out hovels the environmental blowback of well-organized ecological "haints" like Katrina or Sandy. (Yes, all those "otherkind" life-forms like elephants and egrets, salmon and bison, ibis and elk may be imagined to have half-lives in zombie-forms, coalescing into climate changes and well-organized rages of comeuppance like hurricanes and tsunamis. We witness today a thousand-thousand-fold rumble of disappearing companion species, becoming extinct at the rate of 200 per day now as their wetland or rain forest or savanna or riverine habitats are fouled and burned into oblivion, their own plant-denizen-supporters uprooted, their Earth unearthed and their seas sullied in the rapine quest for fuel and minerals. Einstein was right: nothing ever leaves the universe; it just changes form!)[7] When we unleash a globalization force of enculturated rapacity, bent on ripping apart the body of the planet for the sake of our thirst for gadgets and comfort, entertainment and oil, and a fatuous hope of figuring out how to avoid death by fashioning a cyborg sheath to carry our entrails and brains, the bodies and ecosystems broken *will*—like a split atom—have their revenge. Science is hard at work trying to measure the resulting "fission" in forms environmental as well as nuclear. I just cut to the chase of indigenous *gnosis*, and name the effect a "ghost."[8] Pick your language, but face the fact!

Hip-hop is a trace of the debacle when it goes visceral in a human body. Obviously, this will quickly be met—especially pew-side—with a sharply sardonic "Huh? I think you have slightly over-read the phenomenon, Jim! Hip-hop is just pop culture entertainment answering to young-people angst. Not a planetary canary in the coal mine of time!" But I say, "Read the signs!" The planet is seething with judgment on our species. And the church marches down the aisle singing hallelujahs and whooping in arcane language about a little thing called a "saved soul" in exchange for dimes in the offering plate. Or in the suburb, croaks out a musty old hymn by Luther and fights off sleep. Mega-pastors meanwhile draft punk and rock into raving accolades to global capital while promising a "good feeling" to the nuclear family as long as it tithes regularly, obeys quietly, and pays taxes. For sure— "ain't no church in the wild!"

But the wild *is* what the church was provisionally created to serve! Only very lately have we begun to extract Jesus as a prophet from his imperial silencing (like umpteen thousands of such figures before and after him who have spit the same vision in every "off the rails" culture that has abandoned its original instructions in the process of aggrandizing aspirations into "civilizing" designs to take over everybody else). Jesus railed and raged *against* every form of organized hubris that presumed to hoard the product and celebrate the loot in 100-dollars-a-plate dinners, while putting the laborers in early graves. And he raged *for* a communalized Sabbath-Jubilee practice of dismantling debt, recirculating assets, and *returning land to its own logic of bounty and blessing, whose epitome was wildness.* We read right over that last part. But it is right there in the text, over and over again: from Genesis—where we may be catching sight of a tenth millennium BCE Levantine Natufian experiment with an early human-tree alliance[9]—through the prophets like Elijah rooting his vocation in the outback of the desert east of Jordan and being fed by ravens—to Jesus frequenting the caves and sands and mountains whenever he needed to recover a sense of mission. Sabbath-Jubilee[10] is a feral tradition of wilderness-provision, enshrining memory of the wild as the *axis mundi* from whence all things living "get" their living, for which they give their bodies as food (including us as humans) when it is time for them to feed others, and to which they are "held accountable" ultimately (Eisenberg, 1999, 69, 76–79, 86, 90). And if the church has lost sight of that basic foundation—then its destiny is the dustbin of things irrelevant in history! There are plenty of other creatures that know the score, live the reality, and now are ringing the bell of warning—even as they perish.

And hip-hop—though obviously only seeing as far as the *urban* hint of the wild (in decayed buildings and broken up streets and abandoned peoples—all in one way or another beginning to be pushed back toward "wilder" organizations of energy)—is struggling with an ancient instinct. Religious studies scholar Monica Miller—in a Huffington Post article of 2012—offers a core city sample from the frequented streets, the prized tat' parlors, the well-worn parks and bars that host a bit of "wildness" in Portland, Oregon (Miller, 2012). In particular, Miller divines between the lines of hip-hop's sonic assault on business as usual—"between the beats and rhymes" of a millennial fascination, that is—sussing out the epiphany of a new life philosophy among the young demography of roving "Nones" (meaning when it comes to a survey of religious affiliation, they check the box called "None"). These are "heads" creating citadels on corners and shrines in clubs, rubbing flesh to find faith in a release un-preached in the Sunday pew. Precisely! This is a new bombastic, rehearsing an old ecstatic—desire as religion. And unapologetic—as long as the ethic is frank and without force![11]

But how far down dare we go? In Detroit, the Do It Yourself (DIY) aesthetic of community urban gardens and tech-savvy innovation outside the corporation and its cheerleading media is already shifting its iris and tongue to scope out the ground. Indie MC Invincible, for example, national in rep but hunkered down in vocation, has changed up her lambasts recently to focus on fruit-bearing trees and land struggles between farming options local and industrial.[12] Burned-up orchards—not merely charred cars—mark the militancy of her concern. (And rappers as far away as Navajo country or even Bolivia bust the same!) Motown land increasingly weighs in with an insect din of report on the pain—not to mention the raccoons and foxes, opossum and even deer that end up as dead fare by the urban roadside—a strange share of city destiny, to be sure. But right there is the hope. The interweaving of urban dwelling and wild incursion. The possibility of a new artifactual/natural hybrid as the city of the future. *The* question of the hour globally is clearly something like regenerativity— what has a ghost of a chance of still being around for our children's children to care about . . . and be cared for by? Hip-hop lip syncs wild style in its lyric fashion and body tattooing—harking back to an ancient indigenous tradition of making skin a living marquee of community identification and recognized values.[13] But actual indigenous folk push the hint way further back.

Across an imploding globe of violence, 360 million strong, they bear near solitary witness to what the hour may well demand. Not a revolution forward, but a return to sanity rooted in what ancestry knew. Humans can't live except with feet on land, noses full of sky, tongues wet with rivers, and teeth chewing the animal and plant "relatives" who alone are the ultimate givers of life and "salvation." "Ain't no way" to take a vacation from either air or water! And we can't eat our computer! (or enjoy its digits without the coltan-based electronics whose extraction literally enslaves Congo-kids in labor camps managed by armed guards ensuring both corporate profits and youth culture markets, and whose "electronic body" is finally cleaned-up after the hard-drive freezes up by Chinese peasant children in out-of-the-way countryside compounds, poisoning their bodies through their fingertips and their homes with the fumes of the plastic they have to burn to get to the chips and wires). The city is dependent on the country and the country, finally, on what is *not* tended or toxified by humans. Kill the wild with disappearance or poison and we are all gone. This is what the original "church" is finally all about. It isn't supposed to be "in" the wild; it actually *is* the sanctuary *of* the wild. Any other church is a rickety provisional shack trying to recover a memory—and a practice—of the real thing. And if it is not, then it *should* disappear! High time to actually listen to both Genesis *and* Geronimo—and to all the other still living relatives of the latter around the globe who actually do know what time it is. If we don't get serious about figuring out the reciprocity with ecologies that native communities lived with beauty and sustainability for multiple millennia, then for real: "ain't no church in the wild—because there won't be any wild left!" And there won't be any humans either.

Hip-hop has its head bopped to the heat at the heart of the global blood-beat, but has not yet augured down to the source of the sound. I think it is "on to" the fist-pound of the imprisoned round of beings whose struggle to be heard today echoes like a reverb over the ground itself. And it reacts with flair to the hint of ungrieved haints ghosting the streets and heaving the soils of this land of unrequited enslavement and genocide. But it hasn't yet gotten serious about *the* primal question that indigenous folk have been throwing down to their colonizers for five millennia now. And that is the question of justice not only for human beings, but for all the communities of things moving and "keening" on the face of the planet. How do we live on the land without actually destroying it? Urban polity has so far everywhere meant enmity and demise for everything else. As already mapped out, the biblical Cain stands forth as city-builder-sign of the 5,000-year-long history of indigenous annihilation by aggrandizing urbanity whose culmination in extinction is only now being played out before our very eyes! Biblically the archetypal city, Babylon, is spiritually composed of all the blood-cries of all the Abels throughout all of time; it throbs with the baseline echo of its crimes like a death-knell awaiting its second-line stompers, chanting down its walls and conjuring a Jerusalem-to-come composed primarily of sparkling rivers and healing trees (Mt 23:29–39; Lk 11:46–51; Rev 18:1–24).

This is the real "roar of the wild" whose head hip-hop has grabbed like a lion by the mane and strains to hang onto without being consumed. But it still needs deep teaching—as we all do inside the global metrodome—by precisely those peoples who could actually look that lion in the eye without faltering, knowing that one or the other would die and be eaten, but also that the day would come when the body of the survivor would return the favor. We merely pretend! And charge pig farms and Krogers with maintaining the fiction and keeping the smells and screams and blood away from our senses. (Gospel truth, Jim—food comes in a can!) But I say the real ferocity that any spirituality must channel at its core is *this* reality: life is eating and everyone, sooner or later, is food for someone else. Getting *clear on and respectful of that reciprocity* is *the* task of spirituality, and it is indigenous communities, not urbanizing empires, that have built actually sustainable cultures, capable of living in the same neighborhood for thousands of years at a time, based *exactly* on *its* truth! This is the real wildness at the core of real respect between all the communities of living beings on the planet. And it is high time we recovered its honesty, honored its vitality, and lived up to its clairvoyant demand. Rather than live a lie.

But enough pontification about our primal condition and dystopic present. Within the ambit of this deep question about eco-sustainability and human/otherkind reciprocity and the fast-coming reality of climate apocalypse that we all face, let me offer a summary sketch of some aspects of the gift hip-hop offers the "Christian" church in our moment.

(1) A Celebration of the Body

Bodies matter. Certainly for a tradition proclaiming that the Ultimate is incarnate—that "God" takes on flesh—the body must be a central site of reflection, as indeed a central *aporia* that both opens and consumes reflection. Just here, in hip-hop's modalities of making skin a cipher of significance (Tupac tags his own flesh with warning: going up against him is meeting 50 N****s full in the face) and making motor muscle control—as gesture, posture, and figure—a depth-domain of life-incubating "oppugnance,"[14] hip-hop stands as a sign of the times. It hides its designs from the blinkered eye of piety. Most of its flesh—as indeed most of its insight—is "dark."[15] It demands decipherment and exegesis. It counsels involvement. It is a form of living scripture, written on a bone in motion. As a body mime for the insider community, it conserves fire under its smoke. And it matters to religion. Whether religion matters to hip-hop, however, remains an open question. In this perspective, the improvisatory idioms of hip-hop's cultural sagacity supply "material confession" for thinking about faith inside urban commodification and imperial sanction and outside the canon.

(2) An Augury of Ecstasy Inside Postindustrial Desperation (With All of Its Contradictions)

Whatever else it is, hip-hop is a creature of the city. Its capacity to convene various modes of community-posse around particular vocabularies of energy builds on its basic "syntax" (referencing a line in Michael

Eric Dyson's treatment of Tupac [2001] where Dyson hails the Makavelian Griot as having himself become, posthumously, a "grammatical" force for the street; 233–236, 243–246). This is a grammar nowhere formalized as such, but only transmitted across bodies in assemblies gathered to "glory" in a certain effervescence of subjectivity and vitality. Its signature is an angular epistemology, laboring percussive movement into a *gnosis* about ultimate matters (Spencer, 1991, 10). Whether lyrically identified as such or not, depth-topics like death, sexuality, oppression, race, gender, and exploitation, animate its braggadocio and undulate its embodiment. As many of these themes exceed the capacity of conventional language adequately to signify, and inundate somatic experience with a surfeit of meaning overwhelming to mere breathing, it is left both to amped up bodies and ramped up technologies to channel the "tsunamis" of implication. "What" is implicated is a certain possibility of "spirited" excess— a capability of the human being to divine and reflect what Charles Long would call an ultimate "Somewhat," a Fearsome and Titillating Mysteriousness, whose murk of significance drives religious expression, whose amplitude of terror exercises ritual exploration, and whose sheer grotesquery exorcizes Enlightenment delusion that it can render phenomenon transparent (Long, 1986, 116). In a word, hip-hop emerges in our time as a "religion of the oppressed," albeit commercialization has incarcerated its *daemon* in a price tag. Whether hip-hop can thereby contribute explicitly to faith-claims, as already indicated, remains a question asked largely *toward* the faith side of the encounter. Certainly the question asked here is *not* resolved by churches adopting re-mixes, packaging hymns and sermons in staccato "raps," and serving up biblical idiom and Christian exclusivism under a beat.

(3) A Call-response Grammar of the Spirit

What this screed lifts up for existential exploration is a peculiar and pulsating *social grammar* embodied as a resource for emergent creativity that hip-hop art stylizes across the four elements. At the heart of that art—borrowing from Tricia Rose's borrowing from Arthur Jafa—is a complex conjunction of *flow* and *rupture*, itself rendered both flowing and eruptive in multi-metered, poly-rhythmic *layering*, whenever the eloquence gets "itchy headed" as DJ Kool Herc once offered after the first time he "took into his psyche" the hotwire vitality of a pounding Herculoid amp (Chang, 2005, 68; Rose, 1994, 38–39). The reference here is to a capacity to induce "voltage" into physicality, literally to re-make a gathering of individuals into a "body electric composite," moving in syncopated trance toward a climax of exuberant aggressivity. Whether that issue of group energy ultimately goes violent or cathartic, hedonistic or political (sooner and/or later), depends on something much more complex and inchoate—and much more contextual—than simply the lyrics offered. (Merely mumbling "Jesus" over a scratch will not a just world make!)

Rather, I would suggest, hip-hop grammar inculcates a basic social posture. The constant crossing and interweaving of flow and rupture—hard clipped consonants chopping a viscous rhyme in MC ciphers, turntable "iggities" interrupting sampled fluidities in DJ battles, b-boy and -girl pops and angularities on top of a well-grooved step-vocabulary—these are not simply "fashion." What has been conserved here is a basic political resource: a formalization of social conflict—condensed as an assimilable template and broadcast across the boundary of bodies—that theologically might be glossed as a content of "crucifixion" and "resurrection" reduced to a micro-structure of living flesh. What Robert Farris Thompson has called "corporeal cubism" I would call a somatic amulet: a mode of urban homeopathy on urban trauma made popular outside the dollar—at least in underground engagements (Thompson, 1983, 219). As Tupac more than once "vorciferated," and I have more than once verified in my own experience and hearing in both Denver and Detroit, "hip-hop saves" (Dyson, 170–171). It has regularly pulled young minds and desperate bodies out of their pirouettes on the highwire of suicidal involvements and projected them into a community constituted in a percussive antiphony adequate to a depth of pain and height of joy otherwise left inexpressible and unlived .

(4) The Priority of Rupture (Resilience)

In the inner city 'hoods I frequent in Detroit, the sonic cadences of this particular beat encode an entire movement of DIY efforts: adolescents innovating community gardens in the midst of street ruins; entrepreneurial youth building "ghetto" wireless access from tinfoil and recycled electronics; low income artists installing "found objects" (i.e., "waste products") on abandoned houses—rendering them "calligraphic" with a bit of bold paint—as material "signs of the times" (Perkinson, 2011, 10–11; 2013, xiii–xxvii). What is here different from the sonorous hymn-lining in a "get happy" Sunday morning gathering is the privileging of the moment of rupture. No invisible ladder to an "other-worldly pleasure" is offered by this body meme. The code is clearly this-worldly and the "end"—put on psychic deposit in motor memory—a summons to combat. It is simply a condition of neo-liberal existence that the market quickly inveigles such in promises of "getting over." But it is just as evident that the energy of urban struggles, stored as a form of "body lightning" (Thompson, 1983, 211), is also available for insurgence (think South Bronx in the 1970s; think LA in May of 1992; think Detroit under onslaught from white flight and out-sourcing; think Tunisia and Tahrir in uprising!). What it awaits is pedagogy and vision. But it is already in operation, sowing the field of the future with its "underground" mission. Faith (whatever its historical affiliation) is here presented with a radical condensation of its theological formulas and a midnight crossroads. It is presented with a question. Either embrace the corpuscular grace of such a percussive initiation ("re-baptism") and let the new affective structure (Gilroy, 1993, 9, 37–38, 77, 131) of passion re-inculcate a resolve worthy of religion's power for resistance and re-creation (or even "martyrdom" as Dyson hints and Tahrir makes explicit). Or hunker down into the old confessions and disappear into the shadows of history as a relic.

(5) A Body-*Esperanto* Offering the Globe a Chance to Reclaim Its African Ancestry in a Beloved Community Experience of Profound Diversity[16]

It is now patent that hip-hop's advent was not a mere "flash" in the Madison Avenue "pan" of all things glittering and evanescent. Its plan—much like that of Ishmael's Reed's epidemic of "mumbo jumbo" in his epochal send up of white manners going by that name—was inchoate conquest by way of body infection. This is a global virus calling up a recessive gene. Across the span of millennia and across a globe of continents—for whatever irrefragable reason—the evolutionary genealogy of our race has been forcibly disowned wherever polity has drafted color into its hierarchy. That Africa lurks as the root-stock of every family tree is the great terrifying secret of repression inside every racist system (Bynum, 1999, 76, 79). Nowhere on the face of the planet has melanin *not* been politically articulated at the bottom when race organizes domination. We run from our ancestry. Why this should be so is the *koan* of the ages. It is not a mammalian instinct of fearing sundown that came across to the human animal as a rampant phobia of black: indeed, for many of our primate kin, dark was safety and noon the time of terror. Its mystery remains just that: an historical enigma. But even Fanon remarked on the dusky hue of the discontents of dreamtime (Fanon, 101–103). The Algerians he treated during their struggle for independence from France all named their midnight apparitions in deep sleep as "shadow figures" hounding them across the wilds of their unconscious (contrary to the light-skinned enemies actually killing them in daylight). Deep ancestry planetwide shows its disowned face as "dark" when our eyelids close and the imaginary wakes. Whatever the etiology of that dis-ease, the remedy is not brain surgery. It is embrace of home. Hip-hop strangely is our first planetary harbinger of that possibility.

Young people in virtually every country on this blue marble take up its tokes of rhyme and strokes of beat to articulate their pain and refusal to be silenced. And do so in company with similarly animated peers. Yes, Madison Avenue has also come to the game and tried to set the table with its wares and labels. But thus far, the energy remains uncontainable. And its global attraction may well be a hint of the fable that Eve did indeed birth us all, after all. It is just that she stabled in Tanzania or thereabouts, not Canaan. We all came from Africa originally (Bynum, 1999, 81, 85–87, 93–95). And in hip-hop, for the first time, a full sample of all the world's peoples are going tick-tock on their laptops with a pop-and-lock salute to just that fact, whether they know it or not. That alone is worth stopping and staring at. No church can boast the same.

Here is the first inkling of a planetary healing of the gene pool. Against the politics everywhere extant—an entire globe starting to go black under the skin! Yes, bought off in the commercial. Yes, puerile in much of its pomposities and lyrics. Needing profound pedagogy! But for all that, a continuing force of creation, blowing the church off the mike unless it can recover its vocation, cyphering the possibility of a new kind of nation—an embrace of kin under a beat, spittin' local colors of heat, unseating despair, feet chopping rocked out air, raising flared exclamation and spinning exhilaration from the hard concrete, throwing up spare syllables in inimitable repetition of untamable oscillation and brazen soliloquies on the bare walls of poverty, trancing the eye into a mood of fly innovation, climbing sky like a stairway to desire as wide as a galaxy, offering gravity-bound meat a fleet possibility of flying in place, space to breath, a reason to grieve and blare, bellow and care, sigh and share, rare up and throw down like a bear coming out of the lair of winter with springtime hunger to tear up flesh, crunch down bones, feed pups, and live for another year! Do I romance this affair? You bet. Hip-hop on the ground is a ferocious lover and a fierce wrestler, like everything else that is still alive. Its deepest veracity is the truth about our most primal vitality: we are not the well-tamed function of a thing called a corporation, or the domesticated reduction of somebody's interpretation of a pet doctrine, but the beautiful sprout of a wild creation. Everything else to be said most flow from that.

PART V

PERSONAL CONCLUSION:
COMMUNICATION AND SPIRITUALITY
IN POST-COLONIAL PARTNERSHIP

THINKING FROM THE DIASPORA BACK TOWARD THE HOMELAND: READING HUMANITY AT THE CROSSROADS OF SOLIDARITY AND EXTINCTION

Then always, somehow, some way, silently but clearly, I am given to understand that whiteness is the ownership of the earth forever and ever, amen!

—*W. E. B. Du Bois,* The Souls of White Folk

As is by now obvious, this eclectic collection of chapters finds its common focus in crisis. Increasing recognition of the limits and failures of the project of modernity—in this late hour of growing terror—has provoked a "turn to the indigenous" in search of experience and lifeways less destructive. The international cycles of modern economic boom and bust—at least partially manipulated by overlapping interests between finance capital, neoliberal "fundamentalism," and U.S. "green-zone" imperialism rooted in military bases, as indeed, by the blowback from the environment in the form of ever more consequential eco-catastrophe accompanying modern intervention (such as in the Gulf, and more episodically in the rain forest in Ecuador and the tar sands of Canada)—altogether push academic theory toward a much more radical questioning of our continuing romance with modernity, technology, and growth. As a way of rounding out this concern, this last chapter—like the first one—will once again inflect critical theory with personal reflection.

Here we will seek to craft and contextualize a set of questions concentrated on a problematic of reverse hermeneusis: how do we embrace critique coming from those positioned "subaltern" to our own social position and academic training? In particular, the argument will tack back and forth between two different versions of such a demand. On the one hand, we will revisit my own experience of the struggle to internalize critique from Afro-diasporic communities on the ground in the West. But alongside that, we will also track a Filipina partner's struggle to make sense of the displacement of indigenous Aeta from their traditional homeland on the sides of Mt. Pinatubo in Luzon precisely in consequence of her own Kapampangan people's adoption of modern culture (in emulating, even while resisting, U.S. neo-colonialism). The question tracked from various angles through previous chapters recurs in each of these efforts. It emerges at a species level exactly at the juncture where minority and Third World struggles for inclusion in modernity entail cooperation in ongoing expropriation and disappearance of indigenous peoples and plunder of their homelands. Exactly who we are as one species among an almost unthinkable plethora of life-forms can no longer be presumed within the smug certainties of a self-ascribed superiority. White supremacy as the modern offspring of Christian supremacy has its tap root finally in a presumption of *human* supremacy over all else.

How Deep Dare We Look?

At a midpoint in the circuit I run each morning at 6 a.m. on the grounds of what formerly was the Clark Air Force Base, in Pampanga, in the Philippines, history has thrown up a plaque of commemoration. It is July of 2008, my wife and I are hosted by her sister and family in their Clark Development Corp. house, after having attended a conference in Iloilo City on the island of Panay to the south of Luzon, featuring more than 300 indigenous peoples, artists, and academics, asking deep questions of cultural values, and doing so in the muddy wake and desperation of yet another killer typhoon. I run early to avoid the heat, but even 6 a.m. is enough to melt part of the bottom of my Chinese-made, classic sneakers. So wrung out am I with sweat and effort after even just half a lap, the plaque does not even catch my eye. Only through my wife's later commentary—on one of the days when I entice her to join me—am I brought face-to-face with the significance. The sign denominates the drill grounds as formerly a part of the home range of the Aeta, a "Negrito"[1] tribe of hunter-gatherers, living historically all over the sides of Mt. Pinatubo, whose volcanic peaks divide the clouds just a bit west and south. Today, a decade and a half after Pinatubo gained world-historical import in spewing enough ash aloft to disrupt summer expectations all across the Northern Hemisphere, the Aeta can only be found scattered across the region, selling crafts by roadsides, their tattered clothes now a sign of a tattered lifeway.

My wife, S. Lily Mendoza, is a scholar of no mean repute, living a struggling existence as a diasporic Filipina deep inside the United States. We reside just a ten-minute walk from downtown Detroit, epicenter of the Industrial Revolution, "Arsenal of Democracy" by fame and function in the harsh days of the World War II production effort, and now much-maligned stereotype in neoliberal excoriations of labor unions and black governance. The Great Car City today is indeed a battlefield littered with the entropic remains of *rentier* priorities in late capitalism's shift to casino finance. After pulling assets and populace out of the core city to the surrounding "vanilla" suburbs for decades, the business class is now ready to buy up assets on the cheap and repopulate the core in a wave of "gentrification." But the Big-D is equally an astounding incubation chamber for all manner of relocalization projects on the part of hardscrabble "ghetto" denizens. These inner-city dwellers—primarily black, but also brown, Native American, Asian American, and white—are taking city life back into their own hands in the form of more than a thousand community urban gardens, youth-led alternative media initiatives freeing information for grassroots organizing (undergirded by hip-hop backbeats), returning citizens (i.e., former prison inmates) launching restorative justice peace zones in hard-core neighborhoods, and street-hustling artists redeploying junked car parts, abandoned houses, and bright paint as prophetic symbol and social movement mural. Inside such a terror-dome-become-initiation-zone on the margins of capital's palatial estates of privilege and plunder in the exurbs, Mendoza has found resonance for her own continuing initiation into the netherworld of neocolonial predation and struggle.

In an archipelago like the Philippines—latecomer to the more recent stages of settled agriculture's 10,000-year-old conquest of hunter-gatherer social organization across the globe that goes by the seriously ironic moniker of "civilization"—colonial history has engendered a deep conundrum of self-identification for most native dwellers. Cultural traits (shared for eons across the 7,000 islands) that value nuanced negotiation of resources and meanings in a mode of "commons-based" thinking and living now struggle with 500 years of denigration under Western forms of colonial domination and (now) corporatist intervention. The rich delicacy of a deep-culture-orientation of "shared being"—such as that connoted by the Tagalog term *kapwa* discussed in chapter 8—faces continuous erosion in the onslaughts of Hollywood imagery and Wall Street policy. These latter are brokered from abroad by urban elites pimping the populace and leveraging the resources into "wanna-be-like-the-rich-white-folks" lifestyles, granting themselves luxury and closets full of shoes, and conferring on the masses poverty and deep immiseration in ever-burgeoning "slum-cities" or life abroad as a transportable labor force, sending remittances home to support struggling families.

In the face of such, various counter-punching movements of resistance, seeking to co-opt the invading forces of capital and "development" in the direction of a nationalist vision, continually lose the war even in those rare moments when they win a given battle. Mendoza has been a prescient critic of such, arising from her own decades-long personal pilgrimage of decolonization. For more than 30 years, she has been gradually ferreting out and struggling against the depths of her own Methodist missionary-induced spiritual formation and liberal idealist political education. In the process, she has emerged as a recognized (and beloved) scholar *in absentia* among the Manila-based intelligentsia leading the charge in trying to re-invent Filipino national culture at a ground level, accountable to Filipino rather than Western interests. These "indigenization movement" scholars—typically suspicious about diasporic academics who so often down play their own native origins in their fascinations for the latest theoretical fetish of the Western academy—have embraced Mendoza as someone doing estimable out-country battle against the same forces they wrestle within the Philippines proper. Mendoza's English-language tome, *Between the Homeland and the Diaspora: the Politics of Theorizing Filipino and Filipino-American Identity,* has become a virtual classic within the movement at home in spite of the movement leaders' insistence on engaging all things Filipino in Filipino-based languages alone. With sophisticated nuance, Mendoza's text mediates mutual criticism between post-colonial anti-essentialism and nativist strategic parochialism—even as it champions a resolute preferential option for the latter given poststructuralism's current positioning in academic power.

All such homeland embrace to the good, however, over recent years Mendoza has found the cutting edge of anticolonial critique carrying her beyond merely imitative nationalist designs on Western-controlled development. It is now the nation-state itself, and technocratic development as its modern presupposition, that she questions—and does so because of increasing attention paid to the very "indigenes" the indigenization movement invokes. As the prospect of ecological cataclysm intensifies daily, the question pushes deeper in and further back. With concern for sustainability as the plumb line, the historical record of civilization gives rise to profound unease. Almost nowhere over the last 50 centuries of grain-based empires has state-organization ever proved anything other than disastrous for the local ecology and lethal for the 80 to 90 percent of the populace employed as either small farming peasantry or wage-labor proletarians (Rasmussen, 1995, 40 ff). Civilization has nowhere *not* been based on the equivalent of coerced labor and vicious conquest and has nowhere been able to maintain its "achievements" apart from expansionist predation on resources gathered from elsewhere (Scott, 9–11).

Even the supposedly hopeful emergence in the last century of various fractions of middle-class populations in many "developing world" countries has to be held in tension with a growing recognition that middle class lifestyle, in anything even remotely based on the U.S. version of such, is patently impossible for the planet's population, requiring for its realization on a global scale somewhere between three and five more Earths (full of resources and devoid of people) (Leonard, 2007). It is becoming increasingly clear that middle-class lifestyle itself—as the great carrot held out to struggling peoples by the small cadres of global elites (CEOs, G-8 heads of state, international banking wonks, etc.) who actually make policy—is the precise ideal that dooms the planet's ecological infrastructure. That lifestyle serves as cover for those same elites by deflecting desire, through a now globalized mass media, onto what seems a perfectly acceptable aspiration for all. In reality the lifestyle is only attainable by a relatively limited percentage of the world's population, and that only by way of dispossessing others of even a minimal standard of access to resources and living conditions.

WHAT THE ANCESTORS KNEW

And it has ever been the indigenous who have been the first line of expendability for civilization's advance—either killed outright, "disappeared" by way of exile to reservations or highlands or across borders, or forcibly remade in the image of the "civilized" by way of education and religion and remanded to one or another role of menial labor or slavery. But it is also the indigenous—at least those historically living primarily as foragers—who are the standard bearers for sustainability on the face of the planet. Not all hunter-gatherer social orders

maintained viable lifeways. But many did—and it is their centuries-
or even millennia-long witness to such that offers real hope for the
present. We, as a species, are not hardwired into predatory relations
with each other or destructive overuse of environments. There have
been remarkably intricate cultures embodying social checks on self-
aggrandizement and hierarchical domination whose cosmologies and
myths of origin calibrate and mediate the innate responses of their
members' genetic inheritance to the dictates and necessities of their
surrounding ecologies (Reichel-Dolmatoff, 1976). Effective symbiosis between the human community, on the one hand, and the flora
and fauna of their particular environmental niche, on the other,
becomes the governing criteria for their own evaluation of their culture. Restraint in consuming resource stocks and sensitivity to the
viability of the eco-system emerges as the core concern of culture and
ultimately of spirituality. These latter "software agents" of human
social patterns are continuously tested and adjusted to survival needs
not so much in a consciously abstracted mode of self-reflection, but
in a communal and shamanic attentiveness to the constant flow of
feedback from other life forms whose signals of communication and
warning are sensately mediated.

This evolutionary innovation of what might be called "cultures of
limitation" stands as a sign of both caution and possibility for a species
on the brink of overreach. Whatever else the crisis of our time means it
poses a profound question of self-restraint. It is not clear whether we
have the cultural capacity today to entertain the question at its ecological and evolutionary depths. But it would appear that, one way or
another, our seeming success at expansionary adaptation to ecologies
all across the globe now asks us paradoxically whether we are able to
adapt in an "inverse" capacity—one of constraint. Are we that kind of
species that can limit itself in the name of surviving itself? The current
indications are not exactly reassuring.

It is just here that Mendoza finds her own narrative of decolonization taking an ironic turn. Having struggled for years with
an internalized ideal of existence fashioned for her by colonial white
culture, she has gradually begun to unearth and recover a reinvigo-
rated sense of her heritage as Kapampangan. As discussed in chapter
8, decolonization for her has meant recovery of native understandings
of Filipino values and history and ways of being.

Historically, the lowland plain of Pampanga, just north of Manila,
was settled by successive waves of Indonesian (dating as far back as
300–200 BCE), and later on Malay (in a mass exodus of the eleventh
and twelfth centuries) immigrants, pushing the indigenous Negrito

tribes into surrounding highlands. Cut by numerous rivers ("pampang" means river bank), the plain is lush and fertile. The region witnessed its own state-building over the course of two millennia, rooted in river commerce and rice cultivation. Renowned for agricultural, forestry and fishing resources and trade, the area early attracted Spanish interest and was organized as their first colonial province on the main island of Luzon in 1571.

However, Pampanga also was among the first areas to revolt against Spain in the late nineteenth-century independence movement and continued this tradition of resistance into the twentieth century, initially pushing back on local landlord abuses in the early 1900s, then in World War II giving rise to "Hukbalahap" guerilla struggle against the Japanese, which afterwards translated into postwar communist insurgency, and finally birthing the New People's Army campaign against the brutalities of the Marcos regime. Known as hospitable and peace-loving people, Kapampangans nonetheless did not long put up with oppressive behavior. While many of these traits of gentle welcome and pliant adaptability were read by Spanish and later U.S. colonizers as "backward" and "slothful," within native understandings these same tendencies harbored a remarkable resourcefulness and resilience in situations of great adversity.[2] Decolonization has certainly meant returning to a Filipino grasp of values and laboring to disinter Kapampangan culture from centuries of colonial disparagement. But it has also meant learning to recognize the way agrarian Pampanga itself became centered in urban hierarchies converting countryside to crop production and displacing indigenous foragers to unwanted terrain higher up the watershed.

Recognition of the history underneath the history requires a different kind of archaeological effort. The decolonization process here inverts. The question of Kapampangan supercession of the indigenous population whispers its own unknown terrors. Whether in the historical project of displacement or the more recent one of development—the evidence of Kapampagnan disdain for supposed Aeta "backwardness" is palpable. What it might mean for such a one as Mendoza—wrestling through the deformations of Western colonial impositions—at the same time to confess and repudiate her own culture's disregard for foraging "negritos" marks the cutting edge of her concern.

The question posed in the abstract by the global crisis of today—the necessary demythologization of the presumed superiority of civilization over indigeneity, and in particular the revalorization of indigenous "potlatch" or "gift" economies as a serious critique of our own unsustainable economic logic of "growth at all costs"—has a concrete historical agenda. For Mendoza, the issue is not simply about empathy for an "other." In one sense, we can presume that the Aeta are dialectically "internal" to Kapampangan identity as that over-against which they asserted themselves historically and in reaction to which they crystallized some of their own cultural specificity. Here is the hardest work of "archaeological digging" for the kind of historical inventory Edward Said (1978; referencing Gramsci) calls for in his famous work on orientalism. How does one tease out from one's own culturally elaborated sensibility those elements formulated as response to and repudiation of something one now recognizes as quite possibly necessary to existence? How might one face what has been dysfunctional or destructive in one's own deep cultural formation and mythology and work toward an ability to "hear" something radically counter? The resistance to such self-confrontation is deep. Mendoza and I now have continuous experience—in the classroom and in personal conversations—of inordinate and vitriolic reaction, when we try to open up critical discussion about modernity based on indigenous models of sustainable practices. The reaction is often out of all proportion to the posed question. Whence such anger? And how move past its reactive toxicity?

FROM INSIDE THE BELLY OF THE BEAST

In all of this line of questioning, I stand as the face in the mirror to which my own finger and rhetoric most damningly point. Given my white skin, my hetero-normative sex, my masculine engenderment, my middle-class upbringing, and my Western cultural formation, my social positioning on the planet is the least credible "place" from which to sound this toxin of warning. Much as a Global South country (e.g., India) might say back to U.S. insistence that any multilateral protocols regarding carbon emission must be embraced by the developing world if the developed world is itself to sign on, everyone outside of the privileges of Western white supremacy has every right to say back to me, "You have already had your day in the middle-class sun of consumption and plunder; it is our turn now. Go ahead and downsize your lifestyle, it is only just and high time that you reduce your footprint or even disappear like you have 'disappeared' so many other cultures. But it is only now becoming possible for 'us' to enjoy what you have already been wallowing in for 500 years!" At the most fundamental level of any rough calculus of global justice, such a response has merit. At that level, my own response must first of all be one of confession and listening. Beyond that I speak only by way of sufferance of others, not by right (and my wife loves to make note of these words every time I say them!). And I have an ongoing duty to act in any case.

But the confessional work is crucial and it is the awareness and conviction germinated out of my years of battling white racism (within myself as well as in the culture at large) that now guides my own approach to this larger and deeper labor. The questions of that personal battle bear rehearsal here in the form of a partial mapping of the ongoing struggle to step free of the nightmare of modern conquest of the planet and (re)turn to something more viable.[3] White supremacy is in many ways the patina and driver of modern globalization, behind which lie Christian and anthropozoic supremacies, as previous chapters have explored. There is no immediate access to ancestral wisdom that does not entail hard labor on the 500-year-old rock of systemic white power. For me, the relentless reinscription of white skin privilege within the contemporary structures of globalization has meant embracing lifelong responsibility continuously to deepen both awareness and resistance. The scope of the necessary vigilance ranges across the entire theater of what might be called historical white ruthlessness—as the Du Bois epigraph so sharply underscores. It demands that those of us who benefit develop the capacity to name forthrightly, understand clearly, and repudiate actively:

- the comprehensiveness of white rule as a presumption of entitlement to global resources,
- its inchoate power in legitimizing and routinizing the political economy of capitalism,
- its continuing career as a mode of supremacist "certainty" in social judgment,
- its erotic hallucinations and entanglements with the very people it denigrates,
- its historical realization first as a Christian religious ideology in the early colonial era,
- then as scientific racism during the (so-called) Enlightenment,
- and finally, in neoliberal guise, as a supposedly "color-blind" cultural normativity.

Despite Civil rights and Black Power Movement successes in conjuring the reality of racism onto the surface of society and challenging its hegemony publically—white power continues its rule as a default order of institutional practice and cultural habituation. It operates by way of euphemism and innuendo. It continues to organize our social interaction in asymmetrical relations of access and experience across every major domain of existence (no matter that the country has now elected a dark-skinned president; Perkinson, 2012). These include housing, education, incarceration, health care, employment, income distribution and net worth accumulation, among others. As a largely invisible force of systemic privilege and sanction constraining and shaping everyday practices through globalized media and neo-imperial institutions of privatization, militarization, incarceration, for example, white supremacy remains both an active agency and a passive effect, in the present.

In short, being "white" within the neoliberal order of all things global and local—while not fully definitive of my own inner persona—does remain determinative of much of my conditioning and positioning socioeconomically and politically. This is an exigency for which I judge I have irreducible responsibility now as an adult, even though I did not create its reality in the first place—a responsibility that finds its basic mandate in committed noncooperation with the ways race organizes plunder and accumulation or justifies entitlement and right! Embracing such a vocational and existential responsibility, I have then had to ask, "How exactly do I confess what white supremacy has meant historically and how do I resist the way it operates today?" While I embrace the demand for responsibility as entirely dependent upon me, no matter the responses of people of color (whether positive or negative), my *capacity* to respond and resist is *not* simply within my own powers, but requires apprenticeship and tutelage, deep eagerness to learn from communities of color and deep willingness to be checked and corrected by them. And here is the rub for this writing.

I have spent more than thirty years of my time on the planet—much of my primary and secondary school years and most of my adult life—living and working in contexts that were majority African American, initially by accident and then by choice. Over that time I have had to come to grips with how profoundly entangled our respective cultures and identities have become over the course of our history together. Learning for me has not been only about an "other" outside of myself, but even more stridently and confusedly, about the way that "other" has been internalized—both negatively and positively—inside my own white formation and habituation. White culture is at one level, a merely reactive riff on cultures of color—a desperate and dilatory, "Sure glad I am not that," that at the same time inevitably depends upon the very thing it resists, somewhat like a photographic negative inversely imitates the very thing it "negates." Whiteness is profoundly shaped by the blackness it tries to push away in abhor-rence or disdain. Throw in all the convolutions of human desire for the exotically "othered" and fetishically repudiated, and the complex is deep indeed! Unearthing *these* roots of white supremacy gets down into the primordial terrors of sex and death and all things undulating and indistinguishable, fluid and interchangeable, funked up, sweated out, swallowed down, or fawned over.

The typical responses are terror and desire, arousal and disgust, in a menagerie of emotional reactivity and angry confusion that in our age has no clearly demarcated "initiation" process mapped out for its ritual solicitation and naming, and no readily available body of elders, savvy in its taming and integration. Here it is history itself that is initiation chamber, and it is one's own fellow-initiates—if such can be found—who are the source of counsel. Certainly, people of color historically have been made the experts on white supremacy and how it functions socially by sheer necessity. They cannot afford the luxury of not knowing how white people think and operate—and even more crucially, how they embody the regime of assumed superiority and resource-entitlement even at unconscious levels—if they want to sur-vive. But whites dare not shunt onto people of color the burden of white initiation into such a process of self-confrontation and matura-tion as if black or brown or yellow folk were one more time, and in one more way, made responsible for white education and well-being. People like me have to assume the entire responsibility for our own self-knowledge—and for action to redress the damage caused to com-munities of color over the course of a now 500-year history of domi-nation. The summons is a call to enlist in a war of resistance against a social positioning and cultural identification in which we are already profoundly enmeshed (by upbringing and by training)—a kind of self-resistance that is as complex and convoluted as any ancient demand for initiation. In negotiating such a process, the history and experi-ence of people on the other side of the divide of race stands as both "off limits" and as "utterly crucial."

In my particular case as someone who came of age in inner-city Detroit, for example, I can neither assume I have any right to par-ticipate in and learn about black culture nor to abstain from such. The conundrum of a demand to know and change and a proscription against trespass and appropriation exactly demarcates my responsibil-ity. The contradiction implied—with its foreclosure of any possibility of innocence no matter how I choose to act—is itself the pedagogy, a white double bind that is the inverse condition of the racialization white supremacy historically has imposed on bodies of color around the globe. Whatever its geopolitical and cultural particularities, white racialization of dark bodies is fundamentally a structure of binary impossibility. It is a demand historically on the part of white communities that others around the globe prove themselves "human" by adopting white culture and cooperating with Western economic and military priorities. But it is a demand that simultaneously works against the very attempt of such others to qualify themselves for inclusion in the position of privilege (the gated middle class suburb or gated country) and thus access to the resources coercively gathered there over time (through slavery, wage labor, structural adjustment, privatization, debt-imposition, etc.). That is to say, at the most basic level, racialization is an imposition by a militarily dominant group on a dominated group that says, "I will not consider you to be human unless you look and act and live like me," while at the same time saying (under its breath if not outside its consciousness) "and I will never let you be like me because, actually then I would have to share the stuff I have stolen from you." Whatever the contents of any given racialization, this is its basic structure of impossibility. It means no matter how a given target group tries to play the game—whether through trying to refashion themselves as "honorary whites" or repudiating whiteness and maintaining their own cultural difference from whiteness— they lose. Either choice validates whiteness as the normative way to be "human" (the former choice, by way of imitation; the latter in playing into the initial distinction projected by white people on people of color demarcating them as somehow substantially different from and thus inferior to white people). And neither choice secures rights to the goods except on the terms of white power.

The implication for me as white is simple but clear. Until the double bind of racialization is somehow effectively dismantled and eliminated for communities and countries of color around the globe, I as white have no right to try to exempt myself from my own enmeshment in its contradictions. I will need to learn about cultures of color and learn from people of color and at the same time, have absolutely no rights to such cultural participation or such counsel. Only by actually learning about how race operates from the people who have most painfully suffered its consequences and most powerfully forged strategies and practices of resistance to it, can I gain any clarity on my own role and responsibility in seeking to combat its effects as a "co-combatant." All of this implies a deep, slow, thorough-going and lifelong confrontation with the actual meaning and force of white supremacy—by continually probing its effects around me and inside of me, with and without input from communities of color to whom I stand as both culprit and debtor. It is a process that only gradually and in painful self-confrontation will yield insight and comprehension and the possibility of acting otherwise.

UNDERNEATH MODERNITY

But now, in my sixth decade, I have married a Filipina, and in confronting, with her, the multiplying crises of the planet, realize the effort so far described is, at one level, mere scratch-work on the surface of modernity. The real depth-demand of the hour is working back down the phylogenetic line to the place and time in our ancestry where human beings actually lived in a sustainable manner in relationship to their given ecological niches. The work I have been engaged in for more than a quarter century, digging into my own formation as "white" by learning its convoluted contours and machinations from blacks and blackness, gives me at least a foretaste of what might be required for the next step: recovering a more vital realization of my own humanity underneath the "reductions" and domestications of "civilization." Certainly there are all manner of dangers here— a repeat of eighteenth-century European romanticizing of Native Americans as "noble savages" not the least among them. But most of our embrace of modernity and all of its idolatries of growth and development are themselves a romanticization so wildly delusional—so utterly beyond the possibilities of sustainability—as to qualify, today, as seriously insane. Most of us are still in the phase of denial about the terminal prognosis for our way of life. Eco-scientist Gwynne Dyer reports that much of the scientific community is already shuddering with panic that we are not going to be able to stop the heating of the earth that is underway and believes we will have to make the Faustian bargain of reengineering the atmosphere with sulfur dioxide capable of blocking sunlight (even though it takes us further down the path of long-term effects we can't control or understand; Dyer, 2010). Meanwhile (as already mentioned) the Pentagon is deep into preparations for levels of global upheaval in the wake of this heating that they say will make recent warfare seem like a mere sandbox squabble between children. Romance indeed! But in any case, the eighteenth-century "romance" was not merely that. The United States after all did, in fact, learn from, emulate, and incorporate substantive wisdom from native culture, even if it simultaneously dissimulated that precise borrowing (the average U.S. citizen knows next to nothing about where some of our most cherished ideals really came from; Weatherford, 1988, 123, 129–131). Much of our taken-for-granted

notions of personal freedom and the checks and balances of a demo-
cratic vision of politics (no matter how far short the actualization
falls) were imports from the Haudenosaunee (the Iroquois League)
by way of a partial "conversion" of Benjamin Franklin and Thomas
Paine to native prescience (Weatherford, 1988, 125–126; Loewen,
2007, 108–111).

We "moderns" may now be facing the need for a similar conversion at the level of economic viability and ecological sustainability. If
so, the work to be done will require profound interior metamorphosis
away from our addiction to the shallow pleasures of consumption and
zombie-like entombment in the planet-killing machinery of urbanity
and technology, walling us off from the rest of the natural world, and
toward recovery of a much older way of being, symbiotically conversant with and respectful of other life forms. One way or another we
need to recognize in our social forms the reality of the reciprocity that
is our real origin and substance and destiny (our bodies in fact will
become food for others one way or another). Figuring out the way
forward here requires knowing where we have come from—and how
we got "here." There is a history of bloodletting under our feet in
most places on the planet that demands accounting and comprehension, so that we might learn both what to avoid and what to learn
from. And that demand to look ancestry in the eye, pull away the
masks created by our own fears and repudiations,[4] and embrace and
value what finally is not a terrifying other, but is actually "us," is very
much historically specific and culturally concrete.

And just in this regard Mendoza, in her own life and work, is groping intransigently toward a credible future. Underneath all the glitz
of modernization, in her own itinerary of decolonization, she is no
longer content merely to confront the history of white Western domination of her island home in the projects of Spanish and American
colonization. Rather, she is also now allowing herself to be challenged
by the history under the history, the colonization under the colonization, where indigenous lifeways began to be denigrated and disappeared by her own Kapampangan forebears. These latter had already
long before been enamored of the project of settled agriculture in
domesticating plants and animals (including human ones) into an
expansionary aggrandizement of our species at the expense of every
other life form on the planet, and to the elimination of every human
group not willing to submit to a hierarchical social ordering and an
aggressive logic of being. The displaced and tattered Aeta now stand
on the horizon of her awareness as a task of self-confrontation and a
cipher for the future.

Conclusion?

Today every one of the remaining groups of our indigenous (and especially hunter-gatherer) ancestors finds itself under similar assault by
corporate and state interests bent on "development" of the resources
under their feet for the sake of the rapacious appetites for "more and
more and more" that most of us have been socialized (and adver-
tised) into as the supposed birthright of rightly-aspiring, "just-want-
to-be-middle-class-comfortable" global citizens. *Their* prognosis is
patently "extinction." But the deep question they embody as long as
they remain alive is whether civilization is an evolutionary inevitabil-
ity . . . or a mistake whose brief efflorescence on the planet is doomed
(literally) to "burn up" like a streaking comet. The sign on the drill
grounds of the former Clark Air Base is thus stark in its subtle implication: the hunting and gathering Aeta people, as indeed their lifestyle
cousins around the globe, are clearly on their way out, since "we"—
their late sons and daughters—have nearly obliterated any remaining
collective capacity we might have to grasp what they knew, or learn
from what they had proven successful in a 200,000-year crucible of
adaptation. For most of us now, the sign evokes nostalgia at best,
or more likely, a mere shrug of the shoulders. But we should pause
long and hard before the absence it conjures. If we do not learn to
face and decipher the deep text of our own presumed superiority and
the violent history of suppression and unsustainability it encodes, the
absence thus augured could very well become our own. Within a few
decades hence, there may well be no one left to read anything at all.

NOTES

CHAPTER 1

1. And here I am keenly aware that, at one level, framing the question as one of sustainability is already problematic. At the deepest level of our understanding, nothing is sustainable, including the universe itself. Change is ubiquitous and relentless. The battle between synthesis into more complex forms of existence and entropic breakdown into a cold mass of matter flying away from everything else similarly flying away into entropic coldness—the evident destiny of the entirety—is a losing one. Perhaps a better framing of the question would be in terms of something like "generativity." But that too will have its own set of problems. There remains a certain relative valence for the term "sustainability" to the degree it poses a possibility like that in evidence throughout long durations of geologic and human history of ecologies that "held together"—in relatively symbiotic modes of biodiverse equilibrium—for long periods. It is toward such a roughly construed "template of wholeness" that I would refer the term "spirituality" in its popular ascendance today over the term "religious."
2. The process of gradual differentiation and maturation of an organism in relationship to its environment, during which genetic information is modified and translated into the substance and behavior of that organism.

CHAPTER 2

1. Maroon communities composed of runaway slaves and disaffected whites who made common cause with Native Americans in out-of-the-way domains of wilderness, where they could hunt, gather and grow their own food in small-scale, "cut and burn" (swidden agriculture) plots of mixed root crops, while creating their own social institutions, separate from the taxation, conscription, and exploitation of the grain-based, urban-centered state (Loewen, 2007, 107–108, 126–127, 151; Leming, 1993, 37; Scott, 2009, 9–10, 18, 41, 54, 77).
2. See Jim Corbett's commentary on the Exodus account of Moses's struggle to name the Voice that spoke to him out of the bush (Corbett, 2005, 84–87).
3. And even renegade "swidden agriculturalists" doing root crop cultivation in highland zones or desert areas (or other "out-of-the-way" places of revolt), where food production can be carried out beyond the reach of

imperial taxes and plundering, as detailed by James C. Scott in his book, the *Art of Not Being Governed*.

Chapter 3

1. Myers carefully exegetes the flow of sayings here to emphasize that far from trying to cloak what he is saying ("putting a lamp under a bushel"), Jesus is rather seeking to "excavate" ears that can actually "hear." What is entailed is a kind of awakening: breaking the crowds' hearing free ("take heed what you hear") from colonization in simple catchphrases and aphorisms whose purpose is to conform them to the status quo.

2. It is worth noting that Jesus' own favored self-signifying—in oblique, third-person allusions—is what Myers calls the "Human One," translated back into Hebrew as *ben adam*, "Son of Man," itself building from the Genesis 1:26 citation in which God creates the collective "Earth Creature" ("Mud Community," we might say) *adam*, from the ground (Myers, 1988, 37, 64, 243, 248, 391, 405; Gen. 1: 27). Of course, the reference here is especially to Daniel's version, the Human One who comes in apocalyptic vindication of those "warred against" and "worn out" ones who receive (indeed, embody) the kingdom (Dan. 7:11–27).

3. It is likewise worth noting that, in this Lev. 25 vision, everyone is reduced to "gleaning" food like a forager for the duration of time that the fields are allowed to "rest" in a fallow state.

4. As Brandon Scott offers concerning the "expectation of the kingdom under the symbol of the cedar or apocalyptic tree" (Scott, 1989, 386).

5. There is not space to elaborate a full-blown schema for these differing lifeways. But suffice it to say here that I am primarily interested in forms of human dwelling that remain attentive to their dependence on local ecosystems and to a responsibility to the holy embodied in such that is carried out by ceremonial faithfulness to the visions and dreams continuously given to ancestors and community members over time. Forager communities offer the clearest testament to how our species handled this way of living that is quite alternative to our modern ideas, but subsistence agricultural communities, honoring cycles and seasons and limits, or smaller scale pastoral nomadism, reacting to enslavement by going feral and recovering a sense of reciprocity with the wild grasses, also continue the tradition.

6. Indeed, for indigenous peoples, the initial "revolution" from hunting and gathering to settled agriculture, and then from that expansionist monocultural farming project to industrialization, was not "revolutionary" at all, but calamitous! Listening close to the ground around the globe today, I have yet to hear any indigenous leaders calling for a "revolution." Rather, I hear an insistent call to remember. Revolutionary discourse itself valorizes a progressivist view of history that demands rethinking from an indigenous point of view.

CHAPTER 4

1. And of course, in reality, every religious tradition—mainstream Christianity included—is already a working hybrid fashioned over time in concrete ecological and historical circumstances, amalgamating influences from a vast array of sources. Identifying particular forms of Christian practice as hybrid is thus, at one level, misleading. But it is worth noting that such nomenclature is used by imperial orthodoxies of all kinds (political as well as spiritual) to claim the high ground of "right" belief/practice.
2. Historically the genre of "gospel" is a piece of Roman political propaganda—a written document lionizing the emperor's latest military triumph or announcing his coming visit to an imperial city.
3. See the anthropological anthology *Limited Wants, Unlimited Means* for a reprise of the argument.
4. See for instance the experience of the CBS with the island-hopping Mokan people following the 2004 tsunami (Leung, 3).
5. I am beholden for this image to a Ched Myer's sermon given in Detroit at the funeral of a friend in 2006.
6. For further treatment of these ideas, see my contributions to *Constructive Theology: A Contemporary Approach to Classical Themes* (Perkinson, 2005, 252–253).

CHAPTER 5

1. In history, "Europe" per se did not actually coalesce a shared identity until it encountered multiple others around the globe in the colonial enterprise. But for the sake of economy of expression, I use the term collectively here, before its time.
2. For a book-length treatment of this section, see my *White Theology: Outing Supremacy in Modernity.*

CHAPTER 7

1. I recognize that "America" is much more accurately a designation of an entire hemisphere—from the top of Canada to the bottom of Argentina and that the tendency of people in the United States to use it exclusively of themselves is typically imperial and supremacist. Here I am choosing to use it that way largely for reasons of ease of reference (as well as rhythmic structuring in a sentence) when characterizing what so often is invoked self-referentially in US dominant culture.
2. Floyd's argument could itself be nicely complemented by social scientist James Scott's notions of "hidden transcripts" and "weapons of the weak" as displayed in his book *Domination and the Arts of Resistance,* nuanced in application to black musics in conjunction with the rather idiosyncratic idea of hegemony worked out by anthropologists John and Jean Comaroff

in their tome *Revelation and Revolution*. Much the same point would come clear as that being offered by Floyd: namely, the capacity of the human body to encode and crystallize—in various structures of perception, habits of gesture, orientations of feeling, and formalities of movement—historical memory and even political resistance, that is the result of quite consciously engaged ideological struggles and material conflicts from an earlier time, but now carried forward not so much in conscious recognition and thematic content, as in subconscious conditioning and cultural form (Comaroff and Comaroff, 1991, 25–41).

3. As a ceremonial vitalization of the amoral (available for either good or evil) life energy known as *ashe* in Yorba traditions, dance ritual, structured by drum rhythm and song melody, functioned to instantiate principles of interdependence and reciprocity between human and spiritual realms, "making understood the unexplainable" (Floyd, 1995, 20).

4. Without making over much of it, Floyd will even cite Joseph Campbell to the effect that ritual enactment of myth in general, in building its dream-like revelations from the specificities of the material world and its local history, solicits the deepest hopes, desires, fears, potencies and conflicts of the human will, that is itself "moved by the energies of the organs of the body operating vicariously against each other and in concert" (1995, 22; Campbell, 1986, 55). If such can be said of myth in general, much more can it be said of African-influenced enactments informed by African rhythmic, polymetric, and heterophonic stylistics (Floyd, 1995, 6, 29).

5. Among the funky butt, buzzard lope, slow drag and grind repertoire of well-loved and liquored dance steps was also to be found the "itch"—a dance move that became the basis for later jazz-dance developments and clearly suggested the advent of Eshu's New World reincarnation, Legba, whose human "horse" regularly "scratched" after being possessed (Floyd, 1995, 66). Eshu likewise finds re-instantiation in the blues-trope of the crossroads, popularized in Robert Johnson and Peetie Wheatstraw mythologies of having acquired their musical skills in a midnight transaction with the Devil, exchanging their souls for such a gift at the requisite fork in the road (Floyd, 1995, 74).

6. See the way Long works with van der Leeuw's notion of sacral experience as an experience of a vague "Something" that imposes itself (Long, 1986, 163).

7. "America" as war-machine could be ranged on a continuum with "America" as Jim Crow lunch-counter in the south, or more to the point, lynch-mob, or chain-gang, or tenant-farmed field of corn. Indeed, at some deep level historically, "America" has never ceased to be at least a low-intensity warfare machine since its founding.

8. In Paris of the 1940s for example, a young boy on the street clings to his mother in terror, crying "Momma, an N . . . . , an N . . . . , the N . . . is going to eat me," before a young Frantz Fanon who is just out walking, and suddenly Fanon feels his skin ruptured and smeared with the blood of his entire ancestry, feels the "burning sky of whiteness" all around him, broiling his bones in an inescapable mythology. Paris is not America, but

it indeed hosts the white supremacy that America incarnates, the force of privilege and power that has organized global wherewithal relentlessly since 1492 and accreted to itself designation as the epiphany of God's viceregency over the rest of reality. "America" here is a revelation of race, but before we attend to that worldwide apparition in any detail (as we will in the next section), there is a particular version of the dialectic that must be remarked in the homeland.

Chapter 8

1. First published in 2013 as "DJ Qbert as Cyber-Maniac Shaman: What Does Hip-Hop Tricksterism Have to Do with Traditional *Babaylanism*?" in *Back From the Crocodile's Belly: Philippine Babaylan Studies and the Struggle for Indigenous Memory*, S. L. Mendoza and L. M Strobel, eds., 207–221. Santa Rosa, CA: Center for Babaylan Studies.

2. The idea that the biblical traditions of Sabbath and parable (among others) can be read as if granting the "eco-subjectivities" of soil and seed emblematic power to "speak" through the texts was more broadly pursued in my 2013 book, *Messianism Against Christology: Resistance Movements, Folk Arts, and Empire*, where I proposed re-imagining Christology in terms of relationship to an entire local watershed "messianically mediated" by one or another hybrid of animal-human or plant-human alliance.

3. Cf. Kristin Lattany-Hunter's discussion of "off-timing" as a survival skill for a mid-twentieth-century generation of African Americans, using various modes of jazzlike "syncopation" to side-step oppressive incursions on the community (Lattany-Hunter, 1994, 172).

4. See the book by the same name tracing the multistoried appearance of this cultural value/relational quality in the lives of numerous Filipino culture-bearers by Filipino psychology professor and outsider scholar Katrin de Guia 2005.

5. With this language I am intentionally invoking a long-standing tradition of "working the spirit" through the body—whether in the form of Joseph Murphy's treatment of Afro-diaspora spiritualities comparing *Voudou, Santeria, Candomble*, Revival Zion, and Black Church (USA), Daoist imagination of a kind of alchemy of the energies of *chi*, heated in the kidneys to rise along the spinal column finally to "flower" through the cranium, similar Hindu ideas of *kundalini*, or Egyptian "dream schools" where initiation followed a similar biophysical mapping of trance induction resulting in "vision" or alternative consciousness (Murphy, 1994, xi, 5, 36, 71; Fisher, 1997, 98–99, 188; Bynum, 1999, 74, 79–83, 91). It is especially interesting that these latter conceive of the process as "serpentine."

6. Cf. for instance, the thought experiment I offered in a 2009 publication reading Tupac Shakur as a manifestation of Ogou (Perkinson, 2009, 63–65).

7. This is a reference to William Gibson's 1984 Cyberpunk classic, *Neuromancer*, exploring the cyborg revolution engulfing the social order and

splicing human being into the globalizing machine matrix that is rapidly inverting the relationship between flesh and technology (243–244).

8. See the work of Philippine studies scholar Nenita Pambid Domingo on the way the colonial battle over meaning ended up encoded on the face of the bronze *Infinito Dios* amulet now available in markets like the one outside Quiapo Catholic Church in Manila (Domingo, 2013, 47–67). Amulets and charms of various kinds were objects infused with magical/mystical power and aura-ed with the potencies of the *anitos*-ancestors, whose significance is articulated in deeply rooted indigenous mythology, where they are deemed useful for warding off evil or invasion and for promoting healing and economic sufficiency. According to indigenization historian Ray Ileto, they were used extensively in the Philippine Revolution by various leaders and participants as protection against the enemy—which though not effective in warding off bullets, did infuse a high level of confidence that contributed to the ultimate success of the revolution (Ileto, 1979, 22–27; Domingo, 2013, 62).

9. Jesuit anthropologist Albert Alejo details the role of *agongs* (gonglike metallic hand drums that have long been used in indigenous ceremonies around the islands) in rekindling a sense of communal identity and cultural pride that served as a precursor to political struggle over ancestral land and rights on the side of Mt. Apo in Mindanao in the 1980s (Alejo, 2000, 80–121, 254)

Chapter 9

1. The name of one of the early hip-hop breakdance crews.
2. Bambaataa named his organization the Universal Zulu Nation.
3. Reference to Grandmaster Flash of the Furious Five, otherwise known as Joseph Saddler, one of the best known early DJs, renowned for his style on the wheels of steel (turntables), one of the innovators of backspin technique, punch-phrasing, and scratching.
4. Jean Michel Basquiat, famous Manhattan tagger anchoring the graffiti group known as SAMO in the 1970s, who by the 1980s had become a recognized solo artist exhibiting and collaborating as well as continuing to rupture convention.
5. See the comment on the DVD by KRS-One regarding getting down on the ground in break-dancing (QD3 Collective, 2002).
6. Du Bois's famous beginning of *Souls of Black Folk*, "Between me and the other world," and his lifetime elaboration of the "gift of second sight" with which blackness is forcibly installed by its experience of double-consciousness, hints that that entire social positioning is like a shamanic initiation rite of old, dismembering and reassembling social being behind a veil of insight whose irresistible effect is a profoundly unending mode of seeing beneath and under and around things, in a world that has been warped and violated by the operations of race (Du Bois, 1961, 16–17).

7. For a sustained exploration of the relationship between the biblical language of "principalities and powers" and modern scientific discourses tracking the pursuit of the elemental building blocks of physical matter, whose violated integrity may well spell disaster for the biosphere, see the chapter entitled "Elements of the Universe" in Walter Wink's *Unmasking the Powers: the Invisible Forces that Determine Human Existence* (Wink, 1986, 128–152, esp. 141, 152), or my own work elaborating on Wink in *Messianism Against Christology* (Perkinson, 2013, 93–126). Cf. also, the way Zimbabwean churches have adapted their traditional understanding of the *ngozi*—the aggrieved spirit of someone violated or murdered—to the ecological destruction that tree-cutting has wrought on their landscape. The *ngozi* presence returns to haunt and trouble the community of the living until restitution has been made in the form of a "marriage" between the unrequited spirit and that living community (including constructing an actual hut for that spirit that is regularly maintained and cleaned). Today, these churches believe that the trees themselves are returning as *ngozi* and so they now offer tree-planting as part of their liturgy to try to redress the situation and inculcate a new mentality among their folk (Daneel, 259–260).

8. For an example of this kind of thinking, see the Derrick Jensen interview with Tzutujil Mayan-trained educator Martín Prechtel entitled "Saving the Indigenous Soul" (Prechtel, 2001, 4).

9. See Evan Eisenberg's treatment of the evolutionary history of human-perennial and human-annual alliances, one of whose experiments early on in the process of domesticating the wild for human use is the human-arboreal alliance just mentioned (Eisenberg, 1999, 7).

10. Cf. Myers, 2001, 10, 18, 23, 30; 52; Corbett, 218, 220.

11. Cf. Kanye's lines in "No Church in the Wild," in which he hints: "We formed a new religion/No sins as long as there's permission/And deception is the only felony."

12. At the time of the original drafting of this piece, the Detroit City Council was convening a hearing on a proposal to sell—very cheaply—more than 1,000 tracts of land on the east side to Hantz Woodlands (formerly Hantz Farms), an organization committed to bringing industrial farming into Detroit, trying to bump up land prices by making it scarce (i.e., rendering it available only to capitalized buyers, not to poor and working class folk), wiping out numerous community gardens, doing little to create new jobs, and privatizing a huge chunk of the city for the typical corporatized operation of commodity production that is so much a part of the problem with how we handle the earth today. Local artists including Invincible were weighing in through various media to publicize the way corporate interests were being given privileged access to the decision-makers and to counsel community resistance. The deal has since been concluded and the land cleared for a Christmas tree farm, with even larger tracts now under threat of a similar fate.

13. Cf. for example, Lane Wilcken's *Filipino Tattoos: Ancient to Modern* (2010) for the importance of tattooing traditionally in connection with initiation, hunting, social conflict, and so on.

14. Historian of religion Charles Long's term for the "hardness of life" and density of signification colonial conquest forced indigenous folk into globally (Long, 177–178, 197).

15. Though it has indeed become a rainbow reality globally, a black cultural code promulgated by a multi-ethnic posse of devotees (Chang, 2005, 418).

16. I have written about this at greater length in the Abdul Karim Bangura edited *Pan-Africanism Caribbean Connections* and the Anthony B. Pinn and Monica R. Miller edited volume of *Culture and Religon*'s special issue on hip-hop and religion (Perkinson, 2007, 67–69, 75–76; 2009, 66–69).

CHAPTER 10

1. An anthropological term in the islands used to designate the earliest certain wave of immigration that left a settler population still living today.

2. A case in point is the commonly shared Tagalog term *Bathala na,* meaning something like "*Bathala* already," where *Bathala* references a Filipino equivalent of a "high god" and "*na*" is a particle emphasizing immediacy. Read by Spanish and U.S. colonizers as a shoulder-shrugging invocation of fate when circumstances seem impervious to change, on the ground in local culture, the phrase could as equally be read as a term relativizing "irresistible force" with a shrug and a laugh that is actually a counsel of continuing on "in spite of." In an eco-zone of historically regular volcanic upheaval (with tsunamic consequences), as well as regular typhoons, developing a cultural capacity to honor what is "irresistible" as a mode of Divinity, and *yet keep on living,* is actually "creative adaptation" rather than the spin of "irresponsibility" given by miscomprehending colonizers.

3. For a more comprehensive treatment, see my 2004 book *White Supremacy: Outing Supremacy in Modernity.*

4. As in some rites of passage, where initiates are "assaulted" by masked elders impersonating demons or other terrifying forces and must actually reach out in spite of their fears to pull away the masks and face what is behind them. And again, most of the human race shows some measure of fear of "shadow figures" in dream-time, that may represent a kind of historic rupture troubling our ancestral line that has us trying to disown the planet-wide rootage of all of our family trees in Africa (Bynum, 76, 79, 81, 85–87, 93–95).

BIBLIOGRAPHY

Abram, David. 1996. *The Spell of the Sensuous: Perception and Language in the More-Than-Human World*. New York: Vintage Books.

———. 2010. *Becoming Animal: An Earthly Cosmology*. New York: Pantheon Books.

Albrecht, Gloria. 1995. *The Character of Our Communities: Toward an Ethic of Liberation for the Church*. Nashville: Abingdon Press.

Alejo, Albert E. 2000. *Generating Energy on Mt. Apo: Cultural Politics in a Contested Environment*. Quezon City: Ateneo de Manila University Press.

Armstrong, Karen. 1993. *A History of God: The 4000-Year Quest of Judaism, Christianity and Islam*. New York: Ballantine Books.

Armstrong, Robert G. 1997. "The Etymology of the Word 'Ogun.' In Sandra T. Barnes, ed., *Africa's Ogun: Old World and New*, 29–38. Bloomington: Indiana University Press.

Baker, Houston. 1993. "Scene . . . Not Heard." In R. Gooding-Williams, ed., *Reading Rodney King, Reading Urban Uprising*, 38–50. New York: Routledge.

Bakhtin, Mikhail. 1984. *Rabelais and His World*. Translated by H. Iswolsky. Bloomington: Indiana University Press.

Barnes, Sandra T. 1997. *Africa's Ogun: Old World and New*. Bloomington: Indiana University Press, xiii–xxi.

Bechet, Sidney. 1960. *Treat It Gentle*. New York: Hill & Wang.

Blair, E. H., and J. A. Robinson. 1998. *The Philippine Islands, 1493–1898*. Bank of the Philippine Islands (commemorative CD re-issue). Available at http://www.elaput.org/chrmtpar.htm.

Bourgois, Philippe. 1990. "Confronting Anthropoligcal Ethics: Ethnographic Lessons from Central America." *Journal of Peace Research 27* (1), 43–54.

Brennan, Teresa. 1993. *History After Lacan*. London: Routledge.

———. 2004. *The Transmission of Affect*. Ithaca: Cornell University Press.

Brewer, Carolyn. 2001. *Holy Confrontation: Religion, Gender and Sexuality in the Philippines, 1521–1685*. Manila: Institute of Women's Studies, St. Scholastica College.

Brown, Karen McCarthy. 1991. *Mama Lola: A Vodou Priestess in Brooklyn*. Berkeley: University of California Press.

———. 1997. "Systematic Remembering, Systematic Forgetting: Ogou in Haiti." In Sandra T. Barnes, ed., *Africa's Ogun: Old World and New*, 65–89. Bloomington: Indiana University Press.

Brueggemann, Walter. 1996. "The Earth Is the Lord's." *Sojourners* (Oct. 1986): 28–32.

Bynum, Edward Bruce. 1999. *The African Unconscious: Roots of Ancient Mysticism and Modern Psychology.* New York: Teachers College Press.

Cahill, Thomas. 1996. *How the Irish Saved Civilization: The Untold Story of Ireland's Heroic Role From the Fall of Rome to the Rise of Medieval Europe (The Hinges of History).* Harpswell, ME: Anchor.

Campbell, Joseph. 1986. *The Inner Reaches of Outer Space: Metaphor as Myth and as Religion.* New York: Harper & Row.

———. 1990 (1969). *The Flight of the Wild Gander: Explorations in the Mythological Dimension.* New York: Harper Perennial.

Chang, Jeff. 2005. *Can't Stop Won't Stop: A History of the Hip-Hop Generation.* New York: St. Martin's Press.

Charing, Howard G. 2008. "Communion with the Infinite: The Visual Music of the Shipibo Tribe of the Amazon." Available at http://www.ayahuasca .com/spirit/primordial-and-traditional-culture/communion-with-the-infinite-the-visual-music-of-the-shipibo-tribe-of-the-amazon/.

Christensen, Thomas G. 1990. *An African Tree of Life.* Maryknoll, NY: Orbis Books.

Churchill, Ward. 1997. *A Little Matter of Genocide: Holocaust and Denial in the Americas 1492 to the Present.* San Francisco: City Lights.

Comaroff, Jean and John Comaroff. 1991. *Of Revelation and Revolution: Christianity, Colonialism, and Consciousness in South Africa.* Chicago: University of Chicago Press.

Corbett, Jim. 1991. *Goatwalking.* New York: Viking Press.

———. 2005. *A Sanctuary for All Life: The Cowbalah of Jim Corbett.* Englewood, CO: Howling Dog Press.

Cosentino, Donald J. 1997. "Repossession: Ogun in Folklore and Literature." In Sandra T. Barnes, ed., *Africa's Ogun: Old World and New*, 290–314. Bloomington: Indiana University Press.

Crossan, John Dominic. 1991. *The Historical Jesus: The Life of a Mediterranean Jewish Peasant.* San Francisco: Harper.

Daneel, M. L. 1994. "African Independent Churches Face the Challenge of Environmental Ethics." In David G. Hallman, ed., *Eco-theology: Voices from South and North.* Maryknoll, NY: Orbis.

Davis, Mike. 2006. *Planet of Slums.* New York: Verso.

Dayan, Joan. 2003. "Querying the Spirit: The Rules of the Haitian *Lwa*." In A. Greer and J. Bilinkoff, eds., *Colonial Saints: Discovering the Holy in the Americas, 1500–1800*, 31–50). New York: Routledge.

De Guia, Katrin. 2005. *Kapwa: The Self in the Other: Worldviews and Lifestyles of Filipino Culture-bearers.* Pasig City, Philippines: Anvil Publishing, Inc.

Deloria, Vine.1999. *For This Land: Writings on Religion in America.* New York: Routledge.

Deren, Maya. 1953. *Divine Horsemen: The Living Gods of Haiti.* New York: McPherson & Co.

Desmangles, Leslie G. 1992. *The Faces of the Gods: Vodou and Roman Catholicism in Haiti*. Chapel Hill: University of North Carolina Press.

Diamond, Jared. 1997. *Guns, Germs, and Steel: The Fates of Human Societies*. New York: W. W. Norton.

DJ QBert. 2000. "Ahead of the Curve: For Nearly a Decade, Invisibl Skratch Piklz Have Transformed the Battle Jock Arena into a Multi-Million-Dollar Industry. Now They Map Out Turntablism's New Terrain." Interview with Brian O'Conner and Jim Tremayne, *DJ Times Magazine* (May). http://www.djtimes.com/original/djmag/may00/Piklz.htm.

Domingo, Nenita Pambid. 2013. "*Anting-Anting*: Why *Bathala* Hides Inside the Stone." In S. L. Mendoza and L. M Strobel, eds., *Back From the Crocodile's Belly: Philippine Babaylan Studies and the Struggle for Indigenous Memory*, 47–67. Santa Rosa, CA: Center for Babaylan Studies.

Du Bois, W. E. B. 1961. *The Souls of Black Folk*. New York: Fawcett Publications, Inc.

———. 1971. "The Souls of White Folk." In Julius Lester, ed., *The Seventh Son: The Thought and Writings of W. E. B. DuBois*, vol. 1. New York: Vintage Books.

Dunham, Katherine. 1969. *Island Possessed*. Chicago: University of Chicago Press.

Dussel, Enrique. 1995. *The Invention of the Americas: Eclipse of "the Other" and the Myth of Modernity*. New York: Continuum.

Dyer, Gwynne. 2010. "Gwynne Dyer on *Climate Wars: The Fight for Survival as the World Overheats*." Interview with Amy Goodman on Democracy Now! http://www.democracynow.org/search?utf8=%E2%9C%93&query =Gwynne+Dyer+&commit=Search.

Dyson, Michael Eric. 1991. "Performance, Protest, and Prophecy in the Culture of Hip-Hop." *The Emergency of Black and the Emergence of Rap* (A special issue of *Black Sacred Music: A Journal of Theomusicology*, Jon Michael Spencer, ed. Durham, NC: Duke University Press, 12–24.

———. 2001. *Holler if You Hear Me: Searching for Tupac Shakur*. New York: Basic Civitas Books.

Eisenberg, Evan. 1999. *The Ecology of Eden: An Inquiry into the Dream of Paradise and a New Vision of Our Role in Nature*. New York: Vintage Books.

Eliade, Mircea. 1964. *Shamanism: Archaic Techniques of Ecstasy*. Trans. Willard R. Trask. Princeton: Princeton University Press.

———. 1991 (1954) *The Myth of the Eternal Return: Or, Cosmos and History*. Princeton, NJ: Princeton University Press.

Fanon, Frantz. 1967. *Black Skin, White Masks*. Translated by C. L. Markmann. New York: Grove Weidenfeld.

Farmer, Paul. 2004. *Pathologies of Power: Health, Human Rights, and the New War on the Poor*. Berkeley: University of California Press.

Fisher, Mary Pat. 1997. *Living Religions*. 4th ed. Upper Saddle River, NJ: Prentice Hall.

Floyd, Samuel A. 1995. *The Power of Black Music: Interpreting Its History From Africa to the United States.* New York: Oxford University Press.

Foucault, Michel. 1980. *Power/Knowledge: Selected Interviews and Other Writings, 1972–1977.* Edited by C. Gordon. Translated by C. Gordon, et al. Brighton, Sussex.

Frazer, Sir James George. 1922. *The Golden Bough.* New York: Macmillan.

Gebhart-Sayer, Angelika. 1986. "Una terapia estética: Los diseños visionarios del ayahuasca entre los Shipibo-Conibo." *América Indígena 46* (1), 189–218.

Gibson, William. 1984. *Neuromancer.* New York: Ace Books.

Gilroy, Paul. 1987. *There Ain't No Black in the Union Jack: The Cultural Politics of Race and Nation.* London: Melbourne: Hutchinson. Reprint, Chicago: University of Chicago Press, 1991.

———. 1993. *The Black Atlantic: Modernity and Double Consciousness.* Cambridge, MA: Harvard University Press.

Gordon, Avery F. 1997. *Ghostly Matters: Haunting and the Sociological Imagination.* Berkeley: University of California Press.

Gowdy, John, ed. 1998. *Limited Wants, Unlimited Means: A Reader on Hunter-Gatherer Economics and the Environment.* Washington, DC: Island Press, xiii–xxix.

Greene, Graham. 1973. *The Honorary Consul.* New York: Washington Square Press.

Haraway, Donna. 1992. "The Promises of Monsters: A Regenerative Politics for Inappropriate/d Others." In C. Nelson and P. A. Treichler, eds., *Cultural Studies,* 295–337. New York: Routledge.

Harris, Max. 2003. *Carnival and Other Christian Festivals: Folk Theology and Folk Performance.* Austin: University of Texas Press.

Heinberg, Richard. 2014. "How to Shrink the Economy without Crashing It: A 10-Point Plan." Post-Carbon Institute (Nov. 4, 2014), http://www.postcarbon.org/how-to-shrink-the-economy-without-crashing-it-a-ten-point-plan/.

Hemenway, Toby. 2009. *Gaia's Garden: A Guide to Home-Scale Permaculture.* 2nd ed. White River Junction, VT: Chelsea Green Publishing Co.

Herzog, William. 2000. *Jesus, Justice, and the Reign of God: A Ministry of Liberation.* Louisville, KY: Westminster John Knox.

Hurston, Zora Neal. 1990 (1938). *Tell My Horse: Voodoo and Life in Haiti and Jamaica.* New York: Harper & Row.

Ileto, Reynaldo. 1979. *Pasyon and Revolution: Popular Movements in the Philippines, 1840–1910.* Quezon City: Ateneo de Manila University Press.

Jameson, Fredric. 1981. *The Political Unconscious: Narrative as a Socially Symbolic Act.* Ithaca, NY: Cornell University Press.

Jennings, Willie James. 2010. *The Christian Imagination: Theology and the Origins of Race.* New Haven, CT: Yale University Press.

Jensen, Robert. 2008. "The Old Future's Gone: Progressive Strategy Amid Cascading Crises." *Dissident Voice: A Radical Newsletter in the Struggle for Peace and Social Justice.* http://dissidentvoice.org/2008/08/

the-old-future%E2%80%99s-gone-progressive-strategy-amid-cascading-crises/.

Jeremias, Joachim. 1972. *The Parables of Jesus*. 2nd ed. New York: Scribner's.

Jones, LeRoi. 1999. *Blues People: The Negro Experience in White America and the Music that Developed from It*. New York: William Morrow.

Kaufman, Robert. 1961. "Hawk Lauler: Chorus," *New Directions 17*, 225–228.

———. 1965. *Solitudes Crowded with Loneliness*. New York: New Directions.

———. 1967. *Golden Sardine*. San Francisco: City Lights.

Kogi Mamas Speak. http://tierra-y-vida.blogspot.com/2006/09/kogi-elder-brothers-warning.html.

Kohli, Amor. 2002. "Saxophones and Smothered Rage: Bob Kaufman, Jazz and the Quest for Redemption" *Callaloo 25* (1), 165–182.

Lattany, Kristin Hunter. 1994. "'Off-timing': Stepping to the Different Drummer." In Gerald Early, ed., *Lure and Loathing: Essays on Race, Identity, and the Ambivalence of Assimilation*, 163–174. New York: Penguin Books.

Lee, Richard. 1998. *Limited Wants, Unlimited Means: A Reader on Hunter-Gatherer Economics and the Environment*. Washington, DC: Island Press, xix–xii.

Leming, Hugo P. 1993. "The Ben Ishmael Tribe: A Fugitive 'Nation' of the Old Northwest." In R. Sakolsky and J. Koehnline, eds., *Gone To Croatan: Origins of North American Dropout Culture*, 19–60. Brooklyn: Automedia.

Leonard, Annie. 2007. *The Story of Stuff*. www.thestoryofstuff.com.

Leonard, George. 1978. *The Silent Pulse: A Search for the Perfect Rhythm That Exists in Each of Us*. New York: E. P. Dutton.

Leonard, Neil. 1987. *Jazz: Myth and Religion*. New York: Oxford University Press.

Loewen, James W. 2007. *Lies My Teacher Told Me: Everything Your American History Textbook Got Wrong*. Rev. ed. New York: Touchstone.

Long, Charles. 1963. *Alpha: The Myths of Creation*. Atlanta: Scholars Press.

———. 1986. *Significations: Signs, Symbols, and Images in the Interpretation of Religion*. Philadelphia: Fortress Press.

Luna, Luis Eduardo. 1986. *Vegetalismo: Shamanism among the Mestizo Population of the Peruvian Amazon*. Stockholm: Almqvist and Wiksell.

Lyotard, Jean-Francois. 1994. "The Sublime and the Avant-Garde." In *The Polity Reader in Cultural Theory*, 284–288. Cambridge, UK: Polity Press.

Madera, Lisa Maria. 2009. "The Gospel According to Ayahuasca and Santo Daime." *Journal for the Study of Religion, Nature, and Culture* (The Religious Lives of Amazonian Plants) *3* (1), 66–98.

Markus, Robert A. 1990. "From Rome to the Barbarian Kingdoms." In J. MacManners, ed., *The Oxford Illustrated History of Christianity*, 62–92. New York: Oxford University Press.

Marx, Karl. 1967. *Capital: A Critique of Political Economy*. Vol.1. Edited by F. Engels. Translated by S. Moore and E. Aveling. New York: International Publishers.

Marx, Karl. 1963 (1852). *The Eighteenth Brumaire of Louis Napoleon*. New York: International Publishers.

Mendoza, S. Lily, and Leny Mendoza Strobel, eds. 2013. "*Pasakalye*/Introduction." In *Back From the Crocodile's Belly: Philippine Babaylan Studies and the Struggle for Indigneous Memory*. Santa Rosa, CA: Center for Babaylan Studies.

Mendoza, S. Lily. 2000. *Between the Homeland and the Diaspora: The Politics of Theorizing Filipino and Filipino-American Identity*. New York: Routledge.

Mennell, Stephen, and Johan Goudsblom, eds. 1998. *Norbert Elias: On Civilization, Power, and Knowledge: Selected Writings*. Chicago: University of Chicago Press

Merwin, W. S. 2011. Interview by Sarah Gelder. *Yes! Magazine* (Nov. 2). www.yesmagazine.org/issues/new-livelihoods/w.s.-merwin.

Metraux, Alfred. 1972 (1959). *Voodoo in Haiti*. New York: Schocken Books.

Miller, Monica R. 2012. "'No Church in the Wild': The Youth's Unrecognized Spirituality Between Beats and Rhyme." The Huffington Post. http://www.huffingtonpost.com/monica-r-miller-phd/no-church-in-the-wild-spirituality-between-beats-and-rhymes_b_1756187.html.

Mills, Charles. 1997. *The Racial Contract*. Ithaca, NY: Cornell University Press.

Muller, Richard. 2012. Interview on *Democracy Now* (Aug. 2, 2012). http://www.democracynow.org/2012/8/2/climate_skeptic_koch_funded_scientist_richard.

Murphy, Joseph, M. 1994. *Working the Spirit: Ceremonies of the African Diaspora*. Boston: Beacon Press.

Myers, Ched. 1988. *Binding the Strong Man: A Political Reading of Mark's Story of Jesus*. Maryknoll, NY: Orbis Books.

———. 2001. *The Biblical Vision of Sabbath Economics*. Washington, DC: Church of the Savior.

———. 2005. "The Bible and Anarcho-Primitivism." In B. Taylor, ed., *Encyclopedia of Religion and Nature*. London & New York: Continuum.

———. 2013. *Buffalo Shout, Salmon Cry: Conversations on Creation, Land Justice, and Life Together*. Waterloo, ON: Herald Press, 109–126.

Nader, Laura. 1972. "Up the Anthropologist—Perspectives Gained from Studying Up." In D. Hymes, ed., *Reinventing Anthropology*, 284–311. New York: Pantheon Books.

Narby, Jeremy. 1998. *The Cosmic Serpent: DNA and the Origins of Knowledge*. New York: Jeremy P. Tarcher/Putnam.

Oakman, Douglas. E. 1986. *Jesus and the Economic Questions of His Day*. Studies in the Bible and Early Christianity, vol. 8. Lewiston, NY, and Queenston, Ontario: Edwin Mellen Press.

Otto, Rudolph. 1950. *The Idea of the Holy*. Translated by John W. Harvey. London: Oxford University Press.

Perkinson, James. W. 2001. "Ogu's Iron or Jesus' Irony: Who's Zooming Who in Diasporic Possession Cult Activity?" *Journal of Religion 81* (4), 566–594.

————. 2002. "The Gift/Curse of Second Sight: Is 'Blackness' a Shamanic Category in the Myth of America?" *History of Religions 42* (1), 19–58.

————. 2004. "Reversing the Gaze: Constructing European Race Discourse as Modern Witchcraft Practice." *Journal of the American Academy of Religion 72* (3), 603–630.

————. 2004. *White Theology: Outing Supremacy in Modernity.* New York: Palgrave Macmillan Press.

————. 2005. *Shamanism, Racism, and Hip-Hop Culture: Essays on White Supremacy and Black Subversion.* New York: Palgrave Macmillan Press.

————. 2007. "Postcolonial Pan-Africanisms and Caribbean Connections: Behind Du Bois' Veil is Fanon's Muscle on a Herculoidian Trip." In Abdul Karim Bangura. ed., *Pan-Africanism Caribbean Connections*, 64–75. New York: iUniverse, Inc.

————. 2009. "Tupac Shakur as Ogou Achade: Hip-Hop Anger and Postcolonial Rancor Read from the Other Side." *Culture & Religion: An Interdisciplinary Journal 10* (1), 63–79.

————. 2011. "The 2010 US Social Forum as Sign of Martin King's Beloved Community: Ecumenism in the Hour of Planetary Crisis." *The Ecumenist 48* (2), 8–15.

————. 2012. "Theology After Obama—What Does Race Have To Do With It?: A Racial Prolegomenon to American Theological Production in the 21st Century." *CrossCurrents 62* (1), 89–109.

————. 2013. "DJ Qbert as Cyber-Maniac Shaman: What Does Hip-Hop Tricksterism Have to do with Traditional Babaylanism?" In S. L. Mendoza and L. M Strobel, eds., *Back From the Crocodile's Belly: Philippine Babaylan Studies and the Struggle for Indigenous Memory*, 207–221. Santa Rosa, CA: Center for Babaylan Studies.

————. 2013. *Messianism Against Christology: Resistance Movements, Folk Arts, and Empire.* New York: Palgrave Macmillan Press.

Prechtel, Martín 2001. "Saving the Indigenous Soul: An Interview with Martín Prechtel." http://www.thesunmagazine.org/issues/304/saving_the_indigenous_soul.

QD3 Collective. 2002. *The Freshest Kids: A History of the B-Boy.* ID1647QD-DVD. Chatsworth, CA: QD3 Entertainment, Inc. and Brotherhood Films.

Quinn, Daniel. 1992. *Ishmael.* New York: Bantam/Turner Books.

————. 2007. Interview in *What a Way to Go: Life at the End of Empire.* A documentary by T. S. Bennett and S. Erickson. VisionQuest Pictures.

Raboteau, Albert J. 1978. *Slave Religion: the "Invisible Institution" in the Antebellum South.* Oxford, UK: Oxford University Press.

Rackham, H., W. H. S. Jones, and D. E. Eichholtz. 1938–63. Natural History. 10 vols. L. c.L. Cambridge: Harvard University Press.

Rasmussen, Larry L. 1995. *Earth Community, Earth Ethics.* Maryknoll, NY: Orbis Books.

Reichel-Dolmatoff, G. 1976. "Cosmology as Ecological Analysis: A View from the Rain Forest." *Man 11* (3) (Sept.), 307–318.

Rose, Tricia. 1994. *Black Noise: Rap Music and Black Culture in Contemporary America*. Hanover, NH: Wesleyan University Press.

Royster, Philip. M. 1991. "The Rapper as Shaman for a Band of Dancers of the Spirit: 'U Can't Touch This,'" *The Emergency of Black and the Emergence of Rap* (A special issue *of Black Sacred Music: A Journal of Theomusicology*), Jon Michael Spencer, ed, Durham, NC: Duke University Press, 60–67.

Sahlins, Marshall.1998 [1966]. "The Original Affluent Society." In John Gowdy, ed., *Limited Wants, Unlimited Means: A Reader on Hunter-Gatherer Economics and the Environment*, 5–41. Washington, DC: Island Press.

Said, Edward. 1978. *Orientalism*. New York: Vintage Books.

Sawicki, Marianne. 2000. *Crossing Galilee: Architectures of Contact in the Occupied Land of Jesus*. Harrisburg, PA: Trinity Press International.

Schaberg, Janes. 1987. *The Illegitimacy of Jesus: A Feminist Theological Interpretation of the Infancy Narratives*. San Francisco: Harper & Row.

Scott, Bernard Brandon. 1989. *Hear Then the Parable: A Commentary on the Parables of Jesus*. Minneapolis: Fortress Press.

Scott, C. James. 1990. *Domination and the Arts of Resistance: Hidden Transcripts*. New Haven, CT: Yale University Press.

———. 2009. *The Art of Not Being Governed: An Anarchist History of Upland Southeast Asia*. New Haven, CT: Yale University Press.

Shepard, Paul. 1973. *The Tender Carnivore and the Sacred Game*. Athens: University of Georgia Press.

———. 1982. *Nature and Madness*. Athens: University of Georgia Press.

———. 1998. *Coming Home to the Pleistocene*. Washington, DC: Island Books.

Snyder, Gary. 1990. *The Practice of the Wild: Essays by Gary Snyder*. San Francisco: North Point Press.

Spencer, Jon Michael. 1991. *The Emergency of Black and the Emergence of Rap* (A special issue of *Black Sacred Music: A Journal of Theomusicology*). Durham, NC: Duke University Press, 1–11.

Spivak, Gayatri. 1988. "Can the Subaltern Speak?" In C. Nelson and L. Grossberg, eds., *Marxism and the Interpretation of Culture*. 271–313. Chicago: University of Illinois Press.

Stannard, David. 1992. *American Holocaust: The Conquest of the New World*. New York: Oxford University Press.

Taylor, Mark Lewis. 2011. *The Theological and the Political: On the Weight of the World*. Minneapolis: Fortress Press.

Taylor, William B. 2003. "Mexico's Virgin of Guadalupe in the Seventeenth Century: Hagiography and Beyond." In A. Greer and J. Bilinkoff, eds., *Colonial Saints: Discovering the Holy in the Americas, 1500–1800*, 277–298. New York: Routledge.

Thomas, Gregory V. 2002. "The Canonization of Jazz and Afro-American Literature." Wynton Marsalis interview in *Callaloo* 25 (1), 288–308.

Thompson, Robert Farris. 1983. *Flash of the Spirit: African and Afro-American Art and Philosophy*. New York: Vintage Books.

———. 1996. "Hip Hop 101." In William E. Perkins, ed., *Droppin' Science: Critical Essays on Rap Music and Hip-Hop Culture*, 211–219. Philadelphia: Temple University Press.

Townsley, Graham. 1993. "Song Paths: The Ways and Means of Yaminahua Shamanic Knowledge. *L'Homme 2* (4), 449–468.

Weatherford, Jack. 1988. *Indian Givers: How the Indians of America Transformed the World*. New York: Fawcett Columbine.

Wells, Spencer. 2010. *Pandora's Seed: The Unforeseen Cost of Civilization*. New York: Random House.

Wilcken, Lane. 2010. *Filipino Tattoos: Ancient to Modern*. Atglen, PA: Schiffer Publishing Ltd.

Williams, Florence. 2012. "Take Two Hours of Pine Forest and Call Me in the Morning." *Outside Magazine* (November). http://www.outsideonline.com/fitness/wellness/Take-Two-Hours-of-Pine-Forest-and-Call-Me-in-the-Morning.html.

Wink, Walter. 1986. *Unmasking the Powers: The Invisible Forces that Determine Human Existence*. Philadelphia: Fortress Press.

Wolff, Richard D. 2012. *YouTube* video. https://youtu.be/jtAiFji_9uU

Wright, Richard. 1957. *White Man Listen!* Garden City, NY: Doubleday.

Wright, Robin M. 2006. "The Brazilian Ayahuasca Religions." *Fieldwork in Religion 2* (2), 177–186.

Zerzan, John. 1999. *Elements of Refusal*. Seattle: Left Bank Books.

INDEX

Lightning Source UK Ltd.
Milton Keynes UK
UKOW06n1902170715

255381UK00005B/59/P